FAST FADE

FAST FADE

DAVID PUTTNAM, COLUMBIA PICTURES, AND THE BATTLE FOR HOLLYWOOD

Andrew Yule

A DELTA BOOK
Published by
Dell Publishing
a division of
Bantam Doubleday Dell Publishing Group, Inc.
666 Fifth Avenue
New York, New York 10103

For Patricia, Pamela, and Judith

ISBN: 0-385-30006-9

Reprinted by arrangement with Delacorte Press

Design by Richard Oriolo

Printed in the United States of America

Published simultaneously in Canada

January 1990

10 9 8 7 6 5 4 3 2 1

BG

Grateful thanks are extended to the following interviewees (and to the others who preferred to remain anonymous), whose kind cooperation helped to make this book possible:

David Bailey, Roy Battersby, Fred Bernstein, Andrew Birkin, Frank Bloom, Robert Bolt, Don Boyd, Lenore Cantor, Jim Clark, Nat Cohen, Robert Colesberry, Philip Collins, Ray Connolly, Bob Dingilian, Terence Donovan, Robin Douet, Brian Duffy, Jake Eberts, Adam Faith, Bill Forsyth, Brian Gilbert, Hara San, Gilly Hodgson, Hugh Hudson, Derek Hussey, Roland Joffe, Anthony Jones, Valerie Kemp, James Lee, Tom Lewyn, Sandy Lieberson, Robert Littman, Lord Low of Tribeca, Margaret Maguire, Alan Marshall, Sarah Miles, David Montgomery, Robert Montgomery, Lynda Myles, Michael Nathanson, David Norris, Steve Norris, James Park, Alan Parker, Uberto Pasolini, David Picker, Patsy Pollock, Lyndsey Posner, Susan Richards, John Ritchie, Bruce, Sophie & Lily India Robinson, Stanley Robinson, Marion Rosenberg, Alan Sapper, Anthony Smith, Iain Smith, Lynda Smith, Michael Stoddart, Jeremy Thomas, Francis T. Vincent, Jr., Paul Weiland, Colin Welland, Alan Yentob, Alex Ying.

Particular thanks also to the Puttnams—David, Patsy, Marie, Debbie, and Sacha.

The following books were consulted in the research process: *National Heroes* by Alexander Walker (UK Harrap), *Reel Power* by Mark Litvak (William Morrow), *Dustin Hoffman* by Iain Johnstone (Hippocrene), *The Real Coke, The Real Story*, by Thomas Oliver (Random House), and *Indecent Exposure* by David McClintick (William Morrow). *Variety*, *The Hollywood Reporter*, and *Screen International* all provided useful background information.

Wherever dialogue is quoted, this represents the recollection of at least one person present when the conversation took place.

A special "thank you" to all the critics and their journals mentioned in the book, together with my indefatigable secretaries Hattie Forrest and Eunice Sweenie.

INTRODUCTION

If all had gone according to script, David Puttnam's tenure as head of film production at Columbia Pictures would be viewed in retrospect as the golden culmination of an already outstanding career. His films, including *Chariots of Fire*, *The Killing Fields*, *Midnight Express*, and *Local Hero*, had won numerous awards, among them an Oscar for Best Picture. He was widely recognized as a man of charm and intelligence, a shining light in the world of cinema, one of the most successful and charismatic figures ever to emerge from the British film industry. His appointment as head of Coca-Cola's Columbia Pictures in 1986 therefore seemed a logical step, one that should have enhanced David's reputation and further strengthened an already powerful Hollywood studio.

Unfortunately, events followed a different scenario. What began on a high note of optimism and enthusiasm quickly turned sour. Reality replaced fantasy as small differences led to major confrontations, and arguments turned into outright war. Just a little more than a year after taking over as head of Columbia, David Puttnam was out. In moviemaking terms, it had indeed been a fast fade.

I first spoke with David by phone in 1986 while researching my book on the Cannon movie company, *Hollywood-a-Go-Go*. Following my later suggestion of an "in-depth profile" on David himself, we eventually arranged to meet face-to-face on August 30, 1987, a date with special significance, marking as it did the end of David's first year at Columbia. The date would gain additional significance, however, for it also came on the very eve of his overthrow as head of the studio.

Our first meeting took place in David's rented villa on Coldwater Canyon Drive in Hollywood, once the home of Greta Garbo. That actress's legendary shunning of publicity was the exact opposite of the approach David had taken to the press. In Britain he had indulged in skillful manipulation of the media, and he had continued to attempt the same thing in the U.S. Ultimately it would all be turned against him.

After we had talked for several hours at that first meeting, David's wife Patsy joined us. I could not have been more impressed by them. They make a striking couple—both of medium height, both with gleaming blue eyes. Patsy has shoulder-length flaxen hair, and a classic cheekbone structure that emphasizes her Nordic beauty. David's boyishly handsome appearance is belied only by an increasingly grizzled beard.

As I got to know them better over the ensuing weeks and months, I began to realize that underneath the delicate porcelain facade that Patsy Puttnam presents to the world is a core of strength and resilience. When talking about her husband and children she is always on guard, always protective. In debate she can be dogmatic and utterly unyielding, forthright and uncompromising—to Patsy a spade will forever be a spade. But with all this strength comes a disconcertingly effervescent sense of humor, allied to an air of vulnerability.

All the couple's many charms were on full display during our first meeting, and their sincere affection for and support of each other came shining through. What also became apparent, however, was that despite a year's struggle as head of a major American studio (the first ever for a product of the European film industry), David still viewed himself very much as a self-employed independent filmmaker. Even in the glow of that first session, his perspective seemed naïve.

In his discussion of his year at Columbia, certain names—powerful, legendary names—kept reappearing. David described the many trials and tribulations he had undergone at the hands of Ray Stark, Herbert Allen, Marty Ransohoff, Barry Diller, Bill Cosby, the *Ishtar* actors, Bill Murray, Dan Aykroyd, superagent Mike Ovitz, and others. Throughout, he spoke with a sense of righteousness, with the dedication of a man with a divine mission. He talked of his struggles and of the ongoing battles. Although many of the injuries he had suffered would turn out to be self-inflicted, David's plight was clear even then. By taking on so many of Hollywood's most powerful players, he had isolated both himself *and* the studio he was supposed to be running. He had sealed his own fate as well.

The next few days witnessed the dismantling of what many had hoped would be Hollywood's Camelot, a David Puttnam production based at Columbia's Burbank studios. For the faithful, it was a stunning loss. For those who knew him best, however, David's fall was the tragic but absolutely inevitable finale to a program of self-destruction that had its roots in the man's history, buried beneath the layers of complex motivations that characterize the enigmatic David Puttnam.

I

1

In 1931, Len Puttnam met a pretty Jewish girl, Marie Goldman. Two years later, they had married and settled down in the North London suburb of Southgate. Both Len and Marie were children of broken homes, each set of parents having separated during the 1920s. Their first child, David Terence Puttnam, was born on February 25, 1941. A sister Lesley was born two years later.

During this time, there was, of course, a war on. Len Puttnam had become a top Fleet Street photographer by the 1930s, and he was one of the first five photojournalists to enlist as a war correspondent when war was declared. Marie was left alone to tend to the two children during the German bombing blitz, a strain that eventually took its toll. After the war, Marie was diagnosed as suffering from nervous exhaustion and was confined to bed for six weeks with an ulcer. Len, like many of his wartime comrades, also suffered to a degree from shell shock, aggravated by the impotence he had felt in his position as war correspondent, since recording the evidence of man's inhumanity to man was not a role Len had relished.

David, however, apparently emerged from the wartime experience unscarred. He attended kindergarten for a few years until he was seven, then was enrolled at a private boys' school. After Marie took one look at what she considered the hooligan element at the fee-paying institution, he was transferred to the local Oakwood primary. His grades at Oakwood were good enough to lead to a scholarship to Minchenden coeducational, which was considered the foremost grammar school in North London.

Also at the age of seven, David saw his first film, *Pinocchio*, at the Classic Cinema in London's Baker Street, just around the corner from Madame Tussaud's. He was absolutely entranced and remembers consciously thinking that making films was an amazing way for anyone to spend their life, although for a while David thought *all* films were animated cartoons. Soon he learned otherwise, and he became a fanatical filmgoer, imagining that one day when a name came up on the screen, it would be his. The main theme from *Pinocchio*, "When You Wish Upon a Star," remains one of David's favorite pieces of music, providing him a perfect metaphor for the cinema and his dream of breaking into its world.

David remembers Saturday matinees at the local Odeon not so much for what he saw as for the mere fact of being there, and he was there as often as possible. These busy Saturdays were rounded off either with Len, who was taking wedding pictures to supplement the family income, or in a local shop selling tea towels for a friend of Marie's. His mother reports that she would do "anything to keep him away from the local Saturday hangout, the Mayfair Cafe." Despite her strictures, David ended up at the Mayfair whenever he could. His sister Lesley remembers him from the age of ten trying to commandeer the best-looking girls. "He always had a twinkle in his eye and liked female companionship," she says. "And the back room of the

Mayfair, where the glamorous crowd congregated round the jukebox, was like Mecca for him. He was always the smallest boy of his crowd, but quite able to keep up with his glam pals."

Marie enrolled David and Lesley for ballroom dancing lessons. They earned bronze and silver medals, then retired when David was twelve. "I was upset at the time—I wanted them to go for their gold," Marie says. "But the dancing school wanted them to give demonstrations, and they were both too shy, so that was that."

David remembers the end of his ballroom dancing days a little differently, laughing: "I didn't want to be thought of as a pansy." For Lesley, it ended the problem of getting back home after the classes. "David wouldn't take me home. He was too busy meeting his girlfriends, and I had to phone my parents to collect me."

At thirteen, David took up tennis for his school. He represented Minchenden on the summer circuit when everyone else he was up against was three or four years older. Hopes were nurtured that one day he might represent England at the game.

Excel though he might at whatever he undertook, David's first love remained the cinema. For a long time, his favorite movies were musicals, and if they were from MGM and in Technicolor, so much the better. Marie knew the manager of the Odeon in Southgate, and she would occasionally arrange to meet her son after school to have tea in the theater's restaurant before he caught the four-thirty show. He began to visit the movies two or three times a week. "When choosing which ones to see," he recalls, "and this is really pathetic, I would first of all go for the Technicolor pictures. 'Is it in color? Right, that's the one we'll see.' Then if that left two black and whites, we went to the American one . . . I would see [a British] film only if I'd already seen two other films that week. I would always go for a *Hondo* or a *Flame and the Arrow*—no contest. I remember being amazed that *Genevieve* was any good—it came right out of the blue. That an Earl St. John or Rank film could be any good seemed like a total miracle."

In young Puttnam's eyes, even the women in British films

compared unfavorably with the American and Continental variety. Until he was fifteen he idolized Debbie Reynolds, but all that changed with *And God Created Woman* and David's first earthshaking glimpse of Brigitte Bardot. "I was never quite the same again." He laughs. "I *died*. Let's just say I spent a lot of time 'studying' Brigitte, who was plastered all over the walls of my bedroom. . . . That was when I started creeping up to London each Saturday. How we got away with it I don't know. We'd get in the back of the cinema to all these 'X' films. We used to stand outside the exit with their push-bar doors, and when someone came out—bang, foot jammed in the door!"

David's best friend at school, Derek Hussey, remembers their trips into the metropolis—in particular one occasion, when they sat through three films in one day—*White Christmas, And God Created Woman* (again!), and *Rebel Without a Cause*. When he was in his early teens, David began to realize that there was such a thing as serious, quality films. Movies like Fred Zinnemann's *The Search*, Elia Kazan's *On the Waterfront*, and, later, Stanley Kramer's *Inherit the Wind* made a deep and lasting impression on him.

Although his knowledge of films grew and his understanding of the opposite sex developed naturally he stinted somewhat on his formal education. "I guess I was pretty lazy at school," David admits. "And I certainly wasn't too bright, but I would always get a relationship going with the teachers so they didn't come down on me as hard as they did on others as indolent as I was. I got away with murder." One of his old teachers confirms this, laughing. "I told him one day that he wouldn't always get away with it. Whenever I reprimanded him, he'd look at me with those big blue eyes and my heart would melt, but I told him he couldn't go through life like that."

The strategist in David was pushing to the fore even then. Although he was neither the brightest nor the tallest of his contemporaries, he nevertheless managed to be extremely popular. He had inherited his father's charm and attractive personality; these, combined with a ready wit and a quicksilver tongue, were more than enough to see him through. "A charm-

ing wangler" is how one of his school pals sums him up—
"someone you wanted to run with. He knew how to look out
for himself—not with his fists, he was too small for that—but
by using his wits. And there was never anything ulterior about
his little maneuvers—they were all straight and instinctive."

At around this time, Patricia Mary Jones—Patsy—together
with her twin brother Richard and their parents moved to
Southgate from Islington. Despite Patsy's wish to continue at
her old Westminster School, the commute turned out to be so
arduous for the thirteen-year-old that she was eventually forced
to accept the inevitability of a transfer to Minchenden. There,
sixteen-year-old David spotted the new arrival and walked
briskly by, greeting her. "It can't be me he's talking to," Patsy
thought. But this continued at meetings in the playground and
in the school corridor between classes. Soon after, the couple
started dating in earnest, outside school hours.
    "Baby-snatcher!" his friends teased, but David was unde-
terred. "There's ever such a pretty girl started at our school"
was the first mention Marie heard of Patsy. David had a party
at home the following New Year's Eve, and Marie and Len
went out to spend the evening with friends. When they returned, the party was still going on, and they were introduced
to Patsy. After she left, David asked his parents, "What did you
think of my new girlfriend?" He had already described Patsy to
them as "sort of like a cross between Brigitte Bardot and
Mylène Demongeot." They were suitably impressed.
    David's amorous advances were noted by one of his teachers.
"He preferred girls to work" was the despairing but entirely
accurate verdict. There was a general feeling of exasperation
among his teachers that he was not fully applying himself—at
least, not to his studies. When David returned to school after
the Christmas 1957 holidays, he was sent home on the first day.
He reported to his stunned parents that the headmaster had
told him he was wasting their time. On David's final report, the
headmaster wrote, "After five years I find this boy a *total
enigma.*" David rushed to look up the word in a dictionary. To

his relief, he discovered the headmaster had said he was a person who was "mysterious, puzzling, and ambiguous." Unsure of *ambiguous*, he happily settled for *mysterious* and *puzzling*. Two out of three wasn't bad, he reckoned.

Out of school, David decided to begin to fulfill his vague dream of getting into movies. Its vagueness was confirmed in short order. For months his applications hit a brick wall of indifference, forcing him to the conclusion that the film business was completely nepotistic. Only having an uncle working at Elstree Studios would offer the possibility of a break in, it seemed; otherwise, the doors were closed.

David bought a copy of the *Evening News* and combed the job opportunities section. Early in 1958 he applied for and got his first job with the London publishing house Hutchinsons as a messenger boy. Months later, he found another job, courtesy of his father's influence, this time as a photo-lab cleanup boy at an agency called Service Advertising on Brook Street. Neither job was particularly pleasant or challenging, but his employers noted and admired the zeal with which David applied himself to every task, no matter how unpleasant. If he was cleaning the photocopier, there was no question it would be the cleanest and most efficient photocopier in the business. Once when Len Puttnam casually inquired of his contact at the agency how David was getting on, the reply was a somewhat exasperated, "He drives me mad! He's only been in the bloody department five minutes, and already he says he knows it all and wants to move on."

Patsy heard of his exploits on their occasional dates and at the Sunday teas at the Puttnams', to which she was invited. Still at school, to her this was another world.

The energetic young man enrolled himself in a three-year night school course covering company and copyright law, together with psychology as applied to advertising. His promotion from cleanup boy to messenger (despite the apparent contradiction in terms) coincided with Service's move to Knightsbridge, where David delighted in competing with himself on a regular run he did to the blockmakers in Fleet Street.

He bought a stopwatch and tried to shave a few seconds here and there from the run. To his surprise, this was noticed by the hierarchy. Realizing that David could do the fastest run, they picked him out to do the urgent errands and late runs. David had discovered that it was possible to make his own "luck." The stopwatch had carried out two functions: it got him noticed, and it gave him something to think about.

On David and Patsy's regular Saturday-night outings at this time, they would drive to London Airport in his father's car. They would eat a meal in the cafeteria an hour or two before the evening flight to New York was due to leave. During the meal the young couple would fantasize about actually visiting that city.

When boarding for the flight was announced, they would get up with the real passengers, and make for the departure gate. At the last minute, they would turn with a regretful smile and head for the exit. David's constant diet of American movies was having its effect. He wanted to visit the United States so badly, he could taste it.

A career break came when an assistant account executive at the agency went on vacation and a temporary replacement was sought. David was given the job for two weeks. No sooner had the account executive returned, than David had a further stroke of luck: the second assistant account executive went off for three weeks to get married. David thus worked for the same senior account executive for five full weeks. They got along together so well that David was recommended to another account executive as his assistant.

· Like all the other advertising agencies, David's employers had what was known as a graduate trainee scheme. For unknown reasons—possibly because he was known as the fastest, most alert messenger and the only messenger who wore a suit, or possibly because it was an extraordinary era—someone decided that it would be interesting to have a nongraduate in the graduate trainee scheme. To David's amazement and to his employer's gratification, David did as well in the course as any of the graduates.

After finishing the course, David did a brief stint as assistant account executive. Then he was transferred to the marketing department, which turned out to be interesting if a bit dreary. Also, he had been dating Patsy for a couple of years by now, and they were talking about getting married. But on a salary of £8 a week this was out of the question. David's successful application as an assistant account executive at Greenly's agency brought about a huge salary increase to £14 a week.

Patsy left school at seventeen. She briefly joined British Petroleum as a trainee, then soon after discovered she was pregnant. "Are you sure?" David asked. "Pretty sure," Patsy replied a little bit tearfully. "What are we going to do?" "Why, get married of course," David replied without hesitation.

Oddly enough, it was David—who had never known his parents to go to church—who wanted a church wedding, while Patsy, who had been brought up in a deeply religious Church of England household. felt that it really didn't matter. David said, "No, we're doing this the proper way, this is going to last forever, and we're going to be married in church."

At about this time David became aware of a series of new and exciting advertisements that were originating from a new agency, Collet, Dickinson, and Pearce (CDP). Although he knew of no specific job available there, David drafted a letter of application to the agency. He knew he would have to ask for less income than he was now making. He and Patsy worked out that they could get by—if only just—on £12 a week, and they decided that the sacrifice of £2 a week would be worth it just to get a foot in the door at this innovative agency.

After a couple of turndowns, David was finally given a series of interviews. The agency had never taken on an assistant account executive before, but they listened to David's explanation that he was prepared to take on a lesser job if necessary. They offered him a job. He negotiated as best he could, but he ended up settling for a salary of "11 for three months and then up to 12." Not until he got the letter formally confirming his new position did he discover that he had successfully negotiated himself a major raise—what David had taken to mean £11 per week was in fact £1,100 per annum!

Once again, David Puttnam had made his own luck—and, of course, this was only the beginning.

2

By the end of 1963, David Puttnam was earning £3,000 a year—an amazing salary for that time, especially for a twenty-two-year old. In January 1962, Patsy had given birth to a daughter, Deborah. After a rocky start on their own, the young parents were eventually able to buy their first apartment, a small place in Elstree, for £4,000.

By his own account, David had become an active player in London's "swinging '60s" scene. Through his job he got to know the top photographers of the day, and through them in turn, some of the people who later emerged as the decade's most celebrated personalities. One of these was Paul McCartney, with whom he developed a friendship that lasted for a number of years. Influenced by his more bohemian friends, David had started wearing his hair long, before it became an accepted style, which created a problem for himself at his still-conservative office. The arrival of the Beatles, however, changed everything. David suddenly found himself being promoted because of the length of his hair rather than being held back by it. He became the company's token "now" man, their conduit to what was happening in the street. He was the guy who understood the new phrases like "disposable teenage income." He was plugged in, switched on, and tuned in. His life at CDP altered significantly.

According to the newspaper *The Guardian,* which did an analysis in 1964, David was one of the first well-paid young executives—in fact the highest-paid executive in his age bracket—in the country at the time. A senior colleague, John Ritchie, was told by one of the company's heads upon leaving the agency for new pastures, "If you ever want to come back, you're welcome. I think by then you might find someone like David Puttnam is managing director." Ritchie remembers being astonished. Those were the days when managing directors were in their fifties; David was still in his twenties!

"He *was* jolly good," says Ritchie, "if a bit strident. What took the edge off his stridency and made it quite acceptable was his willingness to always seek advice and listen to older colleagues. It was an endearing trait unusual in a young man."

A rival agency, Pritchard Wood, once tried to poach David from Collet, Dickinson, and Pearce. The conversation naturally got around to salaries. David told them he was presently earning £3,500 a year, at which point the Pritchard Wood director in charge of the interview turned ashen and exclaimed, "That's more than me!" The interview was over.

The next move for David and Patsy was to look for a home nearer the center of London. A terraced house that they found in Ranelagh Grove, Pimlico, became their home for the next seven years. In September 1965, when they moved, Patsy was again pregnant. A son, Alexander—promptly nicknamed Sacha —was born the following April. David was present at the birth. "Not that he wanted to be"—Patsy smiles—"because he was meant to be going out with Paul McCartney. But he did stay."

It was as well he did, because the doctor they called never turned up. That left David to help the assistant midwife deliver the baby after a nerve-racking all-night vigil.

Shortly after, David was offered a change of pace at work by being given a temporary shift in responsibility to The Thompson Group. David was aware that CDP's motives were not entirely pure, but he went along with the idea anyway, glad for the change of pace and the opportunity for extra experience. Unfortunately, the assignment quickly ran aground. For David, it was his first encounter with corporate politics.

He had been loaned out as managing editor of a new magazine to Mark Boxer, founder of *The Sunday Times* color magazine. It soon became apparent to David, however, that the whole assignment was a political setup to "get" Mark Boxer. Boxer was then a great friend and confidant of Denis Hamilton, editor of *The Sunday Times* as well as managing director of The Thompson Group. By many at The Thompson Group, Boxer was seen as a threatening heir apparent. David was at one point even asked to give evidence that Boxer, of whom he was very fond, "was showing signs of clinical paranoia." He soon returned to CDP, sadder and wiser, having glimpsed the lengths to which powerful figures will go to achieve their ends. It was not to be his last such experience.

In the odd way that situations sometimes work themselves out, the next year at the agency was a wonderful one for David. With David and his colleagues Charles Saatchi, Ross Cramer, and Alan Parker, CDP had an enviable run of highly successful and award-winning ad campaigns. With the energy level high, for a while the young man was content. It did not last long, however, and David soon felt he had reached the point where there was nothing more for him to do at CDP. Despite its success, he was—in his terms—going around and around in the same track, a feeling that was to be a recurring motif in his life.

Nonetheless, David continued to be an innovative force at the agency. Borrowing an idea that had proved successful for American advertising star Mary Wells, David suggested that the agency assume a role in actually guiding their clients in the development of product. The idea met with resistance, but eventually it was suggested that CDP start a new unit to provide such a service, with David Puttnam as its head.

"Great, that would be marvelous," David told them. He recalls, "So we sorted it out, how many more staff we'd need—I was on £4,500 a year, this was 1967, and I was about to be put up to £5,000—and I said, 'I'd like 10 percent of any profits that come in. There could be a big breakthrough.' 'A profit percentage is out of the question,' I was told, it wasn't company policy, blah, blah, blah. They just weren't interested in giving me 10 percent in anything. I was an employee—be grateful and all that. For me, that was the beginning of the end."

The *end* of the end came when David was asked to take on the Benson & Hedges cigarette account, a move he resisted. "That caused a lot of unhappiness too," David recalls. "They didn't feel I should have the ability to choose what I worked on. I'm sure they thought I was being very pretentious, but I've never smoked, I don't agree with smoking, and I just wasn't prepared to spend my life urging other people to smoke. . . . I said, 'Well, I think I'd like to go.' They didn't rush to disagree."

He was made to sign an extraordinarily restrictive termination contract, stipulating that he would refrain from joining any other agency for a minimum of five years. In return, CDP would put up £2,000 of the £3,000 David reckoned he would need to start up his own business. He left many good friends behind, like one erstwhile mentor Colin Millward, together with the copywriters he had befriended, Alan Parker and Charles Saatchi.

David had never lost his ambition to break into films. He had always regarded anything else he did as a means to that eventual end—but how to break in and in what capacity? A clue came from another colleague at CDP, a true English eccentric named David Reynolds, whose advice was "Be like Diaghilev." David had been complaining to him one day that although he had many interests, he couldn't actually *do* anything. "Look," Reynolds said, "Diaghilev couldn't do anything." David said, "Oh, really?"

There was only one problem—he had no idea who Diaghilev was. Reynolds explained he had been the greatest influence on ballet and music in this century, although he himself could neither play a note nor dance a step. David went straight to the library and got a book about him. He became gradually obsessed with Diaghilev. Around the same time, he read a biography of Irving Thalberg. He photocopied a portrait of him in the book that showed him as a twenty-one-year-old, starting at Universal Studios with Carl Laemmle. David was terribly taken by Thalberg's story. He found the idea of someone of his age making such an impact both exciting and challenging. As with Diaghilev, it was the idea that Thalberg didn't actually do anything himself—rather, he *caused* things to be done. Thalberg didn't write, he didn't direct, but he inspired those who could. David had other heroes at this time and acquired more over the years, but these two men and their careers summed up exactly what he wanted to achieve.

With the money from Collet, Dickinson, and Pearce and a £1,000 overdraft facility from his father-in-law, David set himself up in business as a photographers' agent, David Puttnam Associates. Almost from the very beginning the operation was a phenomenal success, as Lord Snowdon, David Bailey, Richard Avedon, David Montgomery, Clive Arrowsmith, and Brian Duffy were signed up in rapid succession. The culture's craving for pop fashion exploded as the 1960s went into overdrive, and David and his clients rapidly became the new "old boy" network, the new elite. The one thing they all had in common was limitless energy and the courage to risk failure.

Richard Avedon turned out a superb series of Beatles photographs, to which David acquired merchandising rights. Posters were produced from the Avedon photographs, and since the group was enormously successful throughout the world, David had to travel extensively in making many merchandising deals. His first visit to New York was magic for David. It was as if he were coming home at last after all the years of anticipation. He still remembers his first sight of the Manhattan skyline and the thrill of picking out the landmarks he had dreamed about for so long, like the Empire State Building and the Chrysler Building. But nothing had prepared him for the heady injection of adrenaline that New York produced. He felt himself responding to the buzz and excitement on the streets and galvanized by the electric atmosphere.

He was struck especially by the informal way that business was conducted, the lack of the starched-collar approach. If someone loosened a tie, there were no disapproving glances. Everybody from the head of the agency down looked relaxed in their shirt sleeves. David's feeling that the rigid British class system had never taken hold here seemed confirmed when the head man distributed the lunchtime sandwiches and coffee. In the evening he saw the sun set down the avenue as the discussions continued until the natural conclusion of the agenda. Wasn't this what it was all about? he asked himself. Once back in Britain, David buttonholed everyone he could find, preaching the gospel of the new age he had glimpsed.

Since the main business of David Puttnam Associates was on the Continent, he was taken away from home for long spells to go there as well. He spent one working week each month in Germany, where the agency was doing an enormous amount of business. For one other spell each month, David would do another city—Stockholm, Paris, or Madrid—trying to open up business there. That left two weeks out of every month at home, frantically trying to catch up with the work that had accumulated in his absence.

"There was one enormous compensation—I was earning a hell of a lot of money. From five grand when I left advertising, I was making £30,000 a year eighteen months later in 1968. Patsy and I couldn't even spend it. We saved a year's money in double-quick time."

Photographer David Bailey remembers this period well. "David was extremely hard to pin down, always dashing about, always on the move. If he had a fault, it was his tendency to pick people up and drop them. There's a lot of that about, of course.

"He was the first person I knew who was antismoking. We

had to go out on the balcony of his house to smoke. I'd always thought of him as straightforward until then. This was the first sign of eccentricity. That, and the fact that he disapproved of my drinking. He's always been a couple-of-glasses-of-wine man at the most and was shocked at what I used to shift. Then he was forever dragging me off to clubs. Once it was a reggae club in Southall, where we had an absolutely terrifying night. There was a dreadful atmosphere of menace about the place—ours were the only white faces there. 'We'll be murdered,' I told him. I really didn't think we were going to get out alive, but he seemed oblivious to the danger. Perhaps because I was born in the East End, I was more sensitive to the vibes than he was, and in the end I managed to talk him into leaving early, thank God."

When asked about his "Hello, he lied" description of David Puttnam, Bailey smiles and shrugs. "You say a lot of things when you're young. It seemed a funny, amusing thing to say at the time, nothing more than that. Who knows why you say things?"

A few years later, in the early 1970s, David Puttnam would tell a colleague, "You know, one thing I never do is lie." When this produced a raised eyebrow, he immediately qualified the remark with, "Well, I always tell at least *half* the truth." Then he grinned disarmingly: "The only problem I have later is remembering which half I've told."

"Photography is quite a bitchy business," says Robert Montgomery, brother of photographer David Montgomery, "but I've never heard David actually lie. He could take certain things and twist them, but you have to remember he was a negotiator. You've got to listen quite carefully to what he has to say, but he never lies. To get where he did in photography, you've got to pull a few tricks, that's for sure."

And you had to work, hard and constantly. As Montgomery remembers, "David was a total workaholic, even on holiday. He never drank, apart from an odd glass of wine. He never took any drugs. And he always had so much energy, he'd charge you up as well."

Despite his enormous financial success, David had a problem: the photographers' agency business simply wasn't where he wanted to be. He still nurtured ambitions to enter the film business. But how? By itself, being a 1960s yuppie was simply not enough. Despite the inspiring examples of Diaghilev and Thalberg, he desperately needed a catalyst.

For Patsy, things were not going at all well. There were no money worries, but she was seeing less and less of David, and when she did, he was invariably surrounded by a clutch of photographers and their models. The modern town house in Pimlico was badly built, with paper-thin walls that afforded little privacy.

With David up to his neck in work, there was simply no time even for such a trifle as illness, as Patsy discovered. After she had been feeling unwell for several days, she went to a doctor for a checkup. The doctor could find nothing wrong and told her to come back for a further examination the following week.

"Sounds like appendicitis," Patsy's mother told her that evening.

"Don't be silly, Mum."

"All right, but you've got all the symptoms."

"Well, I'm going to see the doctor again soon—he'll tell me."

The next time, the doctor had no doubts. "You've got a terrible appendix," he told Patsy. "We'll need to get you straight to hospital."

"You can't," Patsy informed him. "My children are coming home from school."

The doctor exploded. "Your *children* are coming home? What are you *talking* about? You've got—"

"Listen!" Patsy interrupted. "I've lasted this long. Just give me a few more hours."

Debbie and Sacha were picked up and handed over to an au pair girl whom Patsy quickly found. After giving the au pair a lightning tour of the house, surveying the state of the larder, and flinging a few £5 notes at the startled girl, Patsy drove herself to hospital and was readied for the operation. Since

David could not be located, the decision was made to go ahead without his authority.

During Patsy's ten-day stay in the hospital, David visited her once with the children and once in the company of Richard Avedon. Patsy knew there was a big campaign under way, and she appreciated the pressure David was under; still, she had a feeling she had somehow or other ended up with the short straw. She felt shunted aside. What made it especially difficult for Patsy to cope was the fact that she felt disoriented and totally left behind by the tremendous changes that had recently taken place in society. Four years earlier, in 1962, she had been relegated to the status of a nonperson because she had been pregnant outside marriage. Now here she was at twenty-two, feeling as old as Methuselah, with David traipsing through the house at all hours with these bright young things.

"People were living together, weren't getting married, we had David Bailey and the other photographers in and out, I never knew who they were going to bring, there were pop people and stars coming and going. The madness of photography at that time—models, fantastic amounts of money, great Rolls-Royces, and everyone behaving in the most extraordinary way."

Everyone has their breaking point, and Patsy felt that she was close to hers. She was seeing less and less of David and was bitterly aware that he was the sole begetter of the whole situation. "He *could* stop it," Patsy told herself, "but he doesn't seem to want to."

David is unequivocal about this period in his life. "The whole post-Carnaby thing, I really did think I was 'Jack the Lad.' I did it all, and I had it all. Now, if I met the person I was then, I'd loathe him," he says bitterly. "I fell out with most of my clients. There was a feeling around I was just using them, and they were absolutely right. I became a very unpleasant person."

Patsy was losing confidence in herself. Everyone around her seemed to be doing something except her. She felt like a sponge for everything that was coming at her. A whole new world had opened up from which she felt shut out, typified by the "swing-

ing '60s" scene that danced, unbidden, nightly through her par-
lor. She could feel her life and her marriage gradually beginning to unravel.

She had been brought up in a family where everything had
been orderly and methodical; now she found herself in the middle of a maelstrom, running a household that had become a kind
of halfway house for David's clients, or their girlfriends, or for
anyone who was part of that scene. Patsy felt she was expected
to be a mother not only to David's children but to all his friends
as well.

As Debbie, who was still very young then, remembers, "I'd
sometimes go downstairs for no particular reason late at night,
maybe a glass of water or something, and there was this little
marble table in the kitchen big enough to sit and have a cup of
tea at. Mum would often be sitting there talking to someone
who'd be doing their heart-on-the-table act. She mothered everybody, she was always there. Dad was rarely at home for any
length of time—we really were brought up by our mother in a
very straightforward way, despite the fact we lived in such an
unconventional house."

One day, a friend of David's stopped by for a word at the
office. "Make it quick, I'm in a hurry," David snapped, scrib-
bling away at his notes. "All right, I'll make it quick," his friend
replied. "Are you aware, or even particularly concerned, that if
you carry on as you're doing, there might not be a family to go
back home to?"

David paused and put his pen down, then looked up at his
friend. "What the fuck are you talking about?"

"You and Patsy. And take that edge out of your voice. Listen
to me as a *friend.* You're going to lose her, David, if you carry on
as you're doing."

"Go on."

"She can't see past you at the moment, mate, but that's not
going to last much longer unless you start to bring her into
things more. Take her along with you and stop playing the
field, or someone's going to nab that girl."

David stared at his friend, trying hard to remember that he *was* his friend.

"I know it," he finally admitted quietly. "Only I don't allow myself to think about it. Isn't that stupid?"

"For an otherwise pretty sharp cookie, yes, it is," his friend agreed. "Patsy is one hell of an attractive girl, David. It's only a matter of time before someone makes a move unless you start now to make her a full partner in your marriage. Look, David, call it the old antennae, call it what you will. *My* lesson had to be learned the hard way, and I think enough of you as a bloke not to stand idly by and watch history repeat itself."

"If I can help it," David vowed, "it won't."

His friend's counseling left David in a turmoil. "I'm absolutely going to lose everything," he convinced himself. He wanted to talk to Patsy quickly, but he held back for a few days, inventing all sorts of excuses for not taking the plunge. Finally he admitted that it was only the fear of failure that was stopping him. He began to focus specifically on the following Friday evening for what he saw as the make-or-break discussion. When the kids were safely in bed, he promised himself, that would be the time.

On the fateful day, he worked steadily through the considerable work load that he had to finish before the weekend break. Then at four came a call from Germany to say that one of his clients was in transit from Frankfurt and could David arrange to have him picked up at the airport and join him for dinner later? "Fine," David heard himself say mechanically. "The Dorchester at eight-thirty? Fine, no problem." Here was a perfect example of his good intentions being temporarily thwarted, he told himself as he picked up the phone to call home.

"Patsy? Just to let you know I'll be back late tonight, so don't wait up for me."

There was no reply.

"Patsy?"

"I heard you, David," she said quietly. "I'll see you at breakfast, then."

After dinner with his client that evening, David quietly

opened the front door at Ranelagh Grove and made to go up-stairs. He noticed that someone appeared to have left the light on in the kitchen and tiptoed over to put it out. He froze when he saw Patsy sitting at the marble table, an empty cup of tea in front of her. Her head was buried in her hands. She was sobbing quietly; then when she heard him approach, she started.

"Oh, Patsy, I'm so sorry," he said.

"It's not your fault," she told him. "Business comes first."

"Not anymore," he said. Then to her amazement he got up and took the telephone extension off the hook.

"What on earth are you doing?" she asked incredulously.

"I want to talk to my wife," David replied with a nervous smile. "I've been an idiot, Patsy," he continued as he seated himself opposite her at the little table and gently squeezed her hands. "But everybody in life deserves a second chance. From now on I'm going to change, because if I lose you, I've lost everything, and I can't let that happen."

"There have been offers—" Patsy stammered bemusedly, not quite knowing what else to say.

"Really?" he asked.

"—one in particular, but none that I entertained for one split second."

"Patsy, I'll do whatever's necessary. My priorities have been idiotically wrong. Jack the Lad's finished."

"David"—Patsy grasped her husband's hands in hers—"I don't care what you do. I understand you're a creative man. You've got more energy than anyone else I've ever met, but you must understand one thing about me if we're going to go the course. I need to be with you every step of the way, not as an afterthought. I don't care what risks you take, I don't care what hardships we go through, but you have to take me with you in every way. I'm not bothered about anything else, I mean anything, but we have to get our lives back together again once and for all."

In that moment David's mind became crystal clear. He had become so full of self-loathing at the agency, it had distorted his judgment. He realized that now was the time to make the break and do what he had wanted to all along.

Patsy saw that at the photographers' agency David was enjoying the youth he had never had. She could see how tied down he had felt, having risen to his obligations and responsibilities at the age of twenty. He had been knocked sideways by what was happening at the agency, by the swirling hedonism that was going on around him and by the temptations constantly thrown in his path.

For Patsy the episode brought to her the realization that she did have a vote after all, that she was not a complete nonperson, as she had begun to think. As the weeks and months passed, she found that David followed through in a multitude of ways that would have seemed unimaginable before. With this, the clouds of her sense of inadequacy slowly began to lift. She was eventually able to look back even on the appendicitis episode with a smile. "My God, he'll phone me twenty times a day now to make sure I'm all right. But *then*—!

"He realized eventually that everything I said, rightly or wrongly, was how I saw it. I had no ax to grind, I wasn't making points, I had nothing to win or lose with the advice I was giving. I would never tell him something was good if I didn't think so, not then, not now, because I think he's better than that. I've always treated him like that, because I've always felt him to be very special. I still do, I really do think he's extraordinary."

If there are six requisites for a happy marriage, Patsy learned, the first is faith and the remaining five are confidence. The couple was back from the brink.

3

The first experience Sanford "Sandy" Lieberson had of the entertainment business was as a press agent in the United States. He had rakish good looks and tremendous enthusiasm, engagingly laced with just a hint of soulful larceny— qualities that were endearing. These attributes, plus his desire to succeed and to have some fun at the same time, had brought Sandy into the film and entertainment business.

Sandy first met David Puttnam in 1965, when the CMA Agency, later merged with International Creative Management (ICM), decided it wanted to open an office in England. Sandy agreed to run the London office for a limited period of time and moved there in 1965, becoming the agent for the Rolling Stones. It was at this time that David's Avedon Beatles posters were being touted. At their first encounter, Puttnam and Lieberson felt drawn to each other because of the mutuality and the duality of their interests. David didn't know it then, but he had finally met the catalyst he had been looking for to take him into the movie business.

Sandy was constantly astonished by the low quality of the individuals he came across in the British film business. "There's so many idiots making movies," it once occurred to him, "I might as well have a go at it myself." He began by producing a film with clients that he himself represented—co-directors Donald Cammell and Nicolas Roeg, Mick Jagger of the Rolling Stones, and James Fox. The film was called *Performance,* and distribution was to be handled by Warners. That studio, however, was unhappy with the rushes. Warners' unhappiness had nothing to do with the quality of the film, which on its release was reckoned by many to be both brilliant and the quintessential 1960s movie, but rather with a feeling that the whole thing was somehow totally immoral, as well as—the even more cardinal sin—totally uncommercial.

Sandy's next venture was to be *Mary, Queen of Scots,* with director Alexander Mackendrick. Unfortunately, Universal was in the middle of management changes and the movie was canceled. With *Performance* still in trouble at Warners, followed by the cancellation of *Mary* (for which stars Mia Farrow and Oliver Reed had been lined up), life swiftly became something of a nightmare for Sandy. When he had to relinquish the rights to *Mary,* Hal Wallis picked them up and produced the movie. Sandy was well and truly stranded. He was resourceful and resilient, but undeniably stranded.

Meanwhile, having resolved to leave the photographers' agency and pursue his ambition of breaking into movies, David joined his two colleagues Ross Cramer and Charles Saatchi in forming Cramer Puttnam Saatchi.

"We're going to get into the film industry," they told an astonished Alan Parker, who retorted, "Don't be stupid!"

"And you're going to write us a couple of scripts," they added.

"But I've never written anything longer than thirty seconds in my life."

"That doesn't matter, Alan. Look, we believe in you. We know you can do it, and we're going to try and sell it!"

They visited New York in an attempt to raise money. Alan remembers their return and Charles's disillusionment with the film business. "I'm going to open an advertising agency," he told Alan, and so he did. (Charles Saatchi today co-owns with his brother Maurice the world's largest advertising agency.) David, however, became even more serious about succeeding as a filmmaker. To make himself look more serious, he grew a beard, which he saw as suiting his new film-producer image. His next move was to phone Sandy Lieberson and invite him over for a meeting to discuss the possibility of a collaboration.

Eventually in the late 1960s they agreed upon a partnership aimed at making things happen, an association later summed up eloquently by friends as: Sandy brought the phone book, David supplied the cash. Sandy did indeed have the contacts, and David did have a little over £30,000 to invest in films. They dubbed their joint entity Visual Programmes Systems (VPS)/Goodtimes Enterprises Production Company. (*Performance* had been Sandy's first Goodtimes enterprise on his own.) David's hope was that the photographers' agency, of which he retained 60 percent ownership, would keep them in funds while they made their first tentative steps into film production. Through a complicated series of events, the two men finally secured financing through Rothschilds for a company that was to develop film projects, but that also might take advantage of any other opportunities that arose.

Despite his ambition to break into movies, David actually felt at this point that there was no real long-term future in mainstream movie-making. However, since movie-making was the side of the company that Rothschilds decided should be pursued in the interests of cash flow, David went back to Alan Parker. Between the two of them, they came up with the idea for a film called *Melody*, a love story of two young kids who meet at school. "We had also acquired the rights to seven Bee

Gees songs, and I had to incorporate them into this story," Alan recalls. After a few false starts, they managed to get the necessary backing from U.S. Seagram's boss, Edgar Bronfman, who put up $400,000 of the budget. The British firm Hemdale, which was run by David Hemmings and John Daly, added another $200,000; it was their first movie venture.

Alan Parker remembers a meeting at David's house with *Melody*'s production manager and first assistant director to discuss the film's production. Since Alan had previously been involved with commercials, David had invited him to the session to help out. "He sat down and went through the schedule and the budget with such assurance and thoroughness, like someone who'd been doing it for thirty years, with absolutely instant, intuitive understanding of every detail of the process. When the two of them finally left, he leaned over to me and said, 'It's a good way to learn, isn't it?' "

David produced *Melody*, with Ron Kass as executive producer, and Waris Hussein was chosen to direct (following his film, *A Touch of Love*, which David had seen and enjoyed). He also signed *Touch of Love*'s photographer, Peter Suschitsky. Alan took the second unit camera for *Melody* and filmed some of the activities going on in the center of the field for a school sports day scene. Although the filming lasted for only a day, Alan admits, "I did get carried away at the long jump and got the directing bug for the first time!" At that point in his career, Alan had never directed anything, not even commercials. It occurred to David that perhaps Alan's talents lay there as well as in writing.

Melody opened in the States in 1971, just one week before its British debut, to good reviews but nonexistent business. In Britain, the film was dreadfully renamed *S.W.A.L.K. (Sealed with a Loving Kiss)* by the Boultings' British Lion distributors. This time it was largely attacked by the critics, and again it did no business.

They resigned themselves to a financial flop with their first venture. But then unexpected good news came to Goodtimes: the film had gone through the roof in Japan following its sale at

Cannes to Nippon Herald Films. David visited Tokyo for the second time and was greeted by yet another windfall. The negotiator of the Japanese contract had awarded Goodtimes a percentage of the Japanese *gross* revenues, rather than the *net* they had expected. The resulting checks from Japan kept Sandy and David solvent for some time to come.

Nippon Herald had an enormous success with *Melody*, selling an astonishing three million tickets. The soundtrack album nestled at number one on the Japanese charts for months. The film was reissued soon after and has been in almost continuous circulation ever since. David was greeted at Nippon Herald by the company president, Mr. Furukawa. He was introduced to Furukawa's young assistant, Hara San, who is now one of the most respected names in Japanese movie-making and distribution. An enduring friendship was formed.

David basked in the Japanese success of *Melody*. It was a modest start, yet he had gotten his feet wet and the fledgling Goodtimes had taken its first faltering steps. "*Melody* was what it was," Alan Parker summarizes—"a beginning for all of us."

A beginning it was, but David knew that it still would be a long time—if ever—before he could begin to emulate the great filmmakers whose movies had made such an impression on him over the years. He regarded Fred Zinnemann, Elia Kazan, and Stanley Kramer as having dealt with the big issues and as having forged searing yet recognizable aspects of life into films that probed and illuminated the problems of the little man—and always in an entertaining way. Apart from his father's influence, David was aware that much of the ethical basis in his life had been implanted by these films. He had wanted to *be* Montgomery Clift in Zinnemann's *The Search* and James Dean in Kazan's *East of Eden*. Although these pictures were critical of society, to David they illustrated the infinite American capacity for hopefulness, a quality that held great appeal for him both as a man and as a filmmaker.

As a new producer on the British film scene, David was flattered even then to be singled out for press attention. How did he account for the measure of success he had so far achieved?

"Well, I'm thirty," he said, "which is an incredibly good age to be at the present moment, it's perfect timing. Then I've always been married, so I've never had to go out chasing after birds. When you're single, that's all you do. I hear blokes in the office constantly on the phone fixing themselves up for the night and all that. Their lives revolve around it."

For Goodtimes' next venture, David and Sandy decided to attempt a version of the Pied Piper legend, a decision they would both later regret, although David would learn some valuable lessons. The financial deal was similar to that worked out on *Melody;* Seagram's and Hemdale putting up the cash. It was left then only to assemble the talent. A number of directors— among them Milos Forman, Jiri Menzel, and Fred Zinnemann —were approached before French director Jacques *(Umbrellas of Cherbourg)* Demy was signed to direct *The Pied Piper.*

A fine cast of English actors had been assembled to support Scottish folk singer Donovan Leitch in the title role, including Donald Pleasence, Jack Wild, Diana Dors, John Hurt, and Sir Michael Hordern, together with two hundred rats, on whom $7,000 was expended. The money committed to the project was dependent on Donovan's participation, and he was squeezing the film in between absolutely unalterable tour dates, so it was essential that the film start on schedule. If the movie failed to go ahead, all the money Goodtimes had spent on development would be lost. It was this pressure that led to the decision to go ahead with Demy as director.

From the outset, Demy questioned everything in the script. It was the first time writer Andrew Birkin had been offered actual payment for writing, and so he tried to be extremely accommodating to the director. The script soon arrived at the stage, however, where it was no longer the picture Andrew had set out to write. He had envisioned the film as being light on the surface and dark underneath, but Demy seemed to want change for the sake of change and the whole thing to be much more sentimental. Eventually Andrew had had enough. To David he declared, "I just can't work with Demy. For the sake of the project and my sanity, it's better we part company." Since Demy had more or less delivered the same ultimatum, there was no contest. Andrew went.

But when David introduced Jacques to Donovan, the whole affair really turned ugly. Demy seemed to lose faith completely in Andrew's original screenplay, then became more and more dismissive of Donovan's songs. Of ten that were submitted, Demy said he cared for only two of them. As the production lurched along, Demy changed it from a script-led film to a production designer's movie. Soon Andrew's script, which David had considered dense but extremely playable, had gone by the board. David stood by. He realized he was watching a disaster in the making, but he had not the faintest notion how to stop it.

For the first time, David was in the unhappy position of having a film run away from him. *Melody* had been an easy shoot, but by the same token had earned him no spurs. On *The Pied Piper*, at least, some lessons had been learned and some spurs had been earned.

In late 1971, David and Patsy rented a Soho preview theater and ran the film for a group of close friends to mark their tenth wedding anniversary. After the final credits rolled, the lights went up in the little theater. Alan Parker rose to his feet. "That's the worst film I've ever seen," he muttered. Photographer Terence Donovan, a friend, but never a client of David's was shocked at Alan's tactlessness, taking the view that such criticism was inappropriate for the occasion, but David accepted his friend's outburst philosophically. ("He was right," he said later. "It *is* a piece of shit.")

In the United States, Paramount initially planned a Christmas 1971 release for what it perceived as a children's fable. But when Paramount executives viewed the finished movie, there was a swift change of mind. It finally surfaced eight months later in 1972 as the bottom half of a double bill in a few playdates.

The film's varnished tones and doom-laden scenario, which included not only the swarming rats but poverty, infanticide, and the Black Death, baffled most reviewers, who wondered for whom this alleged children's fable had ever been intended.

The failure of *The Pied Piper* was a bitter pill for David to swallow, and it taught him a lesson he was never to forget. He had been made to compromise on his choice of director and had hired someone who was established on the international market and of whom he was somewhat in awe. Intimidated by Demy's reputation, he had given in to him every step of the way. David vowed that in the future as producer he would remain in charge of each project, for the alternative would be one disastrous compromise after another.

Thoroughly disabused of any commercial hopes for the film, Goodtimes hoped that Hemdale would shelve it completely and save the company the embarrassment of a press showing in Britain. Unfortunately, four months after its U.S. opening, Hemdale took it down from the shelf in time for Christmas 1972. The critics were merciless.

It was clearly time for the Goodtimes partners to move on, their heads bloody but unbowed. In 1971, at the time *The Pied Piper* had completed production, David had been already running pellmell after a third property, whose scale dwarfed anything the company had tackled before. *Melody,* and even *The Pied Piper,* would look like easy calls beside the monumental problems *Inside the Third Reich* would provide.

4

Despite his horrific experience on *The Pied Piper*, Andrew Birkin latched on to another project he thought would make a fascinating film, one that he wanted to make with Puttnam. The inspiration was an interview with Albert Speer in *Playboy* magazine in which the author of *Inside the Third Reich* expanded openly on how he had joined the Nazi Party as a young man. A product of the middle class, not particularly a Nazi and not particularly a Communist, Speer had recognized that he was only a second-rate talent as an architect and that if he were going to succeed, he would need a patron.

At dinner one evening with David, Andrew declared that he had just found the subject he wanted to do next. "So have I," replied David. Then they both produced the same issue of *Playboy* and the Speer interview. The same point in the interview had struck both David and Andrew, the point where Speer stated, "The following day I joined what became the Nazi Party and a week later it was my twenty-third birthday." David had thought, "To spend the rest of your life haunted by a decision you made at twenty-three . . ." That interested him very much, for he had always wanted to make a film about second chances in life.

When Speer's book was brought to Sandy Lieberson's attention, it made a tremendous impression on him as well. "I saw it as an amazing revelation about Nazi Germany," he says. "It was the first thing I'd ever read that brought into focus the mentality behind the Nazi movement and the fascists. There was nothing I'd ever been exposed to that had such a powerful effect on me, particularly being Jewish. We all of us ended up with a passion to make a movie of Speer's book."

With Andrew engaged to write the screenplay, the three associates flew to Germany and talked with Speer's publishers. Then David and Andrew flew to Heidelberg to see Speer himself, to discuss their hopes of adapting his book for the screen. Every major company in the world had also made a bid for the book, it seemed, but Speer selected Goodtimes.

The acquisition was a great coup for the small company. David swore he could feel the earth move under his feet. Could they rise to the occasion? While Andrew developed his script, David hammered out a deal with Paramount—for a fee of $150,000, Goodtimes would produce the film for worldwide release. This represented the first whiff of big money for the team, together with an awesome responsibility.

In the process of script development, David and Andrew came to know Speer well, and a rather close working relationship developed among the men. Certainly the two Englishmen came to understand Speer and to sympathize with him—perhaps too much.

When the finished script was delivered, Paramount was divided between those who thought they had a wonderful project and those who considered the film either anti-Semitic or at the very least "soft on the Nazis." Andrew contended that he had tried to reflect Speer's point of view that if Hitler were painted as the devil, no one would recognize other Hitlers as they came along, since they were only human beings and not necessarily given to chewing carpets. In an effort to gain support, Andrew proudly submitted his script to film director Carol Reed, his cousin and mentor.

"Andrew," Reed told him on the phone, "it's wonderful, you've done a wonderful job. You've shown us what it was like to live in the Depression after the Great War, inflation rampant and the rest of it, and this young man, with his head full of dreams, meeting Hitler. They plan for a new Germany to-gether—it's just tremendous and it's all going so well for them too, it's all going *so* well—and then tragedy! They lose the war."

Andrew felt his balloon well and truly punctured. David shared his concern, for they both realized the enormous respon-sibility they were carrying, not only financially but morally as well. Then there was the problem of finding a suitable director. Stanley Kubrick, with whom Andrew Birkin had worked on *2001,* was approached—and declined. He obviously felt it was an impossible subject, for how indeed did one arrive at the right approach?

After Kubrick, the man everyone except Paramount was most enthusiastic about was Nicolas Roeg, who had codirected Sandy Lieberson's earlier *Performance.* At a meeting with David, Roeg seemed to favor a Bertolucci-esque approach. Paramount plumped for the safer choice of Peter Yates, who would give a somewhat more pedestrian reading of the project, while David fought to have Constantin Costa-Gavras considered. This idea was squelched after six months, when Costa-Gavras himself lost his enthusiasm.

David's intuition had for some time been telling him that the film was losing favor at Paramount. It was off the boil, no longer the hottest subject around—or perhaps it was too hot. It was one of those pictures that never had an actual death knell. There never was a particular time when anyone said the project was shelved, but time passed without a resolution to the mani-fold problems.

In the end, the option on the book simply ran out. David

regretted the loss of what could have been a reputation-making project and the enthusiasm that had sustained him daily since first reading the *Playboy* interview. For Andrew, the demise of the project represented his second failure with David. Many of his friends uncharitably suggested that he had been taken advantage of by Puttnam, then dumped, first on *The Pied Piper* and then on *Inside the Third Reich*. The fact that in the process Andrew had risen from gofer for Stanley Kubrick to an accredited and respected screenwriter appeared to have been somewhat overlooked. Andrew's own feeling was that although David may have seduced, it was no case of rape. As a mark of the esteem in which David held Andrew, he now offered him a guaranteed £10,000 a year to write two scripts. Ultimately Andrew declined, opting for a quicker, more lucrative rewrite project, but the breach was at least somewhat mended.

Despite their loss of the rights to the book itself, David and Sandy were nonetheless determined to make something at least of the research material they had come up with during the long delays on *Inside the Third Reich*. When Paramount behaved impeccably and handed over their $150,000, it was decided to use the money to produce two documentaries. This was because two directors had been involved in the research, Lutz Becker and Philippe Mora; although they got along, each wanted to make his own film. Moreover, there was far too much material garnered for a single project. Both of the films that were eventually made, *The Double-Headed Eagle* and *Swastika*, were widely praised and ultimately proved to be very successful ventures. With the money Goodtimes realized from the two films, it commissioned another documentary, *Brother, Can You Spare a Dime?*, from Philippe Mora, covering the Great Depression of the 1930s. It turned out to be another fine piece of work.

Next, David and Sandy were approached by Tony Elliott, who ran the London listings magazine, *Time Out*. With the advent of nightly TV and instant news, the old Movietone and Pathé newsreels shown in the theaters had disappeared. Elliott's idea was to produce for theatrical release a *Time Out* newsreel, something along the lines of the old *March of Time* series, tackling subjects the media normally shied away from. The proposed first subject was internment in Northern Ireland.

Again, Andrew Birkin was brought aboard, this time to handle research and to co-produce. One noteworthy and telling event occurred when David accompanied Andrew in covering a march in protest of conditions in the McGilligan internment camp. On the march, David got into a heated argument with a Royal Ulster Constabulary (RUC) man, who ordered him back in line. David stood up to the officer, by now ominously beating time into his palm with his billy club. He was a citizen of the United Kingdom, David pointed out, and there was no law that said he couldn't stand there—he wasn't going to budge.

Andrew could scarcely believe his eyes and ears when he saw this new side to David, utterly defiant and fearless. He felt both intensely proud of him and sick with fear at the same time. He saw the officer take in David's *Time Out* press badge—not the RUC's favorite—and groaned inwardly. All he could think was "Back off, David. For God's sake, back off!" Luckily, the officer's attention was diverted then by a scuffle taking place farther down the line and the incident passed off, leaving David white-faced and shaking with rage and Andrew even whiter and shaking with relief and admiration.

Unfortunately, the footage garnered for the film proved less exciting than they had hoped. When it was finally released theatrically, *Bringing It All Back Home*, as the film was called, proved a disappointment. Plans for other *Time Out* ventures were shelved.

The next film in which the rather unlucky combination of Andrew and David was involved was a proposed remake of *The Secret Garden*. For this, Andrew again wrote the script. David was very enthusiastic and threw his full support behind it, but the project foundered when MGM announced it had a claim to the story and threatened a lawsuit if Goodtimes proceeded.

Although the failure of their projects together had been neither man's fault, Andrew still felt a certain distancing from

David. It reminded him a little of a story the author of *Inside the Third Reich* had told him. "Speer told me that he might join a line of ten people on any given morning waiting to see the Führer. If he had a roll of architect's plans in his hand and Hitler saw them, he would summon him to the head of the line, treating him with especial favor. When Speer became armaments minister or was slightly out of favor, he just had to join the line. He still got the half hour of the Führer's time, but it wasn't the same. That was rather the way with David, and I imagine remains the way. If it's something that's his number-one project at the time, you get to jump the line, whereas if he's moved to something else, he's still very kind and polite but you join the line."

For Andrew the bottom line with David is this: "I criticize him sometimes, yes, and we haven't always seen eye to eye. But if someone else criticizes him in my presence, I leap to his defense!"

Sandy reestablished contact with a London lawyer he had once worked with at CMA and asked him to represent Goodtimes. Frank Bloom agreed and was immediately struck by Puttnam's presence.

"When I first met David," says Frank, "he obviously loved being a film producer, and was in love with the *idea* of being a film producer. I'm not sure he ever structured his career, setting out with any positive ideas or goals. What he had instead was boundless, infectious enthusiasm and the energy to carry his ideas through."

Once they were in business together, Frank discovered that David was also an extremely competent desk man, as well as a stickler for formalities. Frank's law firm was sending a plethora of letters to Goodtimes on expensively printed stationery, replete with full lists of partners and other recurrent data. Frank suggested to David that they devise a plain memo-pad system to use instead. "He wouldn't hear of it," says Frank, laughing, "reckoning the idea was cold and unfeeling. He loved the pomp and circumstance of the prestige letter-heading."

Still searching for that elusive mainstream hit, David gave Alan Parker a choice of two sources from which to develop scripts. One was a book, *Calf Love;* the other was a song, "1941," from a Nilsson album. Alan chose *Calf Love*. Early in 1972, when a young writer called Ray Connolly stopped by to borrow a book on Elvis that he needed, David found that Ray knew and liked the Nilsson album, and "1941" in particular.

"Okay, you're a writer," he said. "Do you want to take a crack at writing the film?"

Ray looked at him disbelievingly and replied, "That'll be the day."

"That'll do for the title," David retorted.

5

Now that David was in films, he seemed to have even less time with his family than before. The saving grace was that he was happy, doing what he wanted to do—and Patsy was involved in his every decision.

On the home front, however, most decision making was left to Patsy. She would explain patiently to him that they only had a year and a half to go on their lease; then a year; then that they really had to think about a move. Finally she decided they had to buy a house. The problem was that every time some money came in, David wanted to buy the rights to another book or something. In the end, Patsy had to say, "Look, I need a bit of that!" Then she set off to find their first real home.

What she found was a "handyman's delight" in South Kensington, an old wreck that she personally set about renovating.

Patsy reckons that the scene on the day of the move from

Pimlico sums up David's level of involvement. She had had the movers in and was as organized as she could be. David was about to depart for three months to the Isle of Wight to work on *That'll Be the Day.*

David sat in their bedroom, deeply engrossed in a phone call. Patsy told the movers to clear every other room first. When they finally had nothing left but the bedroom, David was still on the phone.

"Excuse me, ma'am—we've got to go in there now," they appealed to Patsy.

"Okay, take everything except the bed. Take the dressing table, then the chairs."

Slowly the men removed each item of furniture as David, on the phone the whole time, moved from chair to chair to bed. Either he moved or the men moved him, until everything else was gone except the bed.

"Ma'am, we've got to take the bed now," they told Patsy, who nodded hesitantly, then watched as they delicately picked up the pillows. As soon as they began to move the bed itself, David got up, staring at them as if they had just broken into the house. In his best North London cockney, the phone still held in his hand, he yelled, *"Wot's* happening here? Wot *is* going on?"

" 'Bye, David," Patsy said, watching her husband return to his phone conversation. She and the children then got into the van with the movers and drove to their new home. There she helped with the unloading. David locked up the house and left for the Isle of Wight. It was the last Patsy saw of him for two months.

That'll Be the Day became a very personal project both for David and for writer Ray Connolly. Both men shaped key characters in their own younger images, and events in the story were largely autobiographical.

Sandy and David were able to raise financing for the project from Nat Cohen of EMI Films and from Ronco, the record company. To secure the latter's participation, David had to guarantee to feature a minimum number of rock classics on the soundtrack, which Ronco could then release on a double album. Ronco, flush with cash from its compilations of 1940s and 1950s music, agreed and added a further guarantee of a minimum sum that they would spend on cross-promotion of the album and movie. David and Ray went through the script, marking it wherever they could put a record player or a radio in the scene. Characters took to wandering along beaches and through fairgrounds—*anything* to squeeze in the necessary tracks.

Pop star David Essex was hired to play the self-confessed Puttnam role of the school dropout trying to make his way in the world, and Ringo Starr was cast as the streetwise friend he encounters. A director new to films, Claude Whatham, was hired to pilot what had become an extremely personal Puttnam project. In many ways, it was too personal a vision for David simply to have stood back and watch someone else interpret it. And this was David's first mainstream film since the *Pied Piper* fiasco—he had sworn never to allow a situation like that to develop again. David and Whatham did have differences, and at one point Alan Parker was called in to handle a couple of days' shooting for the ailing director.

When the film was in the can and with his producer's muscles well and truly flexed, David found that he had underspent. Proudly he went back to Nat Cohen and handed him a check. "What's this?" demanded the doughty Nat. "It's money we saved on the budget," David explained. Nat handed him the check back. "I allocated the full amount for *That'll Be the Day*. Use it for some aspect of the movie—its promotion, whatever you choose."

That Goodtimes was on the verge of its biggest success was confirmed in 1973 when the film opened to good reviews. The movie's success was heightened by the release and TV promotion of Ronco's double album of soundtrack hits—the company went on to sell over 600,000 units. Despite a disappointing lack of business in the United States, *That'll Be the Day* went on to yield a net profit of over £400,000 against a cost of less than £300,000.

"They'll demand a sequel," David informed Ray before

That'll Be the Day had even opened. Three weeks after the première, Nat Cohen called David. "This film of yours is *unbelievable*," he told him. "It's doing more business the third week
than it did in the first. What about a sequel?"

David would stand outside the ABC Theater on Shaftesbury
Avenue on Friday nights and buy up any remaining seats, for
he had found out that the manager notified only "sold out"
houses to the head office. The head office's method of judging
the following week's bookings and level of promotion was
based on the Thursday- and Friday-night returns, so if a house
sold out on those nights, the film was retained for another
week, with additional advertising money. For weeks after making this discovery, David would spend £20 or so to ensure a
"sold out" return. He regarded it as money well spent. On one
occasion he took Ray along to the ABC just to view the lines of
patrons. Gesturing at the crowd, he turned to his friend and
said, "I've waited four years for this sight, Ray." At last David
Puttnam felt himself master of his own destiny. If the jury had
hitherto been out on his ability to succeed in films, after *That'll
Be the Day* the verdict was in.

David and Ray continued to work together on the movie's
sequel, *Stardust.* Ray acknowledges that working with David on
these two films was unlike any other experience he has had
with producers. So many ideas came tumbling out of David
that even if Ray knocked several of them back, there were
plenty to spare and no offense was taken. The credit on both
films, Ray reckons, should read, "Story by Ray Connolly and
David Puttnam."

Their first choice to direct *Stardust* was Alan Parker, but he
turned it down in favor of Jack Rosenthal's play *The Evacuees*,
which he directed for television in 1973. They then went back
to the man who actually had been their first choice for *That'll Be
the Day*, Michael Apted. They had admired his work on the big
screen with *Triple Echo* and on television in various productions.

David Essex was again signed to play the lead role, but Ringo
Starr declined a part in the sequel. "I lived through it," he told
David. "I don't want to act it."

David turned his sights on ex–pop singer Adam Faith after watching him play a small-time cockney crook on television in *Budgie.* Eventually Faith was signed, but David had to overcome initial opposition from Connolly, Apted, and the film's backers. It was David's fight all the way—another sign of his distinctive vision and of his determination to do things in such a way as to fulfill that vision.

A third major role in the film was that of an unscrupulous American manager. Larry Hagman was eventually signed, playing the part of Texan Porter Lee Austin. Hagman later credited this role as leading directly to his being cast as J. R. Ewing in the *Dallas* television series.

Stardust went on to make a net profit of over half a million pounds against costs of about the same, despite another disappointing U.S. outing. Critics on both continents, however, were enthusiastic in their praise of the film, many of them singling out Adam Faith's performance for special commendation.

For David, *Stardust* was much more than just a look back at the era he had lived through. He had seized an opportunity to emulate his filmmaking heroes, who had often taken supposedly exploitative subjects, and imbued them with revealing insights that illuminated particular eras of contemporary history. It was extremely brave of him to make *Stardust,* which had double the budget of *That'll Be the Day* and eschewed many of the elements that normally spell "smash hit" in favor of a deeper, bleaker statement. David had done it again.

And if he had been fortunate in achieving two hit films in a row in his own country, he was also fortunate in other respects according to the friend who had given him the benefit of his marital experience. "His finally getting into movies saved him —yes, *together* with Patsy's tolerance and influence. When he came to his senses, she was still there for him."

Now Goodtimes began to expand in all directions, going into production, distribution, movies, video, and television. It was truly multifaceted, with an ever-increasing staff and ever-increasing overhead. The name *David Puttnam* on a movie began to have real meaning.

6

Goodtimes now planned a series of six films, each to be based on the life of a musician. They would start with Gustav Mahler and go on to include George Gershwin, Franz Liszt, and Ralph Vaughan Williams. The director for the entire projected series would be the controversial "enfant terrible" of the British movie industry, Ken Russell, known for his flamboyant—some would say "vulgar" and "excessive"—style. Russell's greatest success had been *Women in Love,* but he had already dealt with musicians and composers in programs for British television, a series that had not proved to everyone's taste.

When a complicated finance package collapsed on the first day of shooting and the National Film Finance Corporation withdrew its support, *Mahler*'s budget had to be slashed from £400,000 to £180,000. "Ken was wonderful," says David. "He made the film for less than half the budget we'd planned, he was superb."

The British critics, however, did not find the movie anything like superb when VPS/Goodtimes handled the release on its own in 1974. To David's acute embarrassment, Russell Davies wrote in the *Observer:* "What Ken Russell needs is someone to say nay to him occasionally." The clear implication was that David was too much of a bantamweight to make an impression on the likes of Ken Russell.

David defends the film to this day. "I happen to like *Mahler.* I think it's good," he insists. "Not flawless, but a bloody good picture. Given what Ken put on screen for £180,000, a remarkable piece of work."

When David heard that the president of 20th Century-Fox wanted to see the movie, he excitedly jumped on the first plane for Los Angeles, clutching the precious reels of film. He drove straight from the airport to the studio and arrived five minutes late, to find the president and his colleagues already seated in the screening room. "We ran it," says David, "and it turned out that the guy was just a big Mahler fan who wanted to show the movie to some friends. I'd thought of course that he wanted to *buy* the bloody thing. It was the most dreadful disappointment —a good example of why I sometimes get bitter." Dejected, he caught the first flight home the next day.

An agent named Robert Littman negotiated the deal for the U.S. release of *Mahler.* Bobby had been keen to finance *Melody* in the late 1960s in his capacity as head of MGM in Europe, but the idea had been quashed by the head office. He had moved to Columbia, where he had helped set up the *Stardust* deal for David, then branched out as an independent agent based in Hollywood in 1974.

Mahler's U.S. outing was brief. If the British reviews had been bad, the American verdict was even harsher, led by critic John Simon in *Esquire.* "Collectors of supreme cinematic monstrosities," he railed, "had better keep a sharp lookout for Ken Russell's *Mahler,* which may yet set a quick disappearance record even for a Russell film. This one surpasses *The Music Lovers* and *The Devils*, though in sheer loathsomeness it may fall just a bit short of that emetic duo. The film is of such demented and rotten taste that I do not wish to waste much space on it."

Amazingly, Goodtimes had the last laugh. "In the end *Mahler* was sold everywhere," says Sandy, "and made a tidy profit."

The life of George Gershwin was to be Russell's next outing, with Al Pacino hopefully cast as the composer, but Russell decided otherwise. He had filmed The Who's rock opera *Tommy* after *Mahler* and was full of his own ideas for the second Goodtimes venture, as David discovered to his cost. "He insisted he wanted to do Liszt next, with Roger Daltrey. We agreed. The problem is, he never really finished the screenplay and frankly, he just seemed to go off his rocker."

Rather like a host of a runaway party who is constantly running out of liquid refreshments, David had to beat a path to the liquor store in California no fewer than five times in twelve weeks in search of additional financing. "The film was rocketing over budget, and every time I got back from raising money, the budget had gone up again. I did my best, but it was a nightmare, impossible to keep up with."

Sandy watched as the unstoppable Russell continued. "It was such an unhappy experience for David and myself," he says, "and a real betrayal. He just went off the deep end. Instead of having the film taken over by the completion guarantor, we had to put up our own money to let Ken complete the film the way he wanted to. We decided we didn't want to work with him anymore after that."

The final cost of the *Lisztomania* folly was £1.2 million. *Mahler* had performed satisfactorily on its £180,000 budget, but £1.2 million was insupportable. The losses were significant, despite the Warners distribution deal Bobby Littman had negotiated for the film's U.S. release in 1975. Ironically, the process introduced David to a group of Warner executives, leading later to the "first-look" deal they struck with him at the end of the 1970s.

David had to swallow hard to rationalize the brush with director Russell. "My experience with Ken," he claims, "was a learning process. I learned in that job what I would have had no other way of acquiring—that no producer can afford the luxury of respecting a director overmuch. He was the most naturally gifted director I'd ever worked with, so far as the look of the film was concerned. When he was at his best, he was on the Himalayas, but too often he lost sight of the end to which all this had to be applied. I am a very old-fashioned boy. I believe in the text, the script, the blueprint. Ken took pride in his ability to juggle without these fundamental disciplines."

Once again, as in his Jacques Demy experience, David had allowed control of a film to slip through his fingers. The film was pure Russell, devoid of even the most modest Puttnam influence. Goodtimes was strained to the limit by the subsequent financial drain, although David insists, "It was a partnership I got a lot out of personally," then goes on to admit that his association with Russell "emotionally and financially crucified me."

Sandy was relieved beyond measure that they did not proceed with the George Gershwin project. "We were far better off not doing it," he explains, "because Russell's interpretation of Gershwin would have been so contentious, the man's personal life filled with innuendoes and suppositions. I'm sure it would have backfired—America would never have accepted that, we'd have been slaughtered."

Despite Patsy's interest in and contribution to David's business deals, there was one aspect of the business that he never discussed with her. "He knew that being a bank manager's daughter, I always worried about borrowing money and he never told me how much money it was costing us to finance our business until eventually he came to me and said, 'We're just not going forward, it's crazy.' Then I realized the extent of the burden he'd been carrying and kept to himself. I first read in an interview he gave how he sat in this hotel room in Hollywood and cried his eyes out. He couldn't leave because he couldn't justify having got there and staying there, and he couldn't afford to stay. Now, I never *knew* that. To this day, he doesn't believe in burdening his family when things go wrong."

An offer of a £30,000 advance from Chas Chandler, the manager of pop group Slade, encouraged Goodtimes, now in grave danger of becoming a misnomer, to produce *Slade in Flame*. David produced but never really became involved, making no secret of the fact that he was only doing it for the money. The film was well enough received but proved to be strictly for hard-core Slade fans.

Then followed a strange science-fiction fantasy hybrid, *The Final Programme*, based on a story by Michael Moorcock. The project was Sandy's idea, although David acted as executive producer. The film failed to find an audience at the time, although today it has something of a cult following.

David next went to work on a documentary with Ray Connolly, one that proved highly profitable considering its modest cost. *James Dean: The First American Teenager* was a natural for the two of them, for they were both fascinated by the late actor. Although making a documentary on their hero was fun, David and Ray got too near the real James Dean. "We both came to the conclusion that if we'd ever actually met him, we'd probably never have liked him," says David.

Once again, the job of selling the film in the United States was given to Bobby Littman, who sweated for months in 1976 to find a distributor. When he did, they paid more than the entire production had cost. "If I'd known how cheaply it had been made, I'd never have had the balls to ask for what I did," Bobby says, laughing. "David was desperate to get a deal and get some money in, but neither he nor I expected what we got."

David and Sandy continued to search for the mainstream-hit film that had eluded them since the heady days of *That'll Be the Day* and *Stardust*. They looked first at a property called *Trick or Treat*, a script written by Ray Connolly based on a novel he had published in 1974. It told the story of two lesbians who want to have a baby and how they become tragically involved with a married couple.

David recalls even the beginnings of the venture as an embarrassment. "What has never been said is that I turned it down when it was first written as a book, then while I was away on holiday, Sandy read it and really liked it. "Look," he said, "this is terrific," so it started off with this extraordinary awkwardness between me and Ray, because he knew I didn't like it and that Sandy did. So I stayed back. Not that it would have changed anything if I hadn't."

What followed was a disaster. Bianca Jagger, then the wife of Rolling Stone Mick Jagger, was hired to star in the film. On the strength of her name, financing was secured from EMI and Playboy; Michael Apted was brought in to direct; the production was moved to Rome for location shooting. Then Miss Jagger—due either to insecurity about her lack of film experience or to second thoughts about the nude scenes she had agreed to do—decided she wanted out of the film. In the end, *Trick or Treat* was abandoned, as were finally the ensuing lawsuits and counterlawsuits.

No one was happy with the fate of *Trick or Treat*, especially writer Ray Connolly. He had labored over it in one form or another for more than two years and lived with it until his removal from Rome. Did he hold David responsible for the way he was treated on the movie? "Yes, partly," he admits, "but we were all responsible for the damned thing, every one of us. I am, because I wrote it and never really got it right; Michael Apted couldn't control the actresses, so it was partly his fault. The trouble with David is, he did his job *too* well—he got the money too early, before we were ready to go. Then there was the small matter of Bewanker—sorry, Bianca. I did feel hurt by David because I felt he should have given me more support than he did when things were going badly wrong, but he didn't. That may be the *other* side of David.

"When you work with him, he seduces you and you think he's your very best friend. You're incredibly fond of each other, and you think this is wonderful, it's a great relationship. Then when things go wrong, he withdraws slightly and tends to lose interest a little bit, and if there's something else, he'll go off and do that. When *Trick or Treat* was falling apart, he had something else to go to. He senses the ground is shaky underneath him, and he's off, edging away. You feel really hurt because you've regarded him as your best friend. The truth is he's friendly, but he isn't your *best* friend. He's a producer and you're a writer or director, so when things go wrong, there's no answer, no way out, except animosity."

With the benefit of hindsight, David saw that *Trick or Treat* was a film that should never have been made. "We did it because there's this innate pressure on producers to produce. At the time, Sandy and I were in desperate straits for enough money just to pay the staff wage bill at Goodtimes, and we worked out that if we didn't collect the producer's fee for *Trick or Treat*, we couldn't keep going for another six months. Since we'd other things in the pipeline we thought were really worth making, we made it very much as an expedient picture. When it got into trouble in Rome, I made a very, very stupid error. I tried to be a Boy Scout and thought, having produced a few films, that if I went to Rome, it would be all right.

"When I got there, I quickly found I was dealing with an absolutely irreconcilable situation—an actress who didn't want to act in a lead role, and every other unfortunate thing happening. It would have been a clean and quick decision to have stopped at that point, but it took a long time to persuade the financiers that this could go on forever and could cost them an unlimited amount of money.

"If I were Ray, I'd feel exactly the way he feels, but I really don't think I had any alternative at all. You know, over the years there are certain people I really owe, and Ray is one of them. I've tried to repay my debt to him and I'd like to think that maybe I have, but there's no question, the time in my life I really needed help, he wrote two important films."

Soon after *Trick or Treat*'s conception, Sandy and David had come across another project as they sat in Lew Grade's outer office waiting for an appointment. Sandy had known Lew since his agency days and had asked for a meeting to see if they could work together. As they sat there, a mutual acquaintance, Peter Fetterman, emerged from Lew's office, clutching an armful of storyboards for a film Alan Parker wanted to do.

"Let's have a look at them, Peter," Sandy coaxed. After a

quick scrutiny he turned to David. "Jesus, why aren't *we* doing that?" he asked. "It's a great idea!"

"Well," David said, "Alan obviously wants to work on his own, otherwise he'd have brought it to us, so fuck him." Sandy looked at his partner in surprise, then grinned as he saw the smile on David's face. The storyboards were for *Bugsy Malone*.

7

The interview David and Sandy had with Lew Grade was a pleasant one, but no deals were made. Lew basically wanted people to deliver his projects, while David and Sandy were seeking backing for their own ideas. Since David had come across the *Bugsy Malone* project in Lew's outside office, he felt honorbound to take it back and offer it to the impresario. Grade again turned it down.

After *Melody*, Alan Parker had moved on to direct television commercials, and the hundreds he had turned out for his own Alan Parker Film Company had earned him a reputation as a keen scene-setter, with a sharp eye for period and character detail and a sly sense of humor. Not only that, but together with Hugh Hudson, Ridley Scott, and Adrian Lyne, Alan had completely revolutionized the small-screen commercial art form. Out went the pedestrian, cliched "You'll wonder where the yellow went" jingles; in came luminous images and minifeatures, using real people and real stories and using humor in a way that had never been put across before. It was a case of brain rather than brash, and in many instances the commercials were more interesting than the programs around them.

Alan's partner in the company, a no-nonsense cockney named Alan Marshall, had started in the film business as a messenger boy and had quickly gone on to cutting-room assistant, editor, then picture editor on commercials. He had produced commercials at Collet, Dickinson, and Pearce for a while, meeting David and Alan Parker there. "I wrote the *Bugsy* script as a pragmatic exercise to try to do an American subject," says Alan Parker. "Everything that I'd written up to that point kept coming back with a rubber stamp on it marked 'too parochial.' So I decided to take an American genre in order to make an American success. I didn't know about America, but I knew about American movies, so I took a gangster genre and an American musical and had this idea of maybe doing it all with children. I had four kids of my own, and I'd done a lot of work with kids. Alan Marshall and I had our own little company going, so I told David, with whom I'd become quite good friends at that point, that I badly wanted to do it on my own. We asked everybody, but I just couldn't get it going. . . . Out of sheer frustration, I grudgingly asked David to get involved. He offered me one piece of advice on *Bugsy Malone,* 'I urge you not to do it with children.' 'If I don't do that, David,' I told him, 'I don't know what we've got!' He was *always* full of ideas, most of them crackpot, but he could never be defeated. If David had one thing knocked down, he'd be on to the next thing—there was always something else up his sleeve. His energy and ability to be whacked over the head and climb up again were extraordinary.

"It was never easy for him in these early days. In Britain it was a depressed industry, and the people who were running it were pretty pathetic. It was run mostly by narrow-minded men . . . who knew absolutely nothing but couldn't be told anything, even though the industry was a disaster. In David's trips to America, it was even more humiliating for him. He was treated like a carpet salesman coming from nowhere and no one knowing who he was. They were contemptuous of us being English because our industry had been peopled for so long by second-rate losers. They were very hard times for him, and they left a mark on him.

"He was very unforgiving of how badly he was treated by our own industry, but more so the Americans. He was always thought of as a sort of swift-of-foot spiv, an energetic loony, and no one would ever acknowledge that he might actually be any good, let alone brilliant. The way in which business is done in Hollywood, the fact that you come thousands of miles and the fact that you can't afford the air fare or the hotel room doesn't count. You've got to sit there at the Beverly Wilshire, as he often did, waiting for days for someone to return your call. Then you find out they haven't even bothered to read your script!"

Once David accepted that Alan was determined to press ahead with his cast of kids, he went on to sell *Bugsy Malone* with all the zeal of someone who thought it the best idea in the world. He convinced himself to enable him to convince others.

During a trip to the United States, David ran into songwriter Paul Williams in A&M Records' office. (A&M was releasing the *Lisztomania* soundtrack at the time.) Williams was promptly force fed the *Bugsy Malone* script. When he agreed to compose original songs for the movie, David steered Alan Parker and the project to Paramount through Bobby Littman. They were offered $300,000 in exchange for the U.S. negative pickup rights. "A terrible deal," Alan Marshall says, "although if hadn't been brought off, the film would never have been made at all. But Paramount had no commitment to promote the movie or support it in any way. The studio spent more money on their clients' lunches than they did on *Bugsy*."

The balance of the budget still had to be found, so it was back to Britain and meetings with the Rank Organisation, who—with misgivings—agreed to help finance it. Polydor Records joined in, putting up $50,000 for soundtrack album rights. Finally they needed only an additional $50,000, and the movie would be a definite "go." After much waiting, Barry Diller, Paramount's new chief, came through with the funds.

The whole exercise furthered a growing disenchantment in David's mind. The National Film Finance Corporation, Rank, Paramount, and Polydor—all had contributed to *Bugsy*. But David increasingly wondered as he sought outside investment, Where did the Rothschilds stand in all this? "I was hassling around," David points out, "raising money privately from different sources, when the people who held the bulk of Goodtimes' equity weren't prepared to come up with some of it. It was the fight for the last $50,000 that really crazed me. I was running about all over the place, when the directors of the company, who had millions, didn't have the courage to come up with it."

Almost as soon as shooting at Pinewood had started, David recalls, the unit was presented with Rank's first surprise. "They would give us the studio resources to build only *one* side of the street on our main set," he maintains. "It was a terrible betrayal —they knew we needed both sides. We had to put it up ourselves. Alan Parker had to mortgage his house to cover it, £80,000. Then there was the hydraulics. Everything was built on hydraulics because we needed cellars for people to vanish into, and Alan Marshall had made a deal with the studio that since these hydraulics were lying idle, they would let us have them free. Two weeks after we started shooting, they told us they were afraid they were going to have to charge us for the hydraulics. When Alan Marshall and I asked why, they explained it was because there was another film that wanted them, and either we agreed to pay their charges or they would have to remove them. We said, 'You can't do that, our fucking sets will collapse!' They said, 'Well, we'll need to charge you for them.' We settled it in the end, but only after a terrible row. From start to finish their involvement was a nightmare. They were totally negative, and the money was always late. Thank God they stopped production. They've saved people a lot of pain and unhappiness."

Alan Parker, with a wicked chuckle, says this is not entirely true, indeed that David was hardly involved at all in the physical production of *Bugsy*. "With David, he gets a bee in his bonnet about someone, in this case Rank, and he never forgives. They were a pain in the ass about their share of the money because David wouldn't agree to their ridiculously unfair production and distribution agreement, and it caused us a lot of anxiety. But I didn't mortgage my house! Not unless Alan Marshall did it without telling me! There were no hydraulics or trap doors, either—that's all anecdotal. He wasn't there for most of the filming so he probably is confusing it with Alan Marshall telling him about a problem we had with scaffolding rostrums that the whole set was built on. . . . This is David half-hearing things reported to him secondhand. It's anecdotal, theater, not true. . . .

"During the shoot, David was away in the States vainly trying to get Warner Bros. to get behind *Lisztomania*, a pretty well impossible task. It was a terribly hard time for him, and I remember him lying on the couch in our office and putting his head in his hands—he'd had enough of movies and Americans. I think he only got involved with *Bugsy* to help me, and in a way he was probably surprised it worked at all. His own movies were his priority."

David's efforts to get *Bugsy* entered at the Cannes Film Festival were thwarted at first when he was told it was not "esoteric" enough for the festival. "It's a film for *everyone*," he raged, "that just happens to feature a cast of kids." After a storm of publicity, some of it skillfully engineered by David, the film was accepted and put forward as the British entry to Cannes in May 1976. It received one of the most enthusiastic receptions of any film that year.

During the time *Bugsy* had been shooting, David's old friend David Picker had been appointed head of Paramount. Picker flew to Cannes to see *Bugsy* and enthusiastically renewed his relationship with David. Cannes was turning out well. Of *Bugsy*'s screening, David recalls, "It was just an unbelievable triumph. Alan Parker was literally chaired shoulder high. It had been a particularly bloody Cannes, there'd been violent movies all over the place. That evening a special dinner was held. . . . David Picker gave a speech and said something lovely about *Bugsy*—that he'd been waiting to see a film like that for the last fifteen years.

"Later that evening he said to me, 'Have you got any more guys like this? I mean, Parker really knows how to shoot a film.' I said, 'Well, as a matter of fact I have.' It was Ridley Scott I had in mind. So I phoned Rid as soon as I could get away and said, 'Get on a plane first thing tomorrow morning.' He did, he got the eight o'clock plane, so by lunchtime we were eating on the beach at the Carlton—David, Rid, and I. We were pitching a picture called *The Duellists* and another called *The Gunpowder Plot*. Picker said, 'Which do you feel more strongly about?' I said, 'Well, basically we prefer *The Gunpowder Plot*, but it's going to cost at least $2 million, but we can make *The Duellists* for $1 million.' He said $2 million was too much, he preferred what he called 'the $1 million one.' That was my first deal with David [Picker] after our years of friendship."

Rank unenthusiastically arranged a West End première for *Bugsy* in July 1976 and sat back, skeptically, to await results. David continued to foot the publicity bill with the money he had raised.

His tenacity and determination paid off. Overall, the English critics loved the film, as did the paying public. "Original, perilous, and marvelously entertaining," wrote John Coleman in the *New Statesman;* similar sentiments were expressed by many others. But American critics were decidedly more mixed in their opinions, and the American public gave the film the thumbs-down. Worldwide, however, the bottom line was a gratifying net profit close to £2 million.

Despite this success, David chose to agonize publicly about his feelings for his production company, Goodtimes. "We have failed," he declared, "because we don't seem to have hit on a style of filmmaking." No one rushed to disagree with him, for the only films that could be said to have offered anything like a personal statement had been *That'll Be the Day* and *Stardust*, both of them partly autobiographical.

"Had we been the kind of success we wanted to be, there would be five other Goodtimes operating here," he continued. "We've also failed because we haven't created an energy. And that pisses me off because it hasn't been for lack of trying. We'll go on, according to our own lights, because I'm too selfish to do it any other way, and hopefully by a process of natural selection there'll come a time, if we keep hanging in there, when what we make will also be popular."

The parting of the ways for David and Sandy had in fact taken place while *Bugsy* was triumphing at Cannes. "We didn't part with any animosity at all," Sandy says, "but with *Trick or Treat* and everything, it just seemed all too much. We were making so little money out of the company, we were by now collecting a £12,000 salary each and all the real profits weren't coming through to us, since Rothschilds invested in the movies personally, rather than through Goodtimes. We got nothing from it, we were in debt, both of us owed money to the tax collector, David had a huge overdraft, and I think the banks were worried about him being able to pay it off. We both still owed Rothschilds the money they'd loaned us for our stock in VPS, so with *Trick or Treat* and all, we just thought, 'Christ, we'd better cut and run.'"

"I didn't feel I was doing what I wanted to do," David states, admitting that he was the one who had precipitated the split, while rather glossing over the fact that Rothschilds, after the shock of a string of setbacks including the *Lisztomania* and *Trick or Treat* fiascos, were about to abandon ship in any event. To them Goodtimes had run the gamut from out-of-control budgets to court actions and project abandonment—incidents that did not comply with their conception of prudent management.

"The company always lived, it seemed to me, from crisis to crisis," says Frank Bloom. "David had to fight tooth and claw for everything he got. He developed good relationships with Thorn-EMI and some of the American majors, but it was always a one-off battle. My own theory was that because of the

continuing office overhead and the difficulty of making enough
productions to pay for this overhead and the salaries, they were
always on a treadmill. What happened was, they would often
make things and then try to sell them in a hurry, like the specu-
lative television ventures. They were under tremendous pressure to sell, and that was more significant when it came to selling off bits of their profits of a film, where they couldn't afford
to wait. Of course, when they produced for the majors, the
majors made the investment and the company earned a producer's fee. But that was all they got unless the film went into
profit, which could take a long time, if ever. Even then, David
refused to compromise. On *Stardust,* he needed to boost American scenes and went along to the financiers and begged them to
give him another £150,000. He had to cut his own fee to get it,
but that's the man—he won't compromise on the screen. He
will wreck his own finances first to get the results he wants.

"In the end the venture just fizzled out because they weren't
getting any money. Patsy's strength helped him enormously
through that difficult time when he had to pick himself up and
start again. She didn't show it then, but she's very strong."

"She's everybody's mother" is Andrew Birkin's affectionate
view of Patsy. But for a while, her real concern had been for
her own children's feelings. She had watched in dismay as David's acquaintances were jettisoned and left behind. "The children used to worry about that a little bit," she admits. "Suppose
their dad did that to them? David never acknowledged the fact
that they were children. When he played Monopoly with them,
he played to win. Maybe it brought out the best in them—then
again, maybe it made them a little unsure of their ground. Both
of them have this thing never to let him down. Nowadays,
David never finishes a phone call to them without saying 'You
know I love you, don't you?' "

David was fully aware of the situation with Patsy and the
children, and now he smiles a little contritely. "Patsy would fall
behind, become frightened, and then suddenly get it together
again. Debbie and Patsy took over Sacha—he didn't have anything to do for himself. When Patsy wasn't bringing him up,

Debbie was. He had an enormously rough time when Debbie first went off to school. For him it was an incredible jolt. But yes, I plead guilty to always treating the kids as people."

Sandy's plan was to continue independent movie-making under the original Goodtimes banner, while David formed a new entity, the appropriately named Enigma Productions, in May 1976. Enigma already had its starter in *The Duellists*, in which Ridley Scott made his directorial debut on the big screen.

"This was one of three pieces of material that were in development as potential directorial debuts for Ridley," David recalls. "But I found that having harnessed David Picker at Paramount and his enthusiasm for Ridley's talents, *The Duellists* was the only one of the three projects that could be made within the parameters that were set. The point worth reiterating here is that the final decision was not a creative one, but budgetary!"

Before shooting began, there was a little housekeeping to take care of. David wanted to move his Enigma offices closer to his home, so when he vacated his Dean Street location, he rented the space to literary agent Ed Victor. A dispute soon arose between the two men that provides significant insight into one aspect of David's personality.

The disagreement developed over a telephone bill for £600 that Victor contended Enigma had left at the Dean Street offices. David, relying on the records of his trusted secretary Lynda Smith, felt that Victor was incorrect.

David consulted Frank Bloom for legal advice but realized that there was little he could do. "If I can't prove it, I'm not going to sue him," he declared. "But I'll get even."

Some ten years later, Bloom encountered Ed Victor and expressed regret over the phone bill dispute. Victor, too, was sorry the problem had arisen. "I put a client of mine on to David, and he turned him down. [David] told him that while he was represented by Ed Victor, he didn't want anything to do with him. He shouldn't have done that. My dispute with David had nothing to do with my client or his abilities."

Alone later, Bloom reflected on Victor's story and the occasionally vindictive, unforgiving side of David Puttnam that it revealed. The agent had crossed the invisible line David kept in his head. Once crossed, there was no going back.

Location shooting for *The Duellists* was to take place in France, followed by the north of Scotland, in late 1976. The cast included Keith Carradine, Harvey Keitel, and Albert Finney. Money was tight, and from Ridley Scott was extracted his agreement to do the picture for next to nothing. David took a leaf out of quickie king Roger Corman's book here, that a new director learns as he works—for free. "We had to make these conditions because we budgeted the picture in March, and when we were ready to start shooting, it was October. By then, Technicolor prices and Kodak stock prices had gone up, and it was going to cost another $60,000. In the end, if you're a producer who wants to make a good film, the amount of money you make at the end of the day can't be your main criterion."

With shooting for *The Duellists* under way in 1976, Alan Parker was in New York on a twofold mission—to promote *Bugsy Malone* and to check out the stage musical *The Wiz*, which Universal was interested in having him adapt for the screen. He saw the show and decided against accepting the assignment.

One day as he was passing by Columbia's 711 Fifth Avenue offices, Peter Guber emerged from the revolving doors. "He's the only man I've ever met who talks faster than David Puttnam," Alan says, laughing. Guber had left Columbia Pictures with a golden handshake and had teamed up with Neil Bogart, of the highly successful U.S. record label Casablanca. The resulting Bogart-Guber concern was known as Casablanca Records and Filmworks, fulfilling Bogart's ambition to break into motion pictures. Guber explained that they had been trying to reach him to consider directing a new project they had acquired, *Midnight Express*.

David, on location in Scotland with *The Duellists*, says he got a call from Guber around the same time. "Very typical of Peter— he tracked me down," says David. "I'd known Guber because he'd been at Columbia when they had *Stardust*. He called and asked what I was doing, and I said, what do you mean, what am

I doing, I'm doing a film. And he asked me when I was going to finish, and I said two weeks. He said, well, did I want to come to Los Angeles and work with him? 'To do what?' I asked. He explained they had a story that the head of Columbia had agreed to do called *Midnight Express*. I said I would need to read it first. He said he'd send me the book."

When Alan phoned David later to tell him his news of the meeting with Guber, David said, "You're never going to believe this. Peter's asked me to produce it!"

Peter Guber does not entirely agree with David's version of this story. After meeting Alan and giving him the galleys of *Midnight Express*, he says he then hired Oliver Stone to work on the screenplay "and agreed with Judy Scott-Fox, Alan Parker's agent, that Alan Marshall would produce the film for me. Sometime after that, I hired David Puttnam to be the president of Casablanca Filmworks, to develop his own films through us. Later he came to me and said he would like to produce *Midnight Express* with Alan Marshall, because he wanted to work with Alan Parker, who he was very close to and because he very much liked Oliver's screenplay."

Although the offer—either to be president of Casablanca, to produce *Midnight Express*, or both—was made in January, the Puttnams deliberated for a full six weeks before making their minds up. There were two elements to consider. One was that Enigma was planning the production of a film called *Agatha*, for which Kathleen Tynan had provided a screenplay and that had Julie Christie and Vanessa Redgrave lined up to star. *Agatha* was set to be David's follow-up to *The Duellists*, and was to be filmed in England. Would he be able to mastermind *Agatha* long-distance when it rolled in the autumn?

The other consideration was plain necessity. To all outward appearances, David was a successful film producer who had made a fortune out of hits like *Melody*, *That'll Be the Day*, *Stardust*, and *Bugsy Malone*. The truth was, David had been paying himself a pittance. As producer of *That'll Be the Day*, he had taken a salary of £10,000, then for *Stardust*, £12,000. From *Mahler* he had taken nothing, and from *Bugsy Malone* he had extracted precisely £6,000 for two years' work. Although additional income was still anticipated from some of these films, David and Sandy had to face the prospect of paying 83 percent of anything that came in over £21,000 in tax. David was already in hock to the bank. The two years out of the country that the Casablanca offer represented, and the opportunity to make half-million dollars, tax free, was the perfect solution.

"What had happened," David ruefully explains, "is that I was ten years into my film career, I'd spent the £30,000 we'd saved through the agency, and I'd been living on an overdraft of £68,000 at our bank. We were totally broke, and worse, I had a tax bill looming on top."

The decision to accept the Hollywood offer may not have been instant, but it was inevitable.

8

"**I** won't go unless you come out too," David declared to Patsy. To this, Patsy, doing what she now calls her best spoiled-brat act, answered that she simply didn't want to live in the United States and agonized, fairly understandably, about the disruption that Debbie and Sacha's education would face. But what won the day was the acknowledgment that the way they were living was becoming intolerable, with David hardly ever at home. "You've *got* to come to America," David told her. "I can't stand all these plane journeys. You've *got* to come—it's the only way we're ever going to crack it!"

David moved to the United States in April 1976, while Patsy stayed and held the fort at home until the summer vacation break arrived and Debbie and Sacha could be organized. David had rented an attractive house overlooking the sea at Aderno

Way, Pacific Palisades, and his family joined him there at the end of June.

The start of production on *Midnight Express* had been constantly put back and was now scheduled for September 1976. They spent a couple of months in Aderno Way that were relatively carefree. "Alan Marshall, Alan Parker, Ridley Scott, Jack Rosenthal, Mike Apted—everyone, they all came to stay with us at one time or another during that period," Patsy recalls. "I was back to running a hotel again, but it couldn't have felt more different from Ranelagh Grove. I was part of a creative community, we were in California, I had help—it was *totally* different. We all used to sit around at these breakfasts—nobody wanted to go to work—while endless supplies of English muffins and tea and coffee were wheeled in. The best ideas would come out then, there was this tremendous atmosphere. David was flying back and forth, but was still there a lot of the time."

David's daily routine at Casablanca, in between location scouting trips, was somewhat different. He hated the constant rounds of committees and the decisions that were made only to be changed by further committees. The precise point at which he became firmly aligned with and co-producer of the *Midnight Express* project must remain a matter of dispute between David and Peter Guber, but when he returned from one particular session, Patsy could tell immediately from his demeanor that something was wrong. "I've got some news," he said, "and I just don't know how to break it to you."

Patsy stared hard at him. "Just blurt it out quickly," she said, thinking she was ready for anything.

David looked very unhappy. "The company has decided—I mean, we thought about it a lot and looked at every other option—but at the end of the day, we're making *Midnight Express* in Malta."

As his words sank in (Malta? *Malta?*), all Patsy could think was "But I could be at home!" The move had been for nothing, it seemed.

"In the end it was good," Patsy now sees, "because it reconciled me to living in Los Angeles, and I got to know my way around with David gone and got to like it. In some ways it was better, for when you're on your own, you have no alternative. So although it was a dreadful blow to start with, in the end it turned out to be rather good." Patsy had learned how to roll with the punches.

During David's first couple of months in Los Angeles, writer Oliver Stone was working in Alan Parker's London office on the script for *Midnight Express*. "On the whole it was a very professional relationship with Stone," Alan recalls with a wry little smile. "All right, it wasn't a bundle of laughs, I didn't necessarily want him to be my best pal—in fact, initially I told David and Alan Marshall I didn't know if I was going to be able to work with this guy. 'Don't worry,' they said, 'let him deliver the script, and that'll be it.' We got the script and within half an hour of reading it, we were all on the phone to each other saying how brilliant it was."

David expressed concern to Oliver Stone, however, that certain sequences in his script, notably those featuring the Turkish prison warden, could not be satisfactorily transferred to film. And even if they were, David argued, they would never get past the censor. Stone sensed it was compromise time. He took another look at his script, especially at those scenes dealing with homosexuality and threats of rape inside the prison. The modifications ultimately made to many of Stone's conceptions are ironic in view of the subsequent abuse heaped on Alan Parker's shoulders for the film's excesses. Alan was making what he regarded as an Alan Parker movie—nothing more, nothing less. "I'm very strong when it comes to making a movie," he says, "and *nobody* tells me what to do. Nobody. One of the frustrations that David has working with me and why he'll probably never work with me again—it's *my* film and no one else's. I'm very egocentric and megalomaniac about that. I believe that the director is the one who makes the film and no one else—not the studio executives, not the producer, no one. The scriptwriter has a contribution to make, but only up to a certain point."

With the filming in Malta about to start, the setup consisted of David and Alan Marshall as co-producers for Alan Parker, the two Alans having worked closely together to prepare the film. Their joint endeavors were supervised from Los Angeles by executive producer Peter Guber of Casablanca and Dan Melnick, Columbia's production head.

The Duellists had meanwhile opened to negligible box-office on its Paramount release. *Sunday Times* critic Alan Brien put his finger on what he saw as the film's malaise: "What appears to be needed is some deeper sense of personal, social, and historical seeds from which the duellists' bizarre enmity must spring." It appeared that David and Ridley Scott had failed to ensure that there would be meaningful background and subtext beneath the highly polished veneer. No warmth had been allowed near the chilly heart of the film, although it certainly *looked* magnificent.

While *Midnight Express* was being shot in Malta, David supervised the pre-production of *Agatha* in England at the same time. Kathleen Tynan's screenplay speculated on the reasons for Agatha Christie's real-life disappearance from her home in 1926, when she was in the middle of her unhappy first marriage. David had Vanessa Redgrave, Helen Morse (in place of Julie Christie, who had broken her wrist), and Timothy Dalton lined up to star in the film. Through his British agent, Jarvis Astaire, the talents of Dustin Hoffman were brought to the project. The actor was having marital problems at the time, which made filming *Agatha* in Britain an attractive proposition for him.

"Out of the blue he phoned me," says David. "I just picked up the phone, and someone said it was Dustin Hoffman. He told me he'd read the screenplay and thought it was a wonderful piece of work. He said he badly wanted to work in England for personal reasons for a week or so, and was there any chance he could become involved? I thought, well, that doesn't seem too onerous. There was a role for a journalist, and we worked out that we could make the proprietor of the newspaper a Canadian, give him a nephew with an accent and make the thing work.

"Dustin then literally arrived in England with a writer, a

very nice man named Murray Schisgal, who proceeded to re-write the script! Now, that wasn't the deal. On the other hand, as I was very quickly encouraged to understand, the reason that Warners were twice as pleased was that they now had a film starring Dustin Hoffman and felt they had a real bargain. And no matter what Dustin did, it became very clear that he was running the film."

Problems on *Agatha* quickly escalated. Dustin Hoffman's role expanded overnight from a cameo to co-billing with Vanessa Redgrave. Someone else's part had to be reduced, and the unfortunate Helen Morse emerged as the main victim. Once again, David found himself in a position where a picture was careering away from him. He recognized that *Agatha* was no longer going to be the production he had planned. It was being transformed into a Dustin Hoffman vehicle. Since Dustin's name meant far more than his own at the box office, it was clear which one Warners would back. David saw himself hopelessly squeezed out between the star and the studio.

He decided that the only way out was to terminate his involvement with the film, and he wrote to Jarvis Astaire accordingly. "I went through agonizing and cajoling," David told a reporter, "and found myself asking if I really wanted to work with this worrisome American pest when I could be having a productive time in Malta on *Midnight Express,*" a quote that would be repeated with relish over the years.

"I gave up a year's development work on a screenplay I had loved very much indeed," says David. "I realize now that some-one had found the 'leading man' clause in Dustin's contract, and a cameo was no good for his purposes. But he didn't *tell* anybody. Instead of telling us the truth, he just took over the set with his own writer. Nobody understood what was going on."

Director Michael Apted stayed on and had to put up with endless delays due to the constant script rewriting. Having originally described the picture elatedly as his "passport to Hollywood," grave doubts were now setting in. Here was one individual who did not appreciate David's point that there can only ever be one head of a successful enterprise: "As soon as Hoffman arrived as producer on the film David just *ran*. I don't think David wanted the competition, he didn't want the fact that he was not going to be the sole producer influence.

"I think this was a ridiculous thing for him to do, for he had been responsible for bringing Dustin into the project. I think if you are taking on a major American star who is bringing the finance with him, you have to acknowledge his existence in other ways than he's just going to turn up in the morning and act. He's going to have his own people round him and his own demands. David would never acknowledge that.

"So there was one horrendous punch-up, and David left the film and left me and Vanessa and the project stranded in the hands of Hoffman, who is very difficult to deal with. It was a very dreadful state of affairs. There is a slight element to David that unless he can run the show, unless he can be the full captain of the ship, then he'd rather not be in it at all."

Although not involved in the *Agatha* project, Alan Parker could see the other side of the coin. He concedes that if he had been in Michael Apted's position, he would have felt let down as well, but he still felt that David had made the only sensible move. "If, after a certain point, he sees it's not going to work, he doesn't hang around, he moves very quickly. He *moves*. Now the rest of the people couldn't move—they had to stay with it— so you can see why they're a little bit resentful. On the other hand, I understand exactly what David was doing because *we* were saying, 'Don't bother with *that*, come over to us. We're having a lot of fun.' So it was comfortable for him to walk away from *Agatha*."

In view of subsequent events, David's decision to leave seems not only eminently sensible but absolutely inevitable. Dustin Hoffman claims that he found to his horror that the revised script, which he was responsible for initiating, was unfinished when shooting began. While Murray Schisgal attended to Dustin's lines, Vanessa Redgrave asked Michael Apted to get Arthur Hopcraft as a writer for her. Communication between the two stars was nonexistent, since Dustin reportedly refused to talk to Vanessa. The entire cast found themselves with fresh script pages being thrust at them each day just before shooting was due to start. A visiting journalist described the atmosphere on the *Agatha* set as the most bitter and frenzied he had ever encountered.

With Christmas approaching, the company responsible for *Agatha*'s financing, First Artists, decided enough was enough. Although Jarvis Astaire and Gavrik Losey were officially the film's producers since David's departure, First Artists nevertheless let Dustin know directly of their decision to terminate production in three days. Multimillion-dollar lawsuits between Dustin and First Artists promptly flew in the Hollywood manner.

"When Dustin found out that as producer I was agreeing with First Artists and not with him, our business arrangement and our friendship were over," says Jarvis Astaire. "It's just a shame that the Hoffman of today isn't the Hoffman I've known in the past nine years. Puttnam was complaining that Hoffman had too much power. He was lucky. Hoffman didn't have as much as he wanted. Hoffman also accused Vanessa Redgrave of refusing to act certain scenes. It's just untrue. It was he who refused to act in the film as originally written."

Many years later, Astaire came up with his own version of David's "feud" with Hoffman. "David Puttnam created this myth," he claims, "but Dustin was not the reason David didn't produce *Agatha*. He couldn't produce the picture because he could only come to England twenty days the rest of the year. He was in Malta finishing *Midnight Express*, and he said his tax accountant gave him the tax reason for not coming to England. He was getting what is called a 'tax breather.'" Astaire had known David since his photographers' agency days. "I can tell you that butter wouldn't melt in his mouth," he says, "but don't stick your finger in it."

David sticks to his guns and denies Astaire's version. "I didn't produce *Agatha*," he insists, "because it became a movie out of control. That was the reason. I saw, in that film, how not to make a movie. How any star can't be allowed to decide what's right for a movie."

Michael Apted and Jim Clark, the editor who had worked
with him throughout all the travails of the movie, were left to
deliver the final cut. "Not one single word was left of the original script by the time we'd finished," Jim says. "We restruc-
tured the whole thing in the cutting room, since it didn't seem
to make too much sense as it was. We had to invent various
devices, like the writing of the diary, to explain things and keep
them moving." Despite everything, he has good memories of
Dustin. "I was fond of him. You can't *not* love Dustin. He's a
monster with directors, though. He's a perfectionist—quixotic,
difficult, bright, a great guy—but not to direct, I think!" As for
David, "Of course he did the right thing—he was right to leave.
Yes, Michael and I were left in the lurch—but I think everyone
got over that a long time ago."

David was indeed wise to get away from the mess *Agatha*
became, but in the light of all the circumstances, he can be seen
as having been overly harsh in his judgment of Hoffman. It
seems a pity that the hatchet has not yet been buried, for both
David and Dustin have proved time and again, each in his own
different way, their talent and commitment to quality filmmaking. Hatchet-burying was not to be, however, and the feud
flared into full battle later, when David made his move to Columbia Pictures.

9

With Brad Davis in the role of Billy Hayes and supported by an international cast including Randy Quaid, Paul Smith, John Hurt, Peter Jeffreys, and Bo Hopkins, work on *Midnight Express* proceeded smoothly and on schedule in Valletta, Malta.

As Alan Parker went off to work every day in the hot Malta sun, he would often humorously refer to David and Alan Marshall, within their earshot, as the "bloody table-tennis brigade." Sure enough, there was a table-tennis room in their headquarters, and it was indeed a game at which David excelled. Alan's inference, of course, is that the table was being used for play by certain parties while he was sweating his guts out on location. David, on the other hand, maintains that he simply could not resist the temptation to tease Alan. He contends that as soon as they heard the unit returning each day from their location filming, he and Marshall would dash into the table-tennis room and start batting the ball back and forth. As Parker passed by, David would yell, "What does that make the score now? Forty sets to me and thirty to you? Oh—hello, Alan. God, you look *exhausted*!"

Alan Parker, however, defends his version of this story: "I think it's the fact I actually caught them playing in the first place. He was so filled with guilt that he came out with that story as an explanation—I mean, as always, David has an explanation, he's the fastest tap dancer in the movie music-hall. I immediately did a cartoon where the film unit is lost in these underground caves, up to their waists in water, this guy's just managing to hold the camera above the water level. They're lost, then finally one of them (me) says, 'I think this must be the way out. I can hear the producers playing table tennis!' In fact, David didn't have a lot to do on the movie as Alan Marshall was doing the legwork, so he had a lot of free time."

Many another gentle tussle was seen between David and Alan on the movie, each fighting for his own opinion in a different way. Parker recalls, "After the film was over, David gave me this beautiful silver cigarette lighter that he had inscribed, 'To the Maestro—from the *Master*,' just to point out that he had a different view of how he saw producers."

It is unrecorded whether David accepts the view that one measure of a master is his success in bringing all men over to his opinions twenty years later. If he does, there still remains time for Alan and him to reach complete unanimity. But what is recorded is the support Alan received on the film from both David and Alan Marshall. "The two of them made the film as effortless for me as they could," Parker admits. "We had this problem with Columbia with regard to the homosexuality in the shower scene, which they didn't want, and we had to fight them over it. What happened was that David took the footage to Paris and Dan Melnick was not very happy. . . . But there was no way I was going to change it or drop it. It was a very tender and beautiful moment in an otherwise relentlessly violent film."

Melnick was under enormous pressure from the head office at Columbia, where the David Begelman chaos was erupting. He felt isolated and vulnerable in Paris and went into a paroxysm of rage when David refused to doctor or remove the homosexuality scene. "You may have lost me my job!" he yelled at David, then jabbed him in the chest with his forefinger. "You're *suspended,* buster. You're *off* the picture!"

Then Peter Guber failed to return David's calls. A telex was dispatched from Paris that David reckons must have turned the international lines blue. The polite version of what David had to say to Peter was, "Every time I need any help, you vanish on me." Things back in Hollywood turned very ugly, and armed guards were placed on David's office door at Casablanca. This situation continued for over a week and was finally resolved only by Dan Melnick's girlfriend, who voiced the opinion that the shower scene was great and should definitely be kept in. David was reinstated, and the armed guards were dispensed with. With such unpaid technical advisers, who needs highly paid professionals?

Midnight Express was finished with only one other major conflict—over the film's freeze-frame ending—and was entered at Cannes in May 1978. Although the film was given a tremendous reception at its festival screening, the following morning the press seemed to turn against the whole enterprise, hurling question after question at Alan Parker about the excesses shown in the picture. At one point Alan was photographed yelling back defiantly at the marauding journalists, with David caught in the background tugging away worriedly at his beard.

When *Midnight Express* opened in London, the critics lay in wait, ready to echo the hostile reception at Cannes. Typical was David Robinson, who in *The Times* reckoned that Oliver Stone and Alan Parker had clearly felt a need to compensate for their somewhat negative hero and that their solution had been to turn Hayes's story into a drama of degradation and then retribution. "The film is more violent as a national-hate film than anything I remember even from the Second World War. The worst trouble is that Alan Parker's direction is facile enough,

Michael Seresin's photography picturesque enough, and Giorgio Moroder's music soupy enough to give an innocent spectator the impression that this unpleasant film has some sort of class."

There followed a debate in the British press over the film's alteration of facts and over the depiction of Hayes as a hero and the Turkish authorities as archvillains. Similar criticism greeted the opening of the film in the United States. Richard Schickel wrote in *Time* magazine that "What we have here is one of the ugliest sadomasochistic trips, with heavy homosexual overtones, that our thoroughly nasty movie age has yet produced."

The public had stronger stomachs than most of the critics, however, and the film went on to become a huge international success. Nor was it ignored in the honors stakes, garnering six Golden Globe Awards, three British Academy Awards, and two Hollywood Oscars—Best Score for Giorgio Moroder and Best Screenplay Adaptation for Oliver Stone. On a total cost of just over £2.5 million, *Midnight Express* went on to return net profits of almost £8.5 million. David had achieved his international commercial breakthrough, but—in his own eyes, at least—at the cost of a humiliating climbdown.

"I discovered too late that Billy had, shall we say, a much more 'complex' background than I'd been led to believe," he states. "At the time it was supposed to be the story of a basically good boy who behaved stupidly and brought inordinate punishment on himself. I think we filmmakers were conned over that one. I went into shock—I thought it was a really good, well-made picture until I saw it with an audience—and then I suddenly realized that as much as anything else, we'd been ripped off. We thought we'd made one film, but in the end we'd made exactly the film Columbia Pictures wanted us to make, a very commercial film where the audience is actually on its feet saying 'Go on!' during the scene in which Billy Hayes bites the tongue off one of his captors. We thought they'd be under their seats, but instead they were cheering! That's the depth of misjudgment I realized I was capable of."

Today David describes *Midnight Express* as a "career move,

made with a certain cynicism which is inescapable. We conned ourselves. There had been love in *Bugsy Malone*; there was not much love in *Midnight Express.*"

"Conned?" Alan Parker asks. "It's irrelevant. That was just David doing his tap dance to justify the criticism we got for it, but I don't run away from that. . . . I am immensely proud of [*Midnight Express*], and much of the criticism has since been seen to be alarmist nonsense. It's one of the most important films in many young people's lives, and I stand by every frame of it. Maybe I'm more protective of it than David because it's more my film than his. He is more critical of it and the attitudes within it because he doesn't necessarily see it as part of his body of work. It was something he helped me to do, but it's very much part of *my* body of work, so obviously I'm infinitely more defensive of it."

Something David did gain from the movie was his relationship with Peter Guber. Although their journey together was a bumpy one, their differences reflect to a large degree the enormous value David places on his own independence. "I don't like working for anybody," he admits, "and Peter and I have totally different styles. We often rubbed up against each other the wrong way, and Alan and I got aggravated in that we felt he put little into the actual production of the picture whilst disproportionately rowing himself in on its success. Where I did learn a lot from him was in terms of the subsequent promotion of the film and the energy he put into it. I was influenced a lot by Peter in that respect. I hadn't realized the extraordinary lengths before that you can go to in order to push a film. I watched the degree to which he was able to utilize reviews, making each critic feel as if they had the inside track. He was brilliant at that."

David returned to Los Angeles in 1978 to prepare for Casablanca's new movie, also planned for Columbia release. The subject was teenage suicide: "I found it very interesting that Beverly Hills, which for many people represents the apotheosis of hundreds of years of human striving, should have the highest level of teenage suicide in the world. In looking into it, I stumbled across a tough script by Gerald Ayres about children living in single-parent homes, *Foxes*. I worked on that for about four months and after several false starts got it off the ground, but again I found myself in that old situation. I was working with Casablanca, who had a 'special relationship' with Columbia. After dithering with the film, Columbia didn't want to do it, and Casablanca didn't have the nerve to go it alone. So I was left cobbling together a half-arsed deal with United Artists, having got the script in turnaround from 20th Century-Fox. It was the Goodtimes situation all over again. What on earth was I doing raising funds for a film, when I was supposed to be having my salary paid and working with a company that had money?"

For *Foxes*, David recruited yet another director from the ranks of television commercials, Adrian Lyne. Jodie Foster and Scott Baio from *Bugsy Malone* were cast, together with Sally Kellerman.

Speaking later of *Foxes*, David admits, "We made a hash of it for all the obvious reasons. The first thing we jettisoned was being sensible. I should never have done it in the first place, because I didn't know anything about the subject."

Halfway through production, Casablanca was bought by Polygram Pictures, a short-lived division of the record company. David found himself subjected more than ever to front-office interference. "Why does she have to commit suicide?" he was asked. "I mean, I can see your point, but couldn't she just die self-destructively?" Then it was "Couldn't we spice it up a bit, make it more exciting?" and "How about a big rock soundtrack?" Filming was held up while would-be film executives and their wives were photographed with the actors on the set, and David was obliged, much against his will, to include a skateboard chase scene.

United Artists sat on the picture for a year after its completion, then rushed it out in 1980 in the glare of publicity that surrounded Jodie Foster after the assassination attempt by John Hinckley on President Ronald Reagan. The reviews were mixed: In *New York* magazine David Denby wrote, "After a promising beginning, *Foxes* becomes a maudlin commercial for unhappy youth." In the New York *Daily News*, Katherine Carroll found it a "murky-looking teenybopper soap opera." As against that, David Ansen in *Newsweek* found *Foxes* a "funny, rueful, sexy little movie about coming of age."

In Britain Nicolas Wapshott was perhaps reviewing the timing of the film's release rather than the film itself when he wrote, "*Foxes* is a shabby film which does not deserve to be saved from obscurity by such naked opportunism." His verdict that the film had "no material audience" regrettably proved only too accurate on both sides of the Atlantic.

Toward the end of his first Hollywood tenure, David found himself counting the days until he could return home to England. His visit to the movie mecca had started off badly with the side trip to Malta, then ended disastrously with the *Foxes* debacle. Hollywood had been a dispiriting experience, and he wanted to return home and resume independent production. He felt tired, disgusted, and thoroughly disillusioned.

Dan Melnick was anxious to move on after his holding operation at Columbia following the departure of David Begelman, and David was offered the job of head of production at the studio, first informally by Melnick, then formally by David Begelman's successor, Frank Price. Producer Ray Stark asked him to produce a film with Alan Parker. David found it easy to turn down both offers. "I wasn't tough enough to deal with it," he declares. "It was always going to beat me. Running a studio would have cost me my domestic life, and that would have been a ridiculous price to pay."

Back in Britain, many were of the opinion that the real root of David's unhappiness in Hollywood was the fact that he had been reduced once again to the relatively small fish he had been back in the days of *Melody*. At least in Britain he would be one of the bigger fish around, albeit in a smaller pond.

"Of all of us, we thought he would take Hollywood by storm," says Michael Apted. "I think David met a lot of people in Hollywood who were just like him, people who were just as aggressive but who loved film a lot less and had far fewer scruples than he has."

Alan Parker is far more sanguine. "What happened was this: half of him liked it a lot, more than he would admit. And he hated himself for it. I remember him happily driving down Sunset Strip in his big, flashy BMW. In many ways, I've never seen him happier. It would have been infinitely easier for him to work there than it is in Britain in terms of the kind of money that's available, if he'd been prepared to make certain compromises, which of course he wasn't."

Sometime before he departed Hollywood, while spending a rare day at home, David looked around at the pile of scripts he had spent so much time reading and decided he needed a break. Searching around in a bookcase, he came across a bound volume on the history of the Olympic Games. In the chapter on 1924, it became clear to him just by reading down the lists of medals and times that the British runners had done extraordinarily well. The dark horse in the races had been the Scot, Eric Liddell. Having refused to run in the finals of the 100-meter event, he had amazed everyone by breaking the world record on his way to a gold medal in the 400-meters. David decided to find out more by putting a researcher on the job back in Britain.

It turned out that Liddell had died in a prisoner-of-war camp during World War II, while another gold medalist, Harold Abrahams, was still alive and living in Southgate, just a few streets from David's parents. The more he read about the characters and the events that came in from the research notes, the more enthusiastic he became. Soon he knew he had found his next project. Telephoning Colin Welland, he said, "Listen, Colin, this could really be something."

When Alan Parker stopped by, he was treated to a résumé of this story about the two competing British Olympic runners in the 1920s and the conflict one of them had had with running on a Sunday. "I thought it was a terrible idea," says Alan, "about a load of pompous English twits. I told him to forget it. That's how much I know!"

10

David came back to Britain in 1979 with a bonus in the form of a Warners contract. In exchange for picking up his overhead, the studio was to get first look at any projects he developed. In fact, this enabled it to close down its London office and still left it with a toehold in the market. Still David felt all at sea.

Patsy began to realize that the whole effect of working in Los Angeles had been much worse on her husband and had gone deeper than she had understood. "I knew that he didn't like it, but he had to see his term out. It was brought home to him that when he's not on his own territory, he isn't as strong as he should be. He came back to Britain needing to exorcise the whole process." David felt he had been seriously "out of sync." "You're mad if you don't reflect on that," he says. "How do I avoid that misjudgment again?"

His answer was to spend a year teaching—perhaps on the basis of the idea that to teach is to learn twice over—while Colin Welland labored away on the Olympics script. David was invited by the Australian Film Commission to lecture for six weeks as a script consultant, and he traveled to eight universities in Britain. "I'd come back with a lot of opinions," he says, "and wanted to test them. It was also a test for me, the first time I'd spoken in public."

One worrisome aspect of David's dark night of the soul was his asthmalike attacks of being unable to breathe that left him pale and exhausted. On his doctor's recommendation, David briefly put himself into the hands of a psychoanalyst. But since David felt he spent more time listening to the doctor than he did talking, this idea was quickly abandoned.

Still, he recognized his need for help. Patsy could see that her husband was crying out to find a way to go forward. Through friends, David was introduced to a Jesuit priest, Father Jack Mahoney, with whom he talked many times and whose counseling was to prove a considerable influence. After one visit to Father Mahoney he brought home some books that Patsy even saw him take to bed. Since David had never been a churchgoer, these studies were clearly fulfilling a need and stimulating the dedication he now sought.

David maintains that he is extremely self-analytical and that he constantly questions his own nature—a process he concedes can be painful at times. Father Mahoney told David that he was ten times harder on himself than any objective observer would be.

David gives him much credit for rebuilding his shattered confidence. It was to a great extent through his guidance that David was able to press on with *Chariots of Fire.*

Despite David's acceptance of Mahoney's influence, he made no further move toward Catholicism. "It wasn't the Catholicism in particular," Patsy reckons. "It could have been Buddhism—he just needed someone who was making sense to him, cleansing him, asking him questions and helping him to answer these questions without the usual dogma—just talking the truth. That's when he felt he should stop and take stock of where he was and where he was going."

Alan Parker, totally established in his role of playing Lennon to David's McCartney, sees it in his usual down-to-earth manner: "He was suffering from a touch of the Americas but was embarrassed to go to a shrink like everyone else does there. It was easier to go to a Jesuit priest—probably cheaper too. In his early days, because he was so swift of foot, he wasn't taken as seriously by the establishment as he maybe should have been, which makes him very wary of the establishment now."

As he strove for deeper understanding during this sabbatical, he came to realize the awesome power of movies as a means of mass communication. The welter of criticism he had received for the way *Midnight Express* was slanted had gone deep. He still felt conned. He swallowed the accusations of political naïveté, but the acceptance was not a happy one, and he knew this was something that had to be dealt with.

For the first time, David was truly beginning to understand the impact of movies as a means of communication and the damage that messages of a negative kind can bring. With this dawned an awareness of the responsibility he had as a filmmaker. No longer could it be just a question of finding a commercial project, getting it financed, shooting it, and making it. From now on, there had to be a broader canvas, with wider issues addressed. Cause and effect began to preoccupy him, together with the nagging realization that nothing comes from nothing. He saw that although anyone can get from one point to another, it is *how* it is done that is important.

David Puttnam first approached Goldcrest Films simply because it existed. He left no stone unturned in his search for satisfactory financing for his films. His first meeting with John D. "Jake" Eberts was in 1977. "He was a great one for sniffing out new sources of finance, a tremendous hustler, a relentless pounder of the pavements," says Jake. "He heard I'd put money into some picture, and boy, he was on that phone! He was exactly the same as he is now—nervously pulling at his beard, that slight nervous cough—but you could just feel the *energy* coming out of this guy. I was terribly taken with him, for I could see exactly the sort of problems he was facing, having done the same thing myself a few months earlier. At the time, he wasn't asking for money for anything specific, just generally trying to discover what I was doing and whether my contacts were really serious about putting money into the film business. He came right to the point and was *very* impressive."

Jake was hooked, although, of course, at the time he had no way of knowing he had just spoken to the man who would launch Goldcrest's fortunes with *Chariots of Fire* and who would return the tiny company a staggering windfall of a million pounds on their minute investment of £17,000 seed money in the film. David wanted £17,000 for script and development money, he explained to the Goldcrest committee—an immense amount to them, since it was a big percentage of their total capital. They loved his idea for the film, however, and eventually agreed, on condition that the £17,000 be repaid on the day the film started principal photography—with interest.

With seed money taken care of, there remained for David the small matter of finding *Chariots*'s $6 million budget. He wrote and spoke to every major source of finance—banks, city institutions, film companies, and TV networks—but failed to elicit even a glimmer of interest. Particularly depressing to him was the reason why he was being turned away—the subject of the film, he was told, was "too British for the international market." "You must be out of your mind," one studio executive told David, commenting on the draft screenplay, which he was holding over the wastebasket as he spoke. "I don't understand you. You get an opportunity to produce mainstream commercial movies, and you bring along *this.*" So saying, the screenplay was dropped into the bucket. "Go away and *grow up,*" came the final admonition, "and don't waste our time again in the future."

The encounter would normally have gone beyond humiliation, but even as David's cheeks burned he remained utterly convinced he was right, and that in the end he would be vindicated.

However, he did manage to get partial financing from 20th Century-Fox during Sandy Lieberson's hold-the-fort stint as head of production at that studio. In return, Fox got world rights outside the United States and Canada. Now all he needed was another $3 million.

David Norris had come into the Goldcrest picture in 1979, when he was asked to look after Egyptian shipping millionaire Mohammed Al Fayed. Fayed wanted to invest in films, and since his son Dodi Fayed was a film fanatic, Dodi and his father formed the Allied Stars film company. This was to launch the Fayeds' film career. When Jake Eberts suggested to David Puttnam that Allied might be a source of production financing for *Chariots*, David was naturally enthusiastic but was also concerned that Allied might reject the project on the grounds of parochialism that so many individuals and institutions had already leveled. He decided to establish a fallback position with the submission to Allied Stars by offering it the option of a second project, an East-West drama entitled *October Circle*.

If *Chariots* had not been picked by Allied Stars, David and his chosen director, Hugh Hudson, would have been content to make *October Circle* instead—although there was no doubt which film David's heart was in. "*Chariots of Fire*," he declares, "is about winning on your own terms." Over the years, many would become romantically convinced that David had seen a parallel there with his own life.

Actor-writer Colin Welland was soon exposed to the Puttnam perfection ethic. "Colin did five drafts for *Chariots*," David recalls. "A couple of times he was fed up, and I'm sure he thought I was either pedantic or wrong, but we staggered through it. Some people aren't that lunatic. I suppose you could say I'm exceptionally tenacious." He stoutly defended his choice of newcomer Hugh Hudson to direct the movie. "I don't see it as taking chances," he said at the time. "Hugh has made hundreds of commercials, thousands and thousands of feet of film going through a camera, the equivalent of two or three feature films, learning his trade. Other people don't seem to see that. The real gamble to me is if you just *buy* name directors or stars, because films should be cast technically as well as for the performance. The reason *Midnight Express* worked was that Alan Parker was coming off *Bugsy Malone,* and his greatest desire was to prove he didn't just make kiddies' films. He wanted to make a 'hard' film, so he was ideal casting. My feeling with directors is that each film is an absolute 'horses for courses,' where the best director in the world for one story could easily be the worst director for another. I've never worked to my mind with an unproven director. I've always seen something they've done before. I think that film is a very special language, where within five minutes you'll know whether that man speaks the same language or not. Someone can have a shot for twenty years and never have understood the language of film, while another man can pick it up in a year. It seemed to be self-evident that Hugh Hudson was perfect for this as a director, for his attitude and mine toward the script were very much the same. Hugh understands class, he understands England, and he has an incredible visual sense."

11

In 1980, David was thus poised to begin production on *Chariots of Fire.* He had selected two unknown actors to head the cast—Ian Charleson in the role of Scottish Presbyterian Eric Liddell and Ben Cross as the Cambridge-educated Jew Harold Abrahams. Brad Davis (who had played Billy Hayes in *Midnight Express)* was back as U.S. athlete Jackson Scholz. Ian Holm was set to play the part of Abrahams's trainer, Sam Mussabini, with Sir John Gielgud as the Master of Trinity College and Lindsay Anderson as the Master of Caius College.

The considerable drama in Welland's script revolved around two climaxes. In one, sabbatarian Liddell discovers at the last moment that the 100-meter event for which he has been training is being run on a Sunday, and after much agonizing, he withdraws. He then enters the 400-meter instead and triumphs. For Abrahams, the climax comes after his failure in the 200-

meter event, when he redeems himself by winning the 100-meter event—the race Liddell had dropped out of on religious grounds. The film ends on a note of double triumph with the two men, although fiercely competitive in spirit, never actually competing against each other.

The contrast between the abrasive Abrahams and the dour, modest Liddell reflected how personalized the film had become for David—it seemed to strike at the very depths of his psyche and take him back to the values his father had instilled in him.

"There were elements of *Chariots of Fire* that were deliberately there to exorcise the type of life I feel I've led for the past ten years," David declared at the time. "The film is about people who do not behave in an expedient manner, and for the past ten years my career has led me to behave rather expediently. So it is a wishful film, trying to examine both sides of the coin of my personality. Eric Liddell, an evangelical Scot whose motivation on the track was entirely unselfish, is the kind of person I dream of being. Harold Abrahams, a somewhat aloof, unpopular figure who ran in order to satisfy his personal ambition, is more similar to the kind of person I find myself—a pragmatist, rather than an idealist.

"There's no question that *Chariots* is, as much as anything, a reaction to having been the producer of *Midnight Express*, a film in which I found no sense of identity other than the craftsmanship with which it was made."

The location manager on *Chariots of Fire* was a young Scot named Iain Smith. Iain had worked on a variety of documentaries and commercials before the opportunity came to work with David, whom he had known for several years in his position on the National Film and Television School Board of Governors. Since they had only met every three months or so, their relationship was fairly distant. But Iain was aware of David—and of the fact he was considered a bit of a renegade, with a reputation for toughness that stretched almost to the point of unfairness. He was familiar with David's background in advertising, where the motto is "all or nothing" to achieve the desired ends, and was therefore pleasantly surprised when he got to know

David better. He discovered that although David was indeed all he had heard, he had a great deal more to offer as well.

On the set, Iain would see David stand back, observing the many things that had been well achieved but well aware this was not his main function as producer. Instead, he was constantly on the lookout for danger spots, elements that were out of synchronization or about to head that way. "He throws people in at the deep end, and if they swim they're fine," says Iain, "but if they sink, they sink. That's the hard side to David—he expects the very best, and you've got to give it to him. If you don't, you are never forgiven. It's a mafia thing—that's the best example I can give. He'll draw a circle of influence, and if you stay in that circle, he'll treat you like a brother. You'll never starve. But if you step out of there, you'll probably never work again with him."

For a while, all was harmonious between David and Hugh Hudson. For David, "the sun literally rose and set out of Hugh's arse" is how an irreverent studio observer put it. Iain Smith was one of the eyewitnesses to the differences that soon developed. Hugh rebelled against what he saw as David's rank-pulling. But since total control was an integral part of David's ethos, there could be only one outcome.

"He creates for himself a totally autocratic power base," says Iain, "where he will rule absolutely, and there is no one to second-guess him. Particularly directors. Having achieved that position, he will then rule with enormous kindness and wisdom. That doesn't always work and certainly didn't always work with Hugh, for occasionally situations which crossed came up. Then the dragon arose and terrible conflict resulted. David turns muscular in these situations, horrifyingly muscular, and can become very unkind."

There were several confrontations between David and Hugh, centering primarily on decisions Hugh had made that conflicted directly with David's wishes. Adding to the tension on the set was an awareness of the shortness of funds and of the constant need to economize. Ultimately, the entire script was filmed, but there was little footage that wasn't needed—and used.

When filming and postproduction were finished and David departed for the United States to show *Chariots* to the major studios, David Norris found that he had been working for a financier who wanted to wash his hands of the project. Mohammed Al Fayed ordered him to telex 20th Century-Fox, "We are offering you the opportunity to buy our share in this film for our basic costs, plus interest, plus a 5 percent net profit share." Although the Fayeds had decided they wanted out, Fox was not about to oblige them. The film was shown to the major studios and turned down by all of them, including Warners for the second time. Then Sandy Lieberson rode once more to the rescue, with Alan Ladd, Jr. On Sandy's recommendation, Laddie put up half the $1.2 million advance to acquire the U.S. rights to *Chariots*, which Warners would now release after all, as Laddie's distributors, the *third* time around. The deal negotiated by Norris was that profits on the picture would go into a single pot after Fox and the Fayeds had recouped; then the balance would be split between Fox, the Fayeds, David, and his crew and Goldcrest.

Once again a David Puttnam film was picked to represent Britain at Cannes. The selection of *Chariots*, the sixth film of David's in eight years to be so honored (following the documentary *Swastika, Mahler, Bugsy Malone, The Duellists,* and *Midnight Express)* is in itself probably an unbeatable record.

As he anxiously awaited the film's opening, David elucidated his theory on how potentially good movies can go bad. "They are created by people who are making slightly different films. And as silly as that may sound, I see it time and time again. The writer is writing a film ten percent different from the one the producer thinks he's commissioned, and the director is directing a film ten percent different from the resulting script. Before anyone knows what's happening, you've got a lopsided equation, and a film, being a very frail object, can't survive a twenty percent difference from intent to delivery. So my obsession, if you like, is ensuring that we're all making *exactly* the same movie. Once I'm sure of that, my job is to protect the director and give him everything he needs. This involves a very unique approach as a producer—it's called common sense, the least-applied factor in the entire film industry. My greatest problems have come whenever I've strayed from that."

The film opened in London to enthusiastic reviews over the Easter 1981 weekend. *Observer* critic Philip French pointed out that Hugh Hudson was the third gifted British director of TV commercials and documentaries to be introduced by David to feature filmmaking—"and like Alan Parker and Ridley Scott, he knows how to achieve the maximum emotional impact with the minimum footage, how to bypass the mind without insulting the intelligence, how to beguile." He summed the film up as "immensely attractive, immaculately acted."

Critic Alexander Walker decided to go for a jingoistic tubthump in London's *Evening Standard*. "It is fresh. It is original. It puts you in direct touch with sentiments so long unexpressed publicly you wonder if they ever existed—love of country, fear of God, loyalty to the time, unselfish pursuit of honor, becoming modesty in victory—and that doesn't by any means exhaust the list."

Certainly, the critical acclaim helped. Following the slow holiday weekend opening, the film became a sellout. With the success of the film in Britain, David Puttnam emerged as a Personality, as he found himself picked up and adopted by the media. He acknowledged this reluctantly before the film's U.S. opening, which was scheduled for the fall.

"I've learned a lesson with *Chariots of Fire*," he declared. "I've spent the last ten years trying to sell the idea that filmmaking is a collaborative process. The industry knows this to be true, but with the media it's been a long hard slog, for it suits them to believe that a film is one man's vision. It's convenient copy. Up until now, one had to go along with the fact that it suited them it was a director's medium. What's happened with *Chariots* is that the media decided I was the most tangible thing to hang their copy on. Suddenly *I'm* the one being interviewed, *I'm* the one having to step forward and do my stuff. And I'm doing it because I want the name of the film in the paper. I don't really care—at least, I *think* I don't care—whether they write about me or Hugh Hudson or Colin Welland, so long as they write about the *film*. But the net result is, suddenly it becomes 'David Puttnam's *Chariots of Fire,*' the awful *possessive,* which I've been fighting against for a decade. The truth is it's Colin Welland's film, it's Hugh Hudson's film, and it's my film in just about equal parts."

Alan Parker noticed that that press attention brought about a change in David. "He suddenly realized that if he said something, somebody wrote it in a newspaper. Ironically, years ago, at the end of *Midnight Express,* after all the interviews I did, he said, 'Your trouble is, you're becoming a media figure!' Hugh's hero is Stanley Kubrick, who is very private and doesn't shoot his mouth off like the rest of us. David stepped into the breach for the sake of the film, and he is extremely articulate, extremely charming, able to manipulate others to his point of view. We had no voices in filmmaking except the mundane twits at the British Film Institute, and suddenly David had a point of view, which gave him incredible respectability. If any member of the press wanted a comment on any aspect of filmmaking, they came to him. And he began to rather enjoy it. In fact, he began to feed off it. He *needs* respectability to prove that he's no longer a spiv," Alan says, chuckling. "Maybe he picked the wrong industry! That's why he spends so much time trying to give it intellectual credibility."

Hugh Hudson readily acknowledged his producer's contribution in one of the few interviews he gave. "We all need to identify with certain values," he asserted, "not necessarily out of the past. It was David Puttnam who found this subject and had an immediate positive reaction to it. He thought of me as director because I am familiar with the class conflict and religious values found in the subject. And I was fascinated by his enthusiasm and his faith in *Chariots*—we were in perfect agreement and were complementary. He was so enthusiastic that I felt a personal commitment to make his dream come true." There is certainly no sign in this statement of the backlash that ultimately came from Hugh over what he later came to see as the media overkill on David as producer.

There was concern at the Ladd Company that the G (general) rating that the film was initially awarded—meaning that anyone, even unaccompanied children, could go and see it—was undesirable and liable to put adults off. An expletive was dubbed onto one of the characters to take care of this and gained the film a PG (parental guidance) tag. The Ladd Company had yet to have a hit since its formation, although Laddie had left his previous position as boss of 20th Century-Fox in a blaze of glory. Not only had megahits like *Star Wars* been to his credit there, but also a number of smaller, quality pictures like *Breaking Away, The Turning Point*, and Fred Zinnemann's *Julia*. David felt the film was being promoted by the right company in the States, but he knew he was up against ingrained American prejudice both on the subject matter of the movie and on its foreign source. He anxiously awaited the opening reviews.

There was a band of critics who didn't like the movie, among them Andrew Sarris in *The Village Voice*. Sarris found the film "a surprisingly skimpy entertainment. True story or not," he argued, "there are three false starts to the narrative and half a dozen anticlimaxes at the end." Pauline Kael, in *The New Yorker*, was especially negative and derisive. "The effects calculated to make your spirits soar," she wrote, "are the same effects that send you soaring down to the supermarket to buy a six-pack of Miller or Schlitz or Löwenbräu. The film is bursting with the impersonal, manufactured, go-to-the-mountain poetry that sells products. . . . The picture works, though. It's held together by the glue of simpleminded heroic sentiments. . . . Produced by David Puttnam, who is widely regarded as the major force in the (coming) revivification of the British Film Industry, this movie is in love with simple values and synthesized music. . . . It's retrograde moviemaking, presented with fake bravura. The movie has a mildewed high moral tone, and it takes you back; it's probably the best Australian film ever made in England."

Time magazine, however, provided welcome balance: "Like every element in the picture, the actors look right, they seem to emerge from the past, instead of being pasted on to it, as so many characters in historical movies seem to be. That quality, finally, is what distinguishes the film." Jack Kroll of *Newsweek* agreed, adding, "The large cast provide the kind of sheer acting pleasure you get from Britain's best repertory companies." Kroll discounted any objections his readers might have. "*Chariots of Fire* is a wonderful film. You'll hear it's about runners, British runners at that, and the 1924 Olympics, and you may think you don't want to see it, but you do. *Chariots of Fire* will thrill you and delight you and very possibly reduce, or exalt, you to tears."

A healthy trickle of money from the box office was beginning to roll in from Warners' slow, carefully planned release. *Variety* ran an article that warmed the cockles of David's heart, headed, "Chariots: Slow and Steady Will Win the Race, Per Elated Ladd/WB."

Chariots of Fire went on to take in $1.5 million at the box office in seven weeks of limited release in the United States. Even more important was the fact that it maintained or actually increased its box-office performance with each subsequent week. The Ladd Company and Warners had decided early on to book the film only into theaters that would play it through Christmas 1981 and to adhere to this plan of restricted release no matter how well the picture did. They estimated that the slow buildup and the film's legs would see it through until the following February's all-important Oscar nominations. Then the film could go wide.

By February 1982, the Hollywood Press Association had awarded *Chariots* a Golden Globe for Best Foreign Film. Warners, while pleased with the accolade, went out of its way to emphasize to the Academy members (who vote on Oscar-nomination categories) that *Chariots* was eligible for *all* regular Oscars and should not be limited to the foreign-film category. Terry Semel of Warners spelled out the cost of the company's campaign in boosting *Chariots:* "So far, we've spent $1.2 million marketing the film. By the end of February, with the film entering wider release, we will have spent $4 million and we expect the movie will take in a minimum of $10 million in film rental and perhaps as much as $20 million."

Everything in the U.S. handling of the movie was aimed at making it a commercial success while spending the minimum amount. The rationale was that in many ways the film would sell itself and become its own best advertisement. "Let's treat this as if every penny is important" was the keynote.

With 196 theaters ready to open the movie almost five months after its debut, Warners looked to the February 11 announcement of the Academy Award nominations. "We hope to be going into our second wide weekend with lots of nominations," Semel declared. His hopes were more than justified: *Chariots* was nominated in no fewer than seven Academy Award categories, on top of eleven British Academy nominations. The seven Academy Award categories were: Best Supporting Actor for Ian Holm, Best Original Score for Vangelis, Best Film Editing for Terry Rawlings, Best Screenplay for Colin Welland, Best Costume Design for Milena Canonero, Best Director for Hugh Hudson, and—most coveted of all—Best Picture.

Back in Britain, David felt complete. *Midnight Express* may have been a breakthrough film, but it had not been *his* breakthrough film. Now he had a movie of his own that he was proud to acknowledge.

David and Patsy arrived unheralded at Los Angeles Airport on Saturday, March 27, 1982, weary after the long journey from London. They were recognized, however, as they checked into the Bel-Air Hotel. Everyone knew what they had come for, and soon after settling into their room, the telephone began to ring.

David chose not to attend any of the pre-Oscar parties to which they were invited. Instead, after resting for a while, the couple dressed and dined quietly in the hotel that evening. Next day, David hired a car and they drove to Malibu beach. They reveled in this brief respite, for the pressures and separation of the last few months had been almost overwhelming. Still, there was an underlying tension that could not be shaken off as they anticipated the Oscar award ceremony to be held the following evening at the Dorothy Chandler Pavilion.

Until a few days before, the picture had been considered a rank outsider in the Best Picture stakes. Warren Beatty's three-hour, $43 million *Reds* was the favorite for Best Picture, backed by an enormous campaign launched by Beatty as producer, director, co-writer, and star—together with his distributor, Paramount Pictures. "*Reds* is going to win" had been buzzing on the grapevine for weeks, although both David and Patsy were gradually sensing that *Chariots* was *liked* much more. They had largely shrugged off the few "I voted for you" calls with "Oh yes, but they'll be saying that to everybody!" yet there was a growing feeling that these people actually meant it. Strangers approached them with phrases like "I can't tell you how wonderful your film is," and the British Academy of Film and Television Arts (BAFTA) had presented *Chariots* with its Best Film award. But they still couldn't believe the film was a serious contender.

In the absence of any stars in the movie and since Hugh Hudson was still an unknown first-time director, the media focus had been heavily on David Puttnam as producer. He had, after all, been an increasingly visible presence on the film scene for more than a decade. David *became* the story, as the press finally put it all together. His biography had registered.

Hugh Hudson had begged his producer to take over the promotional interviews, which he reckoned he couldn't handle himself. This made it all the more unexpected when he complained that David had seized the limelight. The friendship between the two had cooled in earnest after Hugh failed to win the Best Direction award in England. So when Hugh and Sue Hudson joined the Puttnams at the Bel-Air, the atmosphere was decidedly strained. The four of them traveled together through the baking California sunshine in a hired air-conditioned limousine and arrived promptly at five at the Dorothy Chandler Pavilion complex. There they took their seats for the award ceremony. To their left sat Warren Beatty, their main rival in several categories, including Best Director and Best Picture, accompanied by Diane Keaton and Barry Diller, the head of Paramount Pictures.

The electric atmosphere in the huge theater and the knowledge that the entire evening would be watched by millions of viewers throughout the world heightened the tension for the contenders. As the evening wore on, there was no clean sweep for any one film, but Patsy was struck by a remark David made to her right at the beginning. He had been going through the program while Patsy was busy looking around at the celebrities in the throng. She knew how he loved to calculate percentages for the sheer exhilaration of seeing numbers work. "I'll tell you something," he said. "If we win Best Costume, that will be the deciding factor."

"What do you mean? How do you know?" Patsy asked.

"Because costume is very important, since we're up against costume. If we win that, we'll win the picture."

"But why costume? Why not production design?" Patsy asked.

"No, *costume,*" David replied.

When Patsy checked the program and the other contenders for costume, she could see his point, for they were indeed up against stiff competition in that category. The favorite was *Reds,* but there were also *The French Lieutenant's Woman, Pennies from Heaven,* and *Ragtime* to contend with.

During one of the intermissions, David observed Warren Beatty and Barry Diller deep in animated conversation. Warren was jabbing away at the program to illustrate his point, and David felt certain that the actor had reached the same conclusion he had.

Patsy could not help but feel how ironic it was, for *Reds* had been in production at the same time as *Chariots of Fire,* and Shirley Russell had commandeered most of the period costumes in London for Beatty. An entire aircraft hangar had been packed with the clothes. Milena Canonero had had to scour the country for any remaining costumes of the same period, then had resorted to her native Italy to have the bulk of the costumes made. The joke in the *Chariots* company had been that if Milena had broken into the *Reds* hangar and stolen the costumes she required, they would not have even been missed. David conceded that Shirley Russell had carried out a mammoth task with extraordinary skill for Beatty's huge-budget production, just as Milena had done for *Chariots,* which had brought him to the conclusion that costume would be the crucial battleground.

Later he learned that Beatty had indeed been arguing the same point with Diller. But for now both Patsy and he were only too aware that although *Chariots* was the popular favorite for Best Picture, the smart money from both cinéastes and the industry was on *Reds.*

The excitement mounted as the first of the seven *Chariots*-nominated categories was reached—Terry Rawlings for Best Film Editing—but this was won by Michael Kahn for *Raiders of the Lost Ark.* For Best Supporting Actor Ian Holm lost out to Sir John Gielgud for the Dudley Moore vehicle, *Arthur.* Five categories to go, and the all-important Best Costume was next. Feelings ran high as the announcement was made that the winner was Milena Canonero for *Chariots of Fire.* If David was correct, the rest of the evening belonged to *Chariots!* Sure enough, Vangelis won Best Original Score against competition from *Dragonslayer, On Golden Pond, Ragtime,* and *Raiders of the Lost Ark.* Next to win was Colin Welland's *Chariots* screenplay, triumphing over *Absence of Malice, Arthur, Atlantic City,* and *Reds.* "Look out, the British are coming!" Colin declared as he held his award high.

Warren Beatty's win as Best Director for *Reds* was a crushing disappointment for Hugh that he was unable to hide. If *Chariots* won Best Picture now, it would be a virtual rerun of what he saw as the British Academy's injustice.

Sentiment won the day as Best Actor and Actress were awarded to Henry Fonda and Katharine Hepburn for *On Golden Pond.* Then Best Picture was next—and last—to be announced. Having scooped the earlier technical awards, Steven Spielberg knew that he was not in the running for Best Picture, although *Raiders of the Lost Ark* had been nominated in that category. He leaned forward to David and Patsy, squeezing David's shoulder.

"It's going to be you—I *know* it's going to be you," he exclaimed, as veteran movie star Loretta Young came out to make the announcement. All eyes were on her as she opened the envelope and looked at the name of the winner. When she appeared to hesitate, David's heart went into his mouth.

Loretta Young had been asked many times before to present the Best Picture award but had turned down every request. There had been no film that she wanted to give the prize to until the arrival of *Chariots*, which she adored. "I prayed for it to win," she told the Puttnams after the ceremony. "That's the only reason I came here tonight." The reason for her hesitation in making the announcement when she first saw the film's name on the card was simple. It was indeed *Chariots*, but she had had to refocus in case she had imagined it, *willed* its name to be there. "Can you imagine an actress making that mistake?" She laughed. Her hesitation had been plain for all to see on the telecast of the event. "I had to take a breath and look again before I said it!"

With her announcement, the theater erupted into applause and cheers. David got to his feet to collect the award, but his legs promptly buckled under him, and he fell into the lap of a priest in the adjacent seat whom he hadn't even noticed until that moment. Tears blinded Patsy's eyes as she watched her husband helped back to his feet by the priest, then briskly make his way toward the stage to receive the coveted award. All she could think was "No, no, it's too *soon*! You can't win things like this yet—you're too young!" Exhilaration was far away as Patsy's mind raced. Oscars were for superstars like Marlon Brando and Barbra Streisand—this was too *early*. She was brought down to earth with a thud as the next thought struck her: "Oh, God, he hasn't thought of anything to say!" Then she was calm, for she knew he would have something sorted out—that was David.

He later remembered walking up the stairs, terrified of tripping since they looked very slippery. On reaching the top, he walked toward the gracious, elderly actress who was waiting to present him with his award. It was like a scene in slow motion.

Everyone had been kissing each other all night, and he thought, "That's not right for this woman, she's a very dignified lady and I don't really know her. I can't just shake her hand, though, that'd be too pompous."

As he walked forward, the solution presented itself as she held out her hand, which he promptly took and kissed. Then he was standing there, looking at what appeared to be a rather tatty velvet cover on the stand—quite different from the glittering facade presented to the audience. He thought to himself, "God, these thousands of people here with everything looking so great from the front—if only they knew how extraordinarily tatty it all is." And he felt unable to enjoy it as much as he had wanted to, too, because it was like revenge after the dreadful time the film had had and its crawl into being. One piece of David was saying, "About fucking time—and thanks for nothing!" It was horrible, he knew, but it was something he felt at least a little bit.

He could hear every word he was saying as he started his speech, but it was like listening to a movie soundtrack, as if someone else were doing the talking. It was a short speech, with only one person singled out, as in an unprecedented departure from the Academy's protocol he declared, "Hugh is the director, and I'd like to have him standing here with me now. I'd like Hugh to come up." Only when Hugh joined him and the Oscar was held high by the two of them did he conclude, "You're the most generous nation. You've taken this little Cinderella of a picture to your hearts." (And he thought to himself, "Cinderella picture? Where did that come from? Why did I say *Cinderella* picture?") His sense of dissociation was complete. The words were echoing in his head, but it was as if someone else had written them.

After the ceremony Hugh Hudson was very glum, and at a dinner party held by Paula Weinstein and attended by the David Pickers and the Michael Apteds, Hugh turned up on his own without Sue. The photographs of the occasion show him smiling, but the struggle is obvious. Patsy has her own view of Hugh's reaction and feels certain he was thinking that if only

David had given him his head, he would have been up there on the stand collecting the Best Director award, not Warren Beatty. If he'd been allowed to spend the sort of money Beatty had, he would have had a real chance at his goal. Paula Weinstein gave her guests a beautiful dinner, but Hugh's attitude put an uncomfortable edge on the whole evening.

When the couple woke up next morning, it seemed that all the world and his wife wanted to interview David. Off he went, promising to be back by lunchtime so they could pack for their late-afternoon flight home. Patsy sat bemused in their hotel room, "gob-smacked" in her cockney parlance, at the patently fraudulent sentiments behind the stream of gifts, cards, balloons, teddy bears, and flowers that jostled the congratulatory telegrams. It all seemed too vulgar and out of place. Fine to have a little note from friends and associates, but all these gewgaws from total strangers struck a decidedly false note.

So choked up did she feel that when David called to say he was having lunch with someone and could she pack, she burst into tears. "What's the matter?" he asked, astonished at her reaction. "What on *earth* is the *matter* with you?" Patsy blurted out. "I can't cope with this, I don't understand this." The struggle had been one thing, the fight to achieve the breakthrough; but what she saw as this incredible display of Hollywood bullshit at the end of it all—that was just too much to take.

Later in the day, Hugh and David said their good-byes and embraced each other emotionally. Hugh was off for a vacation with Sue to the West Indies, while the Puttnams were returning to London. On the plane, someone gave Patsy a present with a Union Jack on it. "Wouldn't it be wonderful to attach it to the Oscar for the press photographers at London Airport?" she suggested. David smilingly agreed.

The photographs were printed, and a comment that Hugh made was relayed to them: that the Union Jack gesture tied to the Oscar was a typical Puttnam maneuver to get all the glory. So sensitive were Hugh's feelings that even Patsy's innocent suggestion held no resonance for him beyond the implication of another small betrayal.

. . .

After the ceremony in Hollywood and the enthusiastic head-lines in the dailies—tying the success of the film in with the prevailing victorious Falklands spirit—the congratulations from many of David's colleagues were disappointingly muted. Many, in fact, seemed reluctant even to allude to the film's triumph. Colin Welland's misunderstood "The British are coming!" declaration at the Oscar ceremony was seen by some as vainglorious and premature. The peculiarly English phenomenon of despising success was quickly settling in.

"I'm very glad for you, David," Lindsay Anderson told him after the awards. "You like that sort of thing."

Alan Parker appreciated a transformation that had occurred in David more than most. "He'd come back from America after *Midnight Express* and said, 'Enough is enough. I'm going to do it on my own terms.' I remember that period very strongly at the beginning of the seeding of *Chariots of Fire*, when he first met Jake. There was a definite change. We've always had the anger, but from the point of view of having been in Hollywood and getting fucked by the system, our only salvation was that we always laughed at it and always knew we'd get them one day. He came back, he was determined to do it differently, outside the system. He wasn't an evangelist yet, but he was certainly someone who wanted to get back his dignity as a person. He wanted to feel good about himself. It was hard for him, for he didn't exactly come back in a blaze of glory. *Chariots of Fire* was the end of the spiv."

Despite Alan's well-intentioned view, many argued that there was still an element of the barrow-boy approach in *Chariots of Fire*, and indeed they viewed the film as being in every way as exploitative as *Midnight Express*. If that film had been exploitative, what about *Chariots*, with its quasi-inspirational, jingoistic message and the many factual distortions its critics had found, poetic licenses David had taken to make the story more dramatic? Had David simply moved on to a classier con game—but a con game nonetheless?

12

The second film David and Hugh Hudson had planned together was never made, despite numerous rewrites. Iain Smith was asked to get involved as an associate producer on *October Circle*, one of the two projects originally offered to the Fayeds, but he found the enterprise oddly lacking in energy. As he saw it, there was insufficient wind in that ship's sails, which he put down to David's not being fully behind it.

Warner Bros. wanted David to follow *Chariots*'s success by producing *Greystoke—Tarzan, Lord of the Apes*, a retelling by Robert Towne of the Edgar Rice Burroughs tale. Despite the fact that Hugh was again to direct, there were many elements of the film David did not like. A major one was the fact that it would be a Warners production, with David acting as a hired-hand producer. He had realized early on that there are two types of films: One is the studio film, in which a studio provides a hundred percent of the financing, but then insists on having its own people crawling all over the superstructure, compiling reports and demanding progress checks—the proposed *Greystoke* system. The idea of this was anathema to David for a multitude of reasons, all of them boiling down to control.

The second type of film is the one David had vowed to make —independently produced, outside the auspices of a studio. The negative side to this approach, of course, is the burden of finding the financing and of dealing with the many demands of investors. But this problem, however horrendous, is justified in David's mind by one light shining at the end of the tunnel—his *total autonomy* over the product. When *Agatha* turned into a Warners/Dustin Hoffman studio effort and autonomy walked out the door, so did David. In many ways his Casablanca period had represented the worst of both worlds; his function there had been reduced to acting as hired hand for an independent company, only tenuously tied to a major studio.

David had now fully defined his own role, and his confidence was restored by *Chariots*'s success. Following the inevitable money-raising traumas (part of which would ideally be solved by the acquisition of his films by U.S. majors as a "negative pickup" on completion), his aim for his next production was to build a wall around his project, a kind of fortress that would protect the creative process going on inside. Once this wall was built, David could then stand back and let the movie proceed, his primary function then being to keep a balance in the production between the twin demands of the creative and budgetary forces. As David viewed it, even a production designer should respect the budget without the feeling his or her artistic integrity is being compromised, while even a production accountant could be expected to make decisions beyond purely money-oriented considerations.

The sum of all his principles and experience told David one thing—not to get involved in *Greystoke*, because he would have no control. Other elements of the film bothered him as well, such as the problem of special effects: "I'm not the producer for this, I can't stand about when I've got a special-effects man telling me he doesn't know if the ape masks will be ready in time," he told Patsy. "Who needs it? And I've told them that while it's budgeted at $18 million, they'll be lucky to get it out for $25 million. In fact, it could easily go up to $30 million."

Despite these reservations, however, one aspect of the *Greystoke* script held enormous appeal for David—the delineation of the love of the ape for the human child. The notion that like does not necessarily have to love like captured his imagination. This one facet of *Greystoke* attracted him, for it held a powerful, elemental appeal, but the question still nagged—was the concept, beguiling as it was, worth the likely $30 million price tag?

David asked Warners to let him have three months to consider the project so that he could conduct a feasibility study. The delay was agreed to, although Hugh waited with increasing impatience. When the study was ready, David took one look at it and concluded that the film's production would be a nightmare in which he did not wish to participate. His decision made Warners angry, and it left Hugh Hudson with a feeling of abandonment. Hugh then elected to become *Greystoke*'s producer as well as its director, letting himself in for the nightmare that the movie's production indeed turned out to be. Still, he had a $30 million movie in his pocket. Later, when David went to Warners to request a fraction of this amount for his own proposed new film, *Local Hero*, Warners—whether piqued, shortsighted, or just plain downright vindictive—chose to turn him down.

Today, Hugh Hudson talks freely of his relationship with David over the years, alternately praising and condemning him: "He voraciously grabbed anything he could for himself from *Chariots of Fire* and denigrated my position many times to the extent that people wondered what I had to do with the film. He capitalized on misquotes that had him as 'director.' Of course he had a lot to do with the film—he initiated it—but I directed it, I styled it. I've heard other things he said, like he chose the music. *I* chose the music for the film, Vangelis was my collaborator on many of my projects, someone I'd known for ten years. It enhances the film, it holds it all together. I've heard David say on the radio that he chose the music and that the film was nothing without the music. That's absolute rubbish and a dishonorable thing to say. It's so patently untrue.

"He should have done everything after the event—as he did during the making of the film and before producing the film—to protect the director. If he is the captain of the ship, his job is to protect and help the people on the ship. He's not a great leader until he can do that. You don't abandon your crew. The great leader—and he may have learned this now—is one who has to deal with all those human issues. They're part of the deal of life.

"I *would* have done interviews if he had asked me. I was nervous a bit of being on TV, especially in the beginning, but I've learned since. I was new at it. If you're a producer or you're in control, you're a father figure, therefore you've got to be a father. You can't take on the position of father and then run away from it and abandon the child. It's very, very immature to do that, and hurtful. He *has* given people wonderful opportunities all his life, for whatever reason or motivation. It's very admirable, but he has at times abandoned them. He's often run away when things got difficult, so he hasn't grown up, he's not totally mature.

"BAFTA [the British Academy of Film and Television Arts] and the Oscars didn't worry me—that had nothing to do with him, that's not the reason I was aggravated. The Americans are taught the only important thing is winning, but we're not taught that in England. Participating is. *Chariots* is about that—participating, not winning, because you can't win all the time in your life. We all play to win, but if you lose, you've got to learn from your losses. There's that great scene in *Chariots* where Abrahams has won and he breaks down, showing how awful it can be to win. It's worse than losing.

"David was determined to grab everything, didn't want to share the glory—that's the truth. But it's all over now, it really doesn't matter anymore. It's only ego and vanity that were bruised, so it doesn't matter. I *made* the film. I know what I did on the film, I know that he initiated it and that a lot of the success and the style of the film was my doing in conjunction with him and all the other people who worked on it—the musicians, the actors, the writer, all of them. *Certainly* he's self-lacerating—I know that. But the reason is guilt. There's a lot of guilt there."

Hugh could be confusing guilt with responsibility, since one cannot exist without the other. Certainly David has never shied from taking full responsibility for his actions. A friend of both men has discussed the feud from both their perspectives: "Hugh maneuvered himself into a position where *Chariots of Fire* was the fallback subject, using *October Circle* as his ticket. He went to David originally saying he loved the book and had tried to buy the rights before he discovered David held them. Perhaps they could do it together? Remember that Hugh was forty now and came from the same background in commercials as the [Alan] Parkers and the [Ridley] Scotts. He'd even seen Adrian Lyne, who was much younger than him, get his chance. So when David failed to get *October Circle* off the ground, he felt honor bound to give *Chariots* to Hugh—who did a very nice job with it, no question. But if ever a film was one man's vision, that film is *Chariots,* and that man is David Puttnam."

Hugh stresses that he still feels enormous affection for David, while disarmingly admitting, "I've been bitchy about him, but there's no point in being bitchy. I've felt slighted by him in many ways. We still share a building in the mews next to his house, and I feel bound to him in the way my career's gone. I wanted him to produce *Greystoke,* but he didn't, for whatever *real* reason. . . .

"If David *had* stayed and produced the film, I think it would have been more successful. I'll say that, which is a great compliment to David, because when I took on both functions, I had to wear two hats. . . . He would have made it work, and it would have come out a better film. Of course I was annoyed when he walked off, because he was a very good partner to work with. He shouldn't have walked off. *That's* my great criticism of him. When you start something, you've got to finish it."

Alan Parker observed the *Greystoke* conflict from a distance. "The Hugh Hudson of *Greystoke* was not the Hugh Hudson who made *Chariots of Fire*. He asserted himself in a way that was not pleasing to David. It was clear that Hugh was going to be very much in the driving seat because of the confidence he had in himself and from Warners after *Chariots of Fire*. David was uncomfortable with that part of it as well as all the other stuff. Hugh had become a maestro. . . . After *Chariots*, there was no mistake that Hugh would be in charge, which I happen to believe is right. David, on the other hand, hates the *auteur* theory, but curiously reinvented the idea of the producer as *auteur*. That's fine for him—but as a theory and a system, it's incredibly dangerous, because there are very few people who have David's ability to understand the mechanics of film and the sensitivities of the creative side. Producers in control are usually a recipe for disaster. Perhaps arguably, for David to be in control it's different, because he is unique and extremely talented—but I call his the Mussolini school of filmmaking.' "

Another aspect of the *Greystoke* saga illustrates, despite the undoubted sincerity of all the other views expressed, just where the bottom line is finally drawn. In the wake of *Chariots*'s success, Hugh Hudson had found himself looking for representation in Hollywood. "Talk to Creative Artists," David suggested, aware of the dizzying rise to power of Mike Ovitz's agency since its foundation in 1975. Hugh was duly taken on as a CAA client.

The original deal that Warners struck with David and Hugh included a fee of $500,000 each for *Greystoke*. Shortly after CAA took Hugh on as a client, Ovitz began to do his job and renegotiated Hugh's fee. Warners agreed to upgrade Hugh to $650,000.

David was informed of this by Warners when the deal was a fait accompli. CAA had done well for Hugh—too well, in Warners' view. Would David help them out by reducing his fee to $425,000?

From that moment, beginning with a burst of outrage that must have rocked Burbank and the nearby Ventura Freeway to their foundations, Warners had effectively blown it. Pride, not money, dominated the equation. David walked away from *Greystoke* without looking back.

. . .

Even before the runaway success of *Chariots of Fire*, an invitation for David to join the board of Goldcrest as a nonexecutive director had been widely discussed, so there was little surprise when the appointment was announced in the wake of the *Chariots* windfall.

David Norris joined the Goldcrest board as director of business and legal affairs in 1982, and found a company in the business of appraising developed product and raising equity against foreign sales. "A film brokerage operation" is the rather unglamorous appellation Norris gave it. When asked what he thought of the operation, Norris replied, "I think you're mad." He cited the cases of ABC, CBS, and NBC in the 1967–70 period, all of which had tried to enter the theatrical motion-picture field, then Lorimar, and Polygram in more recent times. Each had ended up licking its wounds, recording huge losses, and writing off the bulk of its venture capital as an irretrievable loss. But the one thing they had all lacked, Norris noted, was distribution. On this the long-established majors had a stranglehold.

"I *like* your madness," he added, "and I can see how you're trying to contain risk, but you can't expect bonanza business." He nevertheless agreed to join the board, largely because of the presence of filmmakers like David.

Although nonexecutive, David Puttnam ensured that his presence on the board was felt from the beginning. "David was very important to the development of Goldcrest, more important than was fully realized," James Lee reckons. "When we first met, just after I'd become chairman, he'd been involved with Jake [Eberts] in an advisory capacity. He was invited to be the first actual filmmaker on the Goldcrest Films International Board, the company that was the forerunner of Goldcrest itself. At our very first meeting we had to decide whether or not to invest in a picture called *Hopscotch*, with Walter Matthau and Glenda Jackson. Jake had arrived at an understanding with his U.S. partner, Jo Child, who seemed to feel the picture would be put through on the nod. Child was present and was absolutely incensed at David's very forceful argument that *Hopscotch* was not a good bet. David made the point that Walter Matthau was not necessarily a surefire box-office proposition, his audience was getting older with him. The recent trend in Walter Matthau movies had been down, whilst the cost of the films had gone up. In summary, he observed that this was an extremely bad investment to make.

"Coming from the only person round the table with any experience on films—since Dickie Attenborough had yet to join—we decided not to back *Hopscotch*. Jo Child raged, but to no avail, and in the end his IFI (International Film Investments) had to back the film themselves.

"For the first time, Jake could now see he wasn't going to have it all his own way. . . . David was on the board—and I liked the cut of his jib, and continued to do so thereafter. He was never afraid to speak his mind."

There are as many theories about the reasons for David's modus operandi as there are variations of the account of Goldcrest's fortunes. But of one thing there was now no doubt—his unique ability among British producers to generate an idea on his own, a process that by definition puts the producer in the driver's seat. David was free to enjoy genuine collaborative intimacy between producer, screenwriter, and director. Although criticized by friends and enemies alike for making his life too public through his press contacts, what David was telling everyone was, "Look, I have changed. I will be taken seriously!" As a reaction to his 1960s period of self-loathing and to the expediency that had ruled in the 1970s, his attitude now was "That was then, now is now." He was no longer prepared to tolerate the fractious sort of relationship he had had in the past with the likes of Ken Russell.

David has to get pleasure out of a film beyond the mere pleasure of actually getting the film made or indeed of making money. This was evidenced when he was asked if it wouldn't give him a kick to help a "real" director make a chef d'oeuvre—a Visconti, perhaps, or a Fellini. "Quite frankly, no," he replied.

"I don't get any pleasure out of being a banker and making the money available. What's the thrill in that?" Thus, David stands almost alone among producers, who normally are a breed primarily eager just to get any film off the ground, especially if they've managed to collar a certain director or star. David maintains that the main thrill is in *loving* the films he makes and the people he makes them with at the time—and (being all too human) hoping the feeling is reciprocated.

Alan Parker has watched David's system in action but notes its flip side. "His whole way of working is to befriend people. That way he gets the best from them and creates the most enjoyable kind of environment. The moment a project is finished, though, he's no longer their friend, he's on to something else. A lot of people have smarted from that friendship not continuing."

Ever since the Puttnams' return from the United States, Patsy had been chasing a dream she had nurtured over the years. It had been quickened by a visit to Ridley Scott's magnificent Gloucestershire country house in 1977. During the long discussions she and David had had about the pros and cons of making the *Midnight Express* trip, he had spoken the magic words: "Look, it won't be for that long, and when we come back, you can have that house in the country you've always wanted." Patsy had been sold.

And eventually, so was David. They found an old stone millhouse in Wiltshire, a place with charm and lots of possibilities. Patsy fell in love, and so the deal was done—they were landed gentry at last.

13

There are few certainties in the film world, and there had been none at all for David in his career to date. But following the awards for *Chariots,* he was at last able to announce that on April 19, 1982, he would again be standing by a camera producing a film. For the first time, an element of certainty had been introduced: *Local Hero* was about to roll.

David had been advised by Colin Young, the director of the National Film and Television School, to see Bill Forsyth's *That Sinking Feeling,* following its appearance at the Edinburgh Film Festival. A showing in London was arranged, and David responded favorably to the film. At the showing, Forsyth handed over his script for *Gregory's Girl* to David. "Because I'm such a terrific judge of material, I turned it down!" David says, laughing. "I had two reasons. I felt that for him, *Gregory's Girl* didn't represent a major departure from *That Sinking Feeling,* and then

I felt it was a regression for me to *That'll Be the Day*. It was a very stupid decision, and I regret it deeply, but there it is!"

"I owe David a great deal," Bill acknowledges. "Not only did he get me a distribution deal for *That Sinking Feeling,* but he introduced me to my agent, Anthony Jones. So indirectly through David I found my *Gregory's Girl* producers, Clive Parsons and Davina Belling. Then it was David's brilliant idea to double-bill *Chariots of Fire* with *Gregory's Girl,* which brought in more money for my film than it made on its first release. I associate our meeting with a big change in my life, the start of good things happening."

A year after the first encounter, the two men met again, by chance. "David said he wanted to show me a movie," Bill recalls. "We arranged to meet at BAFTA at seven, where he had *Whisky Galore* run. He didn't talk about it there and then, but I got the idea that maybe he had it in mind we should make a film together, and maybe it would be set in Scotland. After a week or so we got more serious and began to talk about it."

David had come across a clipping about a man in the Hebrides who had negotiated a major deal with a U.S. petrochemical company, a better deal than anything the British National Oil Corporation had achieved. The chemistry that had earlier produced *Chariots of Fire* from a study of the 1920s Olympics was at work once again, as David sought to repeat the organic growth that had brought forth that film. Bill agreed to submit a two-page treatment, deemphasizing oil rigs and the hardware of the business and emphasizing the concept of an American petrochemical giant being taken to the cleaners by the supposedly naïve inhabitants of a small Scottish fishing village.

He wrote the script for *Local Hero* between May and September 1981, a year after David's initial approach. Between their meetings, David was enjoying his enormous success with *Chariots,* while Bill's breakthrough film, *Gregory's Girl,* was released. He had plodded on doggedly after David rejected it and had ultimately raised the £200,000 necessary to fund the project. Although still a small-budget film, it was a gigantic step up from the £8,000 that had produced *That Sinking Feeling.* "The odd thing," David points out, "is that when we started working together, neither of us was particularly successful. *Chariots* could easily have been the end of me."

David liked Bill's original script, but he had grave reservations about its length. A second draft arrived two months later, still roughly the same length. Then the money soundings began in earnest, while Bill and newly appointed associate producer Iain Smith (who had been retained following his sterling work as location manager on *Chariots of Fire*) went off to Scotland to find suitable locations and to consider casting. Goldcrest initially agreed to put up £100,000 to enable preproduction to proceed on the basis of Bill's treatment, then agreed to fund no less than half the budget of £2 million when they saw the shooting script. David reckoned the other half would not be too difficult to find at the current stage of his career, but he was in for a rude shock. First Warners, then EMI turned the project down, and then Rank made an offer that would have meant financial suicide.

Only weeks remained before principal photography was due to start. Then finally, on the night that *Chariots of Fire* won Best Film and Bill Forsyth won Best Screenwriter for *Gregory's Girl* at BAFTA, Goldcrest's chairman James Lee said, "Enough fucking about—*we'll* put up *all* the money. Let's just make the film and worry about it afterward."

What followed was a chain of events that David knew only too well. Warners quickly bought the U.S. distribution rights, the second time around, for half the budget—exactly what David had been seeking all along. Why the change of mind? It was apparently a matter of the "Jesus Christ, it's actually being made!" syndrome. A project is all too easy to reject in paper form; it is simpler to say no and thereby avoid responsibility. When a project is actually *rolling*, however, it becomes a different beast entirely, and the same executives who originally turned it down may reconsider.

When it came time for casting *Local Hero* Bill broached the name of the star whom he had in mind for the role of Felix Happer: his dream casting would be Burt Lancaster. David was intrigued, but he had qualms about the effect this might have on the film's budget; at the same time, he was aware of the beneficial effect Burt Lancaster's name would have on cable and television rights. The script was sent out to Lancaster in Los Angeles, and he loved it. He was riding high with his triumph in *Atlantic City*, and was so captivated by Bill's script that he agreed to do his three-week stint on the film for a much-reduced fee up front in exchange for profit points in the picture.

Apart from a week in Houston, Texas, the entire film was to be shot in Scotland over an eight-week period. As usual, David was there from day one and was present for most of the shooting. As David's associate producer, Iain Smith was a key figure on the set, and he quickly established a working relationship with David—a man whose method of operation he generally admired. "David's system was to stay well back from the film during the shooting and the first part of cutting. He then allowed the film to take its form and shape between the director and the editor, then only at that stage would he come back in again and start to look at the film, when everyone else was starting to flag. It's a very clever thing to do, because it gives him the ability to tidy up all the things that are wrong, with a kind of objectivity. And he's doing it when everyone else is saying, 'Oh, Christ, this isn't going to work,' and this is always the case, every single film that's ever made. This always happens after working for fifteen weeks of cutting. You're sitting there watching it, you no longer know what you're looking at, and you think, 'This is really going to bomb, this is terrible.' You sit there and you wonder why on earth you ever tried to make the picture in the first place, and at this low point David arrives, all dapper and spruce. He notes all the dejection and then he'll say, 'Well, I've been thinking about this, and I've made some notes. I think we should take this scene and move it around. . . .' "

David saw *Local Hero* as an ecology piece—a *Mr. Smith Goes to Washington* for the 1980s. Never having produced a comedy before, he admitted he was nervous about the outcome. "What we're trying to make is a modest-budget film that looks like a big film with universal implications," he stated. "I believe passionately that only by being specific do you become global. I hate these films that aim for some nebulous mid-Atlantic market. Cinema is about the transference of personality to that of someone on the screen, and you can only do that if they have a fixed, clearly rooted identity."

Despite Bill Forsyth's tendency toward stubbornness and the occasional friction that did take place on the set, *Local Hero* was one of David's happiest filming experiences. He recognized qualities in Bill that he admired tremendously. "I think he's got a very, very wonderful vision of people. Not so much life as people. Bill has a unique ability to feel out the best in people, and he has an innate belief in the best of people. He's a remarkably uncorrupted and unsoured man. From my point of view, I'm not sure what I give Bill and wouldn't be presumptuous enough to say that it amounts to anything. In terms of what he gives me, I find him an absolutely reliable man, sometimes taciturn so that you're a little unsure as to where you're going or what you're doing, but on the other hand, he's always come through. I've grown to trust him more and more, not less and less, and sometimes it can go the other way. I trust his instincts —that's the most important thing."

Bill in turn is equally appreciative of David. "He's been great," he declared, "really supportive. I was very apprehensive. However, it has been a delight to find out how good producers can be. We did not have a lot of problems. It would have been interesting to have had a couple of big problems just to see how we would have got on."

David was sanguine about the film's prospects. "I think we'll get great reviews and have to fight for an audience like we did with *Chariots*. I think we could have a big hit—it's a film I think the public is waiting for. I've always known it was going to be a good film—recently it moved into the area of maybe it's a great film with cuts and changes we've made. I think we've now got three or four things we did that have made an immense difference to the picture. I am now buzzing with excitement over it. I love it, I absolutely love it. Let's put it this way—it's a ship I'm prepared to go down with."

Part of the deal with Warners had been its commitment to spend $1.5 million on *Local Hero*'s promotion during the first ninety days of its U.S. release in 1983. The movie opened in that market first, since David had to wait a few extra weeks for the availability of the Odeon in London. (Twentieth Century-Fox was in charge of U.K. distribution.) David attended the New York première with Bill Forsyth and felt they were soon off to a good start. "We're on a roll," he declared exuberantly. "I don't know yet how big a hit it's going to be, but I know it'll be a hit. I could watch the film knowing where the laughs should come, and every time they came right on cue."

Then the critics weighed in, and nearly all of them—including those who had disliked *Chariots of Fire*—were charmed. Even Pauline Kael somewhat bemusedly described the film as "misleading in the most disarming way imaginable. Experience in movies has led us to expect a whole series of clarifications, but here they don't arrive. After a while, their non-arrival becomes a relief and we may laugh at ourselves for having thought we needed them. *Local Hero* isn't any major achievement, but it has it's own free-form shorthand for jokes, and it's true to itself."

The reaction in Britain was upbeat as well. Geoff Brown in *The Times* noted a touch of wild natural magic in the film, close to the spirit of some Michael Powell classics, "trying to present the cosmic viewpoint of people, but through the most ordinary things." Another critic, Michael Owen, was even more enthusiastic. "I have only seen it twice and twice is not enough," he wrote. "It is such a joyous experience, bearing the identifiable pedigree of both men, that I predict worldwide success, awards, dollars, and everything else it deserves."

Regrettably, the actual outcome was not so glowing. Although the film turned a very tidy profit with cable and TV sales, it failed to take off in the unpredictable U.S. market. The universality David had felt was within his grasp turned out to elude him. Worldwide, however, it was still a successful outing, and there was no doubt that David had given his battery a thorough recharge.

"I loved *Local Hero*," he said later. "I loved everything about it. Making it, being on location with it, and seeing it. I needed what *Local Hero* gave me—after leaving Hollywood on the Wednesday with an Oscar, there I was in a field in Scotland the following Monday, bargaining with a farmer whose cows we wanted to use. The film is all of a piece, there is nothing artificial jammed into it, it's the opposite of a manufactured film." If the film came across to many as a meander through the Scottish countryside, it was at least a charming meander, with no trace of the manipulative strings that had been suspended so clearly over both *Midnight Express* and *Chariots of Fire*.

14

Jake Eberts dates his involvement in *The Killing Fields* from a telephone call in 1980 from Bob Rehme, who was then the head of Embassy films. "Look," Rehme said, "there is a wonderful article in *Newsweek* about the French Embassy in Phnom Penh and what they did to the Cambodians who tried to leave the country and were denied exit visas. I think the story would make a terrific movie. . . . So why don't you guys develop it, and when the time comes, we'll talk about being your distributor at Embassy?"

At the time, Jake was in New York for a week's visit and was sufficiently intrigued to seek the article out. U.S. journalist Sydney Schanberg and various others had been gathered in the embassy compound with the Cambodians to prepare for the mass departure but were frustrated by the exit visas demanded of them by their native colleagues. Rehme was right, Jake felt—

there *was* a movie there. His next step was to contact David Puttnam. "I called him up and told him the story about Schanberg, explaining that I wouldn't put up the money unless someone like him was prepared to make the film as the producer and would he get involved. He already knew about the story, he said, having read the article and heard it from other sources and said yes, he would like to get involved. The way IFI was constituted, we had to put our funds into someone else's company for development, and an American one at that. So David actually formed a company in Nevada, of all places, called Enigma Nevada, Inc. If David had not agreed to go ahead, I would never have got involved with *The Killing Fields*."

David had already read the *Newsweek* piece and had sought out relevant back issues of *The New York Times*. He saw at once a theme of male friendship that transcended cultures and continents, involving crushing guilt and astonishing tension, set against the huge backdrop of a country in the agony of genocide. Schanberg described his relationship with Dith Pran, a Cambodian interpreter who had saved his life, and how he had been forced to leave Pran behind in 1975 in the flight from the Khmer Rouge after the fall of Phnom Penh. Later, Schanberg had spent four years trying to trace Pran, who had survived starvation, incarceration, and torture while witnessing the systematic slaughter of his people.

When David met with Schanberg, he learned that the story was already committed to *The New York Times Magazine* for an article called "The Death and Life of Dith Pran." David saw the broad canvas in the subject and a larger theme he had long sought. He alerted his American lawyer, Tom Lewyn, to the fact that he wanted the rights to Schanberg's article. David made exhaustive representations to Schanberg, both in person and through Lewyn. Schanberg hired Sam Cohn to represent him, an agent who had always been well disposed toward David; this probably helped his case. David subsequently acquired the rights against stiff opposition from other interested parties, some of whom reportedly offered considerably more money.

As usual, David had very specific ideas for the writer, director, and cast of the film. But Jo Child at IFI had separately talked to Paddy Chayefsky and Sidney Lumet. Not only that, he wanted David to consider Dustin Hoffman to play the role of Schanberg. Clearly, Child was unfamiliar with the *Agatha* tale.

David resisted his pressure. In a stinging reply to Child, he wrote, "In essence, it comes down to this, my enthusiasm for our project stems from the fact that the entire picture exists in my mind, and what I have to find is a writer with whom I can communicate and who can put down on paper the film as I see it. My job has only been worthwhile when I've had along side of me contemporaries whose lives contain the same dreams, resonances and points of departure. This is patently not true of Paddy, and probably not true of Lumet. Further, I have never envisaged the piece as a star vehicle and I think it's fair to say that Dustin Hoffman would be as unprepared to work with me as I most assuredly am to work with him."

David had already assigned the writing of the script to Bruce Robinson, a young actor-turned-writer who had already worked with David on a number of aborted projects. Bruce remembers a breakfast with David in New York where they discussed with French director Louis Malle the possibility of his involvement with the movie. "He was talking about ballets of B-52s in the opening sequence—just nonsense, absolute nonsense, just as if he hadn't even bothered to read the script. He said he would want to rewrite it, after I'd worked on it torturously for a year and a half! We came out of the hotel to get into the limo, David's going back to England on the Concorde, and I was going back to Los Angeles, where I was living at the time, and he asked me what I thought about Malle. I said, 'He's ridiculous, the man's absurd, it's crazy what he's saying.' David listened, then said, 'Look, there's this young English director, never done any films, called Roland Joffe, whom I feel in my balls is right for the film.' I said, 'Yes? Well, for Christ's sake, go with him.'"

In turning Malle down, David wrote to Sam Cohn (who happened to be Malle's agent), saying, "All of my successes have been based on my ability to bring together a group of equals who instinctively wish to make the same movie. Bruce's script, to which I am heavily committed, has gone too far to be turned around and made into what could be termed a Louis Malle film."

For the part of Sydney Schanberg David defiantly cast Sam Waterston, whom he had spotted in producer Don Boyd's *Sweet William*. "I don't want a star who will bring with him all sorts of associations with other films," he declared. "I want all the audience's attention focused on the story."

For the part of Dith Pran, Dr. Haing S. Ngor was cast. Dr. Ngor had been working in Los Angeles as an assistant supervisor for the Indo-Chinese employment program when Roland Joffe discovered him. He had been a gynecologist in Phnom Penh when the Khmer Rouge occupied the city, and like Dith Pran, he had escaped into Thailand four years later. Only he himself and his nine-year-old niece had survived the extermination of their family of mother, father, four brothers, and fiancée.

David had long since decided that the budget for the movie must be on a scale that matched the scope of the project. "The day I decided to make *The Killing Fields* for £10 million," he recalls, "I knew it had to be a big feature film. You can't borrow £10 million of somebody's money and then bugger off and make a personal statement. All I'd have done in making a film that appealed only to a minority would have been to castrate the film business by proving yet again that you can't make serious films popular." Nor was *The Killing Fields* to be loaded with below-the-line costs: "The director's fee, my fee, the rights to Sydney and Pran, the screenplay and two leading actors, totaled less than £900,000."

From its conception to its completion, David saw *The Killing Fields* in highly graphic terms. "Ideas are God-given," he declared. "They don't come from anywhere else. All you have to worry about initially is whether a particular idea has the right dramatic curve. What is wonderful about this story is that it

3

starts off with an exciting relationship which goes down through a kind of visual and energetic period to reach a crisis, a tragedy, a parting of the ways. Then the curve flows up again to a reunion. That curve is as good as you're ever going to get for a movie. You can't ask for more. So long as you hold true to it, you'll end up with something that works emotionally because it's the classic curve of every human being's life—hope passing through trouble and travail to some form of resolution."

David recognized the constant theme that ran through his own work. "All the best of my pictures are, one way or another, about men in moral crises." He added that it was this aspect that intrigued him most—how people act under sometimes intolerable pressure, how much the human frame can stand, how moral issues are argued and resolved or left hanging to await resolution another day, maybe in another lifetime. Even when treated in a gentle, comic way, as in *Local Hero*, the theme was the same, although for him *Chariots of Fire* had been its ultimate embodiment.

Cambodia itself was under consideration for a possible location, but the initial difficulties, together with the potential problems, soon ruled it out. Thailand, just across the border, presented itself as the logical second choice. Thailand had the advantages that it was not virgin territory as far as filming was concerned, and that the cooperation of the Thai armed forces was promised.

The film's budget of £10 million was put up entirely by Goldcrest, save for $3 million from IFI. Warners advanced $4.75 million for North American theatrical rights and a further $4 million for U.K., French, German, and Japanese territories. With a video sale to Thorn-EMI, 80 percent of the budget was thus comfortably covered in advance.

Still, many viewed it as a highly risky venture. One of the people most impressed by David's audacity and courage in casting was Sam Waterston. "When I arrived in Thailand," he marveled, "it suddenly struck me that here was a producer gambling all this money on a movie of high purpose without a major star to carry it. Not only that, but he was using a first-time director and an Asian as one of the two chief characters. Now *that* takes some guts!"

The Killing Fields' first day of shooting in May 1983 was fraught with tension. It could well have turned out to be the *last* day of shooting. The opening scene in the movie had Sam Waterston and Haing Ngor chatting in an outdoor café. Their conversation is abruptly curtailed when a bomb explodes.

To simulate the explosion, the special-effects people had ready a pile of Fuller's earth offscreen, together with an air hose connected to a compressed air cylinder. Purely to alert the actors that the "explosion" was happening, a squib was set to go *bang*, for all that would be produced otherwise was a *whoosh*, followed by large quantities of Fuller's earth flying everywhere. Unfortunately, a local assistant substituted a compressed gas cylinder for the compressed air. When the squib went off, the gas was ignited, creating a horrific fireball that blazed across the set.

Luckily for Sam Waterston, at that moment the action required him to be leaving his table, so that when the big bang came he was already moving. Still, the flames singed the back of his hand and his shoulder, as if he had been caught by a blowtorch. His was the only injury, but until this was established, there was a terrible moment of shock and horror.

"It was *unthinkable*," says Iain Smith, shuddering at the memory, "and it could have been the *end* of the film. We'd been so pedantically careful with all the safety precautions. But still the accident had happened."

David is not proud of his reaction. "I went fucking berserk," he recalls. "My instinct, sad to say, was that Roland is one of those hairy-arsed realists and had somehow done it deliberately. I mean, obviously it was a mistake, but that the situation had been created by Roland in his quest for more realism. I tore into him, and he was so bewildered by my attack, he didn't even defend himself, just looked at me. Of course he was in shock as well. I *pounded* home my attack—how irresponsible he had been. Then it turned out to be an unbelievable error by one of the special-effects men."

A more major confrontation took place between David and Roland over a scene that was set in an opium den. Roland expressed his wish that real opium be obtained for the actors to give the scene an extra edge. "David saw the whole thing as potentially enormous trouble," says Roland. "He too was obviously asking himself what this signified for the rest of the film —was it all going to go like this? I'd been shooting this scene all day without opium and hadn't finished. David was terribly worried because the report would go to Warners on the dailies that we hadn't finished this apparently easy indoor scene and that I'd want to go on shooting it forever—which was quite possible. I *might* have said, 'No, I'm sorry, I think this scene is so important, I want to keep on shooting it tomorrow and the day after.' Who knows what caverns were opening up in David's mind—understandably.

"David called a production meeting. I knew he would scream and shout—he had to do something to get rid of all that tremendous tension. *So I didn't go.* I figured out that if I went and David said an awful lot of things he might regret, that would leave a lot of repair work to be done. If I didn't go, he could say whatever he liked but not to me. So I went to bed instead, whereupon this huge memo arrived. I told the man who brought it, 'The best thing you can do with that is take it outside and fling it into the Chao Phraya River.' The point I conveyed to David was that in his worry over the scene that day, he'd probably put a lot of stuff in his memo that he'd regret. What I would rather he did was take the memo back, read it again next morning, and black out the stuff he didn't really want to say but which was probably necessary to express at the time.

"The memo duly came back—all eleven pages of it—almost *entirely* blacked out except for the beginning, 'Dear Rolie, Yesterday was a very difficult day,' and the last line, which said, 'We are in this together, we are partners. Yours, David.' "

The scene was shot in the end without opium and in any case

was subsequently dropped from the finished film. Roland, however, had made his point.

Other worries surfaced during the three months of filming in Thailand, some brought on by visiting reporters. Surely David realized that the whole basic stand of the picture was anti-American, suggesting as it did that U.S. involvement in Cambodia was a tragic mistake, they asked. Wouldn't this serve to turn off the huge American audience needed to at least earn back the film's cost? "We're certainly at risk," David conceded. "Because of the long gestation period of any picture, you can't really consider what the political climate may be when it is eventually shown. But the United States is not truly represented by either the left or the right. There is a decent center, and we must hope the film plugs in to it."

One irreverent wit at Warners described the production as a simple "boy meets boy" story. David spelled out in his own fashion the rather different angle from which he viewed the picture: "What we're attempting is a film which has the realism of *The Battle of Algiers* but with the operatic quality of *Apocalypse Now*, in order to make it work commercially. That's a difficult thing to achieve. It's always been one or the other in the past. I think we have a very substantial base to build on. I admire both *Algiers* and *Apocalypse* enormously, but neither had a central relationship with which you could identify. Our film has that relationship. But I'm extremely nervous about the ambitions of the project, and it's not made easier by newspaper articles like those which have been appearing recently about *Gandhi* [another Goldcrest-financed venture]. We're dealing with a factual situation in *Killing Fields*, and in preparing the film, we've talked to many of the people involved and read all the books and articles which are available. But in the end we have to tell a long, complicated story in just two hours, and the final criterion is how you make it work as a film. If you get subjected to the undergraduate nit-picking to which *Gandhi* has been subjected—saying this or that is wrong—then you're sunk. The thing I reject is the notion that only newspapers and scholars can make judgment on serious situations and that filmmakers aren't clever enough.

"The kind of thinking that seems to be going on at the moment implies that filmmakers shouldn't tackle serious subjects. Are the people who write these articles saying we should make nothing but musicals and fantasies like *E.T.*? If they are, I think that's very worrying. In my case, I've reached the stage in my career when it would be very easy to say, Sod it—I don't need this aggravation."

Was David saying that filmmakers should be allowed to abdicate responsibility for facts when making what are claimed to be true stories? Isn't to say that "the final criterion is how you make it work as a film" reducing *The Killing Fields* to the level of a melodrama and reprehensibly using a tragic backdrop to "trade up"? Were the manipulative strings still showing? In that case, perhaps it is as well that *Inside the Third Reich* never went ahead when David was ten years younger, since what might have resulted was the ultimate buddy movie featuring the double act of Hitler and Speer with several million Jewish extras in the background. And was he willfully confusing an attack on *Gandhi* with an attack on the man, rather than Richard Attenborough's attempt to portray the man?

If Frank Bloom is right (he sees David's announcements as signals for the future), the purpose of this statement appeared to be to preempt criticism of *The Killing Fields*. David's message came across as: "If it works on a visceral and emotional level, suspend reason and forget the rest. And if you don't agree, I'll leave you to Hollywood's tender mercies."

In any case, a bombshell was dropped at the end-of-shooting party with David's announcement that the movie might be his last as an on-the-spot line producer. "It's probably my swan song," he declared, "for it's got to the point where I feel that I'm competing with myself, and it's time I started to do other things."

When filming on *The Killing Fields* was basically complete and many problems—such as editing—were as yet unresolved, David nonetheless went directly into another project. He traveled from Thailand to Ireland to work on *Cal;* the trip proved a wonderful antidote to the large-scale problems he had encountered in the Far East. Although *Cal* was a small-scale picture, David felt genuine excitement as he saw the film being put together. A great amount of work remained, however, on *The Killing Fields.*

The major problem of the length of *The Killing Fields* was never satisfactorily resolved, although on the eve of the film's release, David reacted with outrage to rumors that he had censored scenes in the film's extended postproduction process. "Not a frame has been changed" was the official story. In reality, a tremendous amount *had* been changed. Bruce Robinson was critical of alterations made to his original script, of which he reckoned about 80 percent survived. He saw himself as having been exposed to David both at his best and at his worst. "Just imagine, you need $15 million to do an American guilt job, you've got an unknown Cambodian as the star and a scriptwriter financiers have never heard of. He held out for me to do it. Puttnam was marvelous. I don't know how he had that kind of confidence. He did dilute a measure of anti-Americanism in the script because he knows what you can get away with in a very expensive film. Anything I wanted, he got for me immediately. He's great in that sense, bloody brilliant. . . . He's a wonderful uncle until he doesn't want you around anymore. Then he's a fucking nightmare. He was always astonishingly kind when I was supplying what he wanted, but as soon as I didn't give him the goods he expected from me, which was acquiescence, then he wasn't very charming anymore. That's just one facet of him, of course. I can be quite unpleasant when I'm doing my job, too.

"David requires one hundred percent loyalty from people, but he doesn't give you it back, he doesn't give you a break. You have to be one hundred percent David Puttnam, not ninety-nine percent—he won't allow you that one percent, he won't forgive you for anything. You get in line and do what he wants you to do. If you step out of that line, you're in trouble.

"Would I work with him again? Like—tomorrow! Why? Because he's a *brilliant* fucking film producer!"

Working together with David over such an extended period gave Roland Joffe a considerable insight into his producer's mind. "He's an enormously complex man—that's part of his delight. The strata of David, the levels at which he works, both psychologically and actively in the world, are always interesting because they are nearly always contradictory. David is a man who has six or seven agendas going at any one particular time. The power of most of these agendas is that he has to be massaged with affection.

"He's not combative in a frontal way, although he very much wants to win. He also wants to be liked, and that sets up interesting dynamics. He's got immense charm, and as a friend that's absolutely wonderful, but that same skill and charm are put to work when he works. I see it operating on other people and it's wonderful. Then I see it operating on me."

David again chose to open *The Killing Fields* in the United States first, in the fall of 1984—just a few weeks ahead of its scheduled British opening. There were many favorable reviews, but there was also harsh criticism. J. Hoberman in *The Village Voice* found the picture "murky and undramatic. It suffers from the *Gandhi* syndrome. The filmmakers are so convinced of their subject's importance that they don't bother to develop characters, sustain dramatic tension or maintain structural coherence."

Variety, however, a key indicator of Hollywood attitudes, found the movie "intelligent, sober, perhaps even too austere. The picture is terrifyingly successful in physically evoking its time and place, and is also the sort of tremendously ambitious project that can only be undertaken when an adventurous producer such as David Puttnam has carte blanche to make it his way."

In Britain, Quentin Falk in the *Daily Mail* described the film as "an epic to move us all, a superbly designed, vividly photographed and confidently directed movie." Philip French in the *Observer* felt the film was "essentially a celebration of the human spirit. In this, it is characteristic of producer David Puttnam, whose films are virtually all inspiring stories of courage in adversity and male friendship, with women relegated to a marginal position or approached from an adolescent perspective."

Especially significant are the views of British journalist Jon Swain, who is depicted in the film: he was in Cambodia, and Dith Pran saved his life as well as that of Schanberg. He confesses to having felt apprehensive when he first heard the film was being made. "Could the mood of a beautiful Southeast Asian country so earnestly and stupidly at war be recaptured in a Western-made film? And, more important, was it possible to make a film about the conflict which would convey the Cambodians' point of view with compassion and understanding and still appeal to Western film audiences?" he had asked himself. "In spite of my uneasiness about these things, I think all of us who lived in the shadow of Cambodia's unimaginable horror wanted this film to be made. For me, personally, *The Killing Fields* represents something which is of great importance, a chance to give recognition to what was a true act of courage by one particular Cambodian. I had been through the war as a journalist and come out safe, where many I knew, Cambodian friends as well as journalists, perished. In the last analysis, I owe my life to Dith Pran, Sydney Schanberg's interpreter. How he saved us from certain execution is scrupulously and flawlessly told in this film."

While he was in the United States to push the movie, David examined his own role as producer and chose to answer a question for the record that he'd been asked many times: Would he consider directing a film himself? "I know I *could* direct," he answered, "but I'd be mediocre. I wouldn't be a bad director in that I would certainly create the illusion of a decent result, but I would be a mediocre director. I like to think I'm a sufficiently good producer to be inclined to fire myself after viewing the first few days' rushes. I really believe that, and if I ever lose that objectivity, then I'll be lost as a producer. I'm proud of my job, and it gives me a satisfactory level of creative employment."

When it was pointed out to him that his pictures generally

depict people with a sense of values and morals, he explained that this was no coincidence. "I genuinely believe that there is wonderful material for filmmakers in the area of people's emotional crises. Cinema offers the ability to sit in darkness, to watch people something like five times life-size on the screen, and to lend them your identity. . . .

"If *The Killing Fields* is a homage to anything, it's a homage to some of the films I saw twenty years ago. *The Battle of Algiers* may not have made back its negative cost, but what it did do was give me the encouragement to produce *The Killing Fields*. Please God, someone will see our picture and be encouraged to make something even better."

The Killing Fields went on to collect nine British Academy Awards, including one to David for Best Film, one to Bruce Robinson for Best Adapted Screenplay, and one to Haing Ngor for Best Actor, as well as Outstanding Newcomer—an unprecedented double honor. The film was then nominated for seven American Oscars (including Best Picture) and went on to win in three categories—Best Cinematography to Chris Menges, Best Film Editor to Jim Clark, and Best Supporting Actor to Haing Ngor.

Meanwhile, *Cal*—the "small" film David had worked on after filming on *The Killing Fields* was finished—proved to be another successful Puttnam entry at the Cannes Film Festival, where the film's lead actress, Helen Mirren, won the Best Actress award.

David set about pushing the film in his usual forthright manner. "I love the picture," he declared. "If pictures like *Cal* don't work at the box office, all we'll be left with is *Ghostbusters*." Rebutting a charge that the story line required a sophisticated audience to understand *Cal*'s Northern Ireland background, he pointed to the example of *Romeo and Juliet*. "No one asks, what's all this with the Montagues and Capulets? You just accept that there's a dispute. Similarly, here you don't need any special knowledge about Northern Ireland."

The film was well received and did decent business in Britain and on video release, but it failed in the vital U.S. market. "No disrespect to Warners, but it was just *thrown* out," said David.

Variety saw it differently. It had forecast "limited box-office prospects in arthouse venues" for *Cal's* U.S. release with deadly accuracy. "It's difficult to imagine audiences, particularly outside the British Isles, becoming too excited by this mute tale."

Rumors were circulating that David would soon be taking a break. He was offered the post of chairman at Saatchi & Saatchi by Charles and Maurice, which he declined despite the considerable financial inducement they offered. David sank into a terrible depression after *The Killing Fields* opened. The experience of shooting the film had left a legacy of two ulcers and the feeling he had peaked as a producer.

Patsy was alarmed. "What happened after the film was that he saw again the huge impact movies can have on people. Despite his earlier agonizing about understanding communications, he still didn't feel he was really qualified to fiddle around in people's brains, since he didn't know that much himself. He was full of self-doubt about everything.

"He felt by this time that *Chariots* was not the film everyone said it was, it was just a nice, honorable picture. He agreed with the people who had called him politically naïve after *Midnight Express*. He was still very much his own severest critic. He was now picking on everything and saying, 'It's only mediocre, and I've gone along with all this glory and all the trumpeting. It's not right—who am I kidding? I've got to stop kidding myself.' I think that what was really happening to him was the final stage of growing up."

Unfortunately, the angst of this process obliterated what should have been elation at what many saw as the triumph he had wrought from Sydney Schanberg's story and from Roland's direction. Although victory may have thus been snatched from the jaws of defeat, the onset of maturity seemed to have made David aware of the ambiguity of success.

Another reason for David's depression was the attitude others in the British film industry had toward him, exemplified by the niggardly response of that organization to British Film Year. This much-touted push to bring the missing millions back to the British cinema was greeted in many quarters with apathy and skepticism.

David dropped his bombshell soon afterward. "I'm planning a sabbatical once outstanding contracts are out of the way," he told a stunned press conference. "And after that, I seriously want to leave the business altogether. Patsy and I may go to New York, then I want to come back to England and possibly teach for five years. I know something about making films, and I'd like to pass on what I know."

Many believed David had just hung a "for sale" sign around his neck.

15

David Puttnam attempted to remain aloof from the day-to-day operations of Goldcrest. He managed to stay uninvolved when Jake Eberts, the head of production and one of his most ardent supporters, left the company to join Embassy Pictures. As Jake recounts, "David's job was not to run Goldcrest; he used to come to meetings and did his best, but he really didn't care about my leaving."

As a replacement for Eberts, David recommended his old friend Sandy Lieberson. Lieberson accepted the job despite grave reservations and only after David's assurances. "It was a nightmare," Sandy says in retrospect, "one of the worst experiences I ever got involved in. Just from day one when I arrived, the atmosphere of the company was so bad, so hostile, that I knew I'd made a dreadful mistake."

Sandy found that he had been thrown in at the deep end. One

of the first decisions he had to make was whether to continue development of John Boorman's *The Emerald Forest,* which Eberts had left in an advanced stage of development. Boorman had been working on the project for eighteen months when Goldcrest decided to pull out.

As far as David Puttnam was concerned, there was a critical difference between the way he went about making a film and the way Boorman was going about it. David, given to extremely orderly methods, was disturbed by reports from the Amazon jungle, where *Emerald Forest* was under way, that the situation was chaos. "In fairness, there may be different ways of making movies," David says. "John Boorman may work one way, while I tend to be extremely orderly. But you can't make a financial judgment based on someone else's way of seeing the world. So, based on the way *we* would have proceeded, it was an easy call, not difficult at all, which was—why don't they get their act together?"

As a result of this decision, David Norris threatened to resign as a member of the Goldcrest board. He had ardently argued in favor of the project, and he happened to be Boorman's lawyer as well.

Ultimately, *Emerald Forest* was completed and released by Embassy, but the contretemps left scars at Goldcrest and further weakened its already-tenuous structure.

Certainly one factor that gave the Goldcrest board pause was the realization that if it went ahead with Boorman's production in the jungles of Brazil while simultaneously financing David Puttnam's *The Mission,* which was set to film in the wilds of Colombia, they would be faced with two potentially problematic and financially unpredictable productions at the same time. Obviously, their loyalty was to David.

At the same time, still another project came before the Goldcrest board, one that was to effectively sound the death knell for the company. Sandy Lieberson presented the script for *Revolution* to the board, declaring, "This has the potential to be the best movie script I've ever read." Sandy today stands by his initial judgment on *Revolution* and argues that it is not what it *was*, but what it *became*, that caused the problems.

As the discussion on whether to proceed with *Revolution* began (with none other than Hugh Hudson slated to direct the movie), David found himself in the most difficult position he had ever been in on the Goldcrest board. He voted that the film be postponed until the script problems were sorted out, arguing that in any case the budget that had been drawn up was not realistic. David said, "Look, I'm a filmmaker. I've worked with Hugh. We've watched the lesson on *Greystoke*, and this is all Goldcrest's money." The board's attitude was largely, "Oh, come on. Your fight with Hudson should be over by now. You should be bigger than that—you should be able to be magnanimous."

David was furious at the implication he was bad-mouthing Hugh. "I do not doubt," he told them, "that Hugh will do the picture brilliantly, but he will *not* do it for that price—he's not that sort of filmmaker." Only Richard Attenborough supported him, however, so David felt he had no choice but to react to the jibes of partiality. "If you won't listen to me as a filmmaker, what the hell is the point of my being here?" he railed. "If you're really foolish enough to believe in this nonsensical vendetta, then I must take myself off the board."

Attenborough was unequivocal. "If you go, I go too," he stated. Now the same pressure that had been exerted earlier on Norris was brought to bear on David and Dickie, that Goldcrest couldn't possibly afford to have two major board members leaving at such a delicate time. But when would it be any different? The two found themselves trapped, unable to leave in case it rocked the boat of the current fund-raising campaign.

With the decision made to proceed with *Revolution* and a percentage of the budget in place through a European consortium, Goldcrest chief James Lee felt confident that there would be plenty of time to get the script right. "There was a lot of delay while Hugh Hudson dithered with the casting," he recalls. "He was very uncertain about exactly what he wanted and only late in the day got around to Al Pacino. We ended up committed to going into preproduction around November 1984, with February 1985 set as the start of filming in Devon. Sandy was an enthusiast, as I was, as were Warners. *The Mission* was going ahead at the same time, together with *Absolute Beginners* and *Room with a View.* Although we sold Warners the package of *Revolution* and *The Mission, Revolution* was the one they really wanted. *The Mission* was carried on *Revolution*'s back, so it was ironical that if David had had his way and halted *Revolution,* he might never have got the go-ahead on *The Mission.* And history would have worked out a little bit differently!"

David had first come across the script for *The Mission* back in 1977 while he was living at Pacific Palisades in Los Angeles. Fernando Ghia was in Hollywood trying to raise money for the project with a finished script by Robert Bolt that David asked to read. David had not only been deeply moved by it, he could not get it out of his mind thereafter. Something about it kept coming back to haunt him, although he could see that there were deep-rooted problems still to be solved. David and Ghia met fairly regularly thereafter. David would invariably find the producer just about to close a deal, or with some prospective deal just broken down.

During his depression after the completion of *The Killing Fields,* David's thoughts once again turned to *The Mission.* Despite everything he had said about pulling out of films, or at least taking a break, *The Mission* somehow represented unfinished business for him. And wouldn't Roland Joffe be the ideal director to be involved in the project?

"It was very odd," David muses. "The man reminded me of the material." To Fernando Ghia he said, "I feel I'm working with the best big filmmaker to come along in many years, a sort of natural David Lean figure, and Roland's qualities seem to coincide with some of the things you said you wanted for *The Mission.*"

The theme of the film hearkened back to the mid–eighteenth century, when the Spanish and the Portuguese were dividing up Latin American territories between themselves. Jesuit missions stood in their way and were eventually overrun and destroyed in the interests of trade and exploitation of the region's natural resources. The wholesale slaughter of the Guarani Indians, who had joined the missions, followed.

The main characters in the story were Gabriel, the Jesuit missionary who has founded the community of Christian Indians in the jungle, and Mendoza, a slave trader who is racked with guilt after killing his brother in a duel. Gabriel accepts Mendoza as a novice; then, when the mission is attacked, the two men take up their own positions. Gabriel opts for passive resistance, and Mendoza once more takes up his sword.

David had intended only to executive-produce the picture, distancing himself from the vicissitudes he had experienced on *The Killing Fields* and leaving the actual location and production duties to Fernando Ghia. Iain Smith was hired to repeat the line production he had handled so capably on *Local Hero* and on the arduous *Killing Fields* location. David was still concerned about certain aspects of the script and met with Robert Bolt to have these ironed out.

Patsy has her own ideas about David's motives in making *The Mission*. "I would say that he wanted to do it because he wanted to do another film with Roland, something that had never occurred before with any of the other directors. I think he was feeling that at his age he was absolutely tired of finding new directors all the time, only to have them pillaged by others. He was going to stick with this one. But truthfully, his heart wasn't in that film like it was in *Killing Fields* or *Chariots of Fire*. They'd been his conceptions from the word go. That isn't to say he wouldn't give *The Mission* his best, but it wasn't his own baby."

With David on board only as executive producer, this was so. But the position changed as preproduction began and Ghia clasped the controls. First he alienated Roland Joffe, then Iain Smith fell foul of him. Word quickly got back to Warners and Goldcrest.

David was left with no alternative but to step in and take over the production reins himself. He did so with a very heavy heart, having vowed after *Killing Fields* never to personally produce a film of that size again. When Roland Joffe declared that he was keen to get Robert De Niro to play Mendoza, David fought him over the choice.

"I'd rather go for a nonstar, not someone who's going to bring their own baggage to the part," he argued, but Roland dug his heels in. Besides, De Niro was interested. He offered to bring his fee down and take a larger part of the profits instead. "It isn't true to say I didn't want Bobby," David insists. "I was just very concerned about the impact on our schedule, for it was extremely tight on this picture."

David, Roland, and De Niro had a long talk late one night at Blake's Hotel in London. "Look, I'm really concerned," David told the star. "You have a reputation for wanting a lot of on-camera rehearsal time. Quite honestly, the film was never set up to accommodate this or the type of actor you represent."

"I understand your problem," De Niro replied gravely, "and I will never delay your picture."

David was surprised at this ready acquiescence, but he had another bombshell ready. "I'm also not totally convinced that you are right for the picture."

This time De Niro was clearly taken aback, but he politely replied, "Nobody has ever said that to me before, David. I'm an actor, and my feeling is that I'm right for anything that I really sincerely feel that I can do."

David felt that it was enormously to De Niro's credit that at all times the exchange was handled with dignity, decorum, and a respect for each other's position. For what he had been trying to enunciate between the lines was, "I'm the producer. These have to be the rules. If you're not happy with them, please, for all of our sakes, don't sign on." It was a cool introduction.

Then Liam Neeson was signed for the supporting role of one of the priests. "It was never enunciated," Patsy says, "but I suspect that Liam was in that position so that if Bobby decided to pull out, he would be available to go straight into his part. Left to David, maybe Liam would have got the job in the first place. This way he had his fallback position, his plan B."

Now Roland flexed his casting muscles further. "He had developed an obsession that he might find a nonactor in the Haing Ngor tradition and turn him into a star," David recalls. "He had several people in mind like Danny Berrigan, a Jesuit priest with whom he spent a lot of time, trying to sincerely convince himself that he would work in the role of Gabriel. When Roland finally decided on Jeremy Irons, it was Bobby's turn to feel unsure. It wasn't really that he did or didn't want Jeremy, but people tend to strike attitudes. He came around marvelously."

For Roland, the working atmosphere was once again positive. "With David and I, we both agreed to totally respect each other's positions. I'm the director and he's the producer—both of us have to create the environment. If the producer and the director find themselves in an adversarial relationship during filming, it's a disaster. Ideally, both men will have agreed on the kind of film they want to make *before* the camera turns. After that, no secrets, unless it's something that would send your partner into terminal shock. . . .

"As much as I love David—and I do—I have to confess, he's unhappy when there isn't a telephone within a hundred yards. He's got a fetish about communication, one not shared by the Colombian Ministry of Communications. So Colombia for him was anguish. 'Roland,' he said to me one day, 'I thought you were sane, but you've now totally taken leave of your senses.' And I said, 'Why?' He said, 'The nearest telephone is sixty kilometers from here. I mean, how can we communicate with the production office?' This is a producer's view of the world. The director's eye is always fixed on what's going right, and the producer's on what might go wrong."

Both Roland and David got close to both their lead actors during the shoot—Irons with his training in classical theater, De Niro the master of the instinctive and improvisational. "Bobby and Jeremy worked out a relationship over the course of the film," Roland said. "Bobby was holding his own in what is really quite a simple film. It was not a film about New York, in which he can use his street-wiseness."

One day, David heard of a disagreement that had arisen between De Niro and Joffe during shooting. It seemed that De

Niro wanted not only to change the lines in one particular area but also to effect a considerable character change. At dinner that evening, diners at adjoining tables were startled to overhear the conversation between David and his star.

"I hear you're unhappy with one of the scenes, Bobby?" David began.

"Yes, I am."

"Is it the lines?"

"No, it's more than that. I feel the character wouldn't react in the way he does here."

The offending scene was discussed in detail, then David delivered his thunderbolt. "Well, Bobby," he said, "you may be right, but if you're not, we stand to lose a lot of money. We're walking into a brick wall here. You know, if *The Mission* takes only as much as *your last five films combined*, we'll lose a lot of money."

"Hey, what do you mean?" De Niro growled.

"Just what I say. You know them as well as I do: *Falling in Love, True Confessions, King of Comedy, Once Upon a Time.* . . ."

What are you saying?"

"I'm saying that the real danger here is that what you've got is a pattern of films where you're quite wonderful, but somehow the film doesn't become the sum of its parts—it's turned into a De Niro *vehicle*. That's why we've got to make sure you fit perfectly into this picture with the overall."

"Mm. I'll have to think about that."

Although the discussion was not acrimonious, people sitting around them could feel crackling tension as the discussion took place. There were no explosions, although there could have been. The rest of the dinner seemed to pass without a return to the topic, and the star and his producer seemed to relax together. The scene was shot as written.

The gamble David had taken had paid off. The consummate artist that De Niro undoubtedly is had been faced with a persuasive argument that he was genuinely unable to ignore. As David had stressed from the beginning, if *The Mission* was not a team effort, it was nothing. Still, he had pushed the point to the very edge—the "face-off," as Iain Smith calls it, of which he is truly a master.

Behind the scenes on *The Mission*, other crises were looming. The financial problems generated by Goldcrest's other commitments began to manifest themselves in the most awful way imaginable in Colombia. Funds failed to materialize in time to keep *The Mission*'s large unit going. David was livid.

"In Thailand with *The Killing Fields*, we were able to lean on a sort of infrastructure that already existed," he says. "While in Colombia there was absolutely nothing—everything was shipped in from Europe, down to the last sandwich. When it comes to the whole issue of what happened at Goldcrest, there are two things that I still resent. One is that they didn't share with me either the initial problems or the true gravity of the situation, and I was supposed to be a director of the company! That's one thing when you're working around the corner, but when you're working in Colombia and paying a lot of people weekly wages, you cannot mess around with Friday night's check—it's not negotiable. I think on more than one occasion we weren't given sufficient opportunity to cover ourselves in ways that we could have prudently organized. That still hurts me. We were given a good deal of unnecessary anxiety because of lack of information and candor."

Then Roland was hospitalized for four days suffering from dehydration, and David was convinced that he had brought Roland's illness about when he had tried to share the financial pressures he was under. Word filtered through to this difficult location about the apparent extravagances being spent on the far-less-vulnerable set of *Revolution* back in Britain and the subsequent cash drain on Goldcrest. This in turn created enormous additional pressure on David and his team, thousands of miles away in the stifling heat of the Colombian jungle. Old friendships were put under terminal strain.

"My resentment," he declared, "is that while we caused our director to become quite seriously ill attempting to conform to the limitations placed on our production, other people were not coping with their crises, not cutting their cloth, not taking re-

sponsibility for the seriousness of Goldcrest's financial situation. That's when I got *very* upset indeed. I feel I took it out on
someone's health, because another group of people had different priorities. That will always leave me bitter. The break in
our friendship came down to the fact that I don't believe Hugh
and Irwin Winkler, *Revolution*'s producer, were prepared to
take onto their shoulders the compromises and pressures that
Roland so magnificently absorbed. That I can never forgive.
When our weekly cash flow was arriving late, first there was
one excuse, then another, then it was the bank's fault, and when
it happened for the fourth week, I just went berserk. I called
Bob Daly at Warners. 'How do you feel about advancing money
here direct instead of sending it all on to Goldcrest when the
film's delivered? Can you advance $200,000? I need some cash—
we're using a lot of extras and we have to pay cash.' He said,
'That's fine, but I have to tell Goldcrest what I'm doing.' I said,
'Fine, you tell them, but I *need* the money.'

"Next thing, I have James Lee on the phone shouting and
carrying on. It wasn't up to me to get money paid direct. I said,
'Okay, *you* pay us the money.' And only then did it all start to
emerge, confirming the stories we'd been hearing. The overrun
on *Revolution* and *Absolute Beginners* was killing them. So my
argument was, *Revolution* was shooting in Devon, *we're* in fucking Cartagena, you *can't* mess around with our cash flow. And
that's where it got very ugly. In a situation like that, I'm probably not at my most tactful. It was dangerous, what they were
doing was positively *dangerous.* At one point the Colombian authorities threatened to hold Iain Smith hostage until the money
came through. I mean, they don't screw around out there, it's
not like sitting in High Wycombe. Goldcrest misled us for three
solid weeks."

In addition to this peril, Iain Smith had to grapple with the
realities of modern-day Colombia. "We made the film in spite of
the Colombians," he asserted. "They don't have any sense of
their endemic history, and they don't have a work ethic. The
cost of everything was largely influenced by the United States
and also by the main export, which happens to be cocaine. At

the same time, Colombia is one of the kidnapping centers of the world, so I was very concerned about security for the crew." The "cocaine capos," it seemed, had just announced that because of the U.S. Drug Enforcement Agency patrolling the coast for traffickers, they would kill any Americans they found in Colombia—a big worry with Robert De Niro in the film. It would have created a major international incident had De Niro been kidnapped or had any attempt been made on his life. Iain Smith managed to enlist the help of the Colombian secret service, who provided the unit with bodyguards to protect the crew and especially De Niro.

The last of Goldcrest's money arrived just before the end of *The Mission*'s shooting, bringing an intense feeling of relief. The Waunana Indians received $80,000 for their work on the film, as opposed to De Niro's $2 million—and the Indians were also allocated a small percentage of any profits that emerged. In addition, and at David's behest, Goldcrest and Warners made a substantial contribution to a fund to buy agricultural equipment and finance an education and health program. "Having worked with them, we now feel a certain responsibility for their fate," said David.

In the early days of the filming, before the difficulties began, David had invited Patsy out to the location to see the breathtaking falls where much of the picture was being shot. Patsy normally makes a point never to attend the shooting of any of her husband's films ("That's *his* province"), but David was especially persuasive and finally coaxed her to fly out to Colombia for a few days. He kidded her constantly about all the time she was spending working on Kingsmead Mill, their country house. "I can make three films—*Local Hero, Killing Fields,* and *Cal*— now I'm on *The Mission,* and you're *still* toiling away on your production," he said, laughing.

Kingsmead Mill had reminded Patsy from the start of a French country house, from the charming original millhouse itself to the two connected cottages, the enormous front lawns, and the big iron gates. In Bristol, the Avon divides into two streams. One flows under the millhouse, which was originally built to grind flour; the other flows into the mill pool. Then the river rejoins and makes its way downstream. Part seventeenth century, part eighteenth century, the sixteen-acre estate now boasts an orchard, a walled garden, a vegetable garden, an Elizabethan knot garden, and a laburnum grove and stone courtyard at the back of the house. With David's support ("I'll make the films—you get Kingsmead sorted out"), Patsy had set about restoring the Mill to something that would survive a few hundred more years. Their plans also included the acquisition of several surrounding fields, for originally the millhouse had included a forty-acre estate, and they wished to re-create this relationship of proportion between house and land. Meanwhile, discussions went on about the renovation of the house and cottages.

A series of builders were interviewed, and Patsy took on some local people from Stroud. For the first time in their lives, the craftsmen were confronted with a client demanding to know not how quickly a job could be finished but how well it could be done. Patsy's keynote was simple—the workmanship had to be fully up to the best of the old standards. Materials were a problem, but if they had to wait for an old barn somewhere to fall down before they could get some of the magnificent old Tetbury roof tiles they required, then so be it.

The workmen found that they were dealing with someone obsessed with getting every single detail correct, and they responded accordingly. Endless conferences followed on such subjects as how to get double glazing installed without destroying the fenestration, which would take the correct period look away.

With joiners working away inside, builders swarming over the outside, and an estate manager appointed, Patsy saw she was going way over budget. "I'd have been fired by any producer," she happily admits.

David probably did not realize it at the time, but *The Mission* marked the end of a major phase of his career. A very significant phase was about to begin. He had spent the last several years toiling away on problematic films in difficult locations. On the home front, all was relatively calm, despite the enormous bills Patsy was running up in reconstructing the house. He needed a change. It was a time for reassessment.

Alan Parker has his own appraisal of David and his career to this point. Regardless of how firmly based the Puttnam and Parker friendship seemed, it was not founded on a mutual admiration of each other's product, except in fairly isolated instances. Their separate views on *Midnight Express* are well known; less so are differences in how they view other efforts over the years. "I don't think I've ever liked anything he's done," Alan says with an almost perfectly straight face. "And he certainly hasn't liked anything I've done, but that's why it's a healthy relationship. I remember once he attended the Cannes showing of *Pink Floyd—The Wall.* We had the sound turned up so loud, there were bits of plaster falling off the ceiling. He left immediately afterward and didn't talk to me for days! We've still never discussed it. We can rely on one another to hate the other person's work, but that's good."

Having got that off his chest, Alan admits, "I did like *Local Hero* very much. I like Bill Forsyth. It didn't completely work as a film, but the parts that are Bill's work . . . Bill's got this incredible humanity—you even like his villains because he really loves people.

"*The Killing Fields* is David's best film, I think, a terrific, very substantial film, the only film of his I've liked without any criticism, except for the John Lennon error—a *terrible* idea [Parker's reference to the use of Lennon's song *Imagine* in the movie's closing scene]. Come to that, most of his ideas are terrible. On the other hand, two out of ten are brilliant and these are the ones you have to look out for. *Chariots?* Extremely well made, but a little too pompous and self-righteous, which is the theme of all his work, a theme that many people admire.

"He's an optimist, David would say, and I'm a pessimist. He wanted to make films which will show how human beings can aspire to being better, while I try to find the things that are

wrong in the human psyche and explore what's rotten with the
world in order to make it better. In his life he's tended to become more pompous and self-righteous because he's gone evangelical. I much prefer the spiv over Jesus!"

16

espite the undoubted millionaire status of Jerry Perenchio and Norman Lear, Jake Eberts learned from his new bosses at Embassy to never confuse people's personal wealth with money available for movies. He spent a year on the road on the toughest fund-raising operation he had ever faced—a depressing experience after his successes in Britain. There were so many routes for U.S. investors who wished to dabble in movies. They could simply buy Coca-Cola shares if they wanted a piece of Columbia Pictures, or Gulf & Western shares for a stake in Paramount. Jake also found that the hits he was associated with—like *Chariots of Fire* and *Gandhi*—were considered small beer in comparison with the *Star Wars, Indiana Jones,* and *Tootsie*-scale hits in which investors were more interested.

"It was probably the worst year of my life, a discouraging experience," says Jake. Once the guiding light behind Goldcrest, the great white hope of the British film industry, he now found himself in the unenviable position of fund manager for American millionaires who were unprepared to risk any of their personal fortunes. Matters came further unstuck in February 1985, when Perenchio and Lear announced that they intended to sell Embassy. To dress the company up before the sale, they would appoint a studio head. Jake could see there was no place for him in the new setup, and he negotiated a settlement. Shortly after he left Embassy, the company was sold to Coca-Cola.

Once he was back in Britain, Jake heard rumors about Goldcrest and its difficulties, but he was too busy setting up his own new company, Allied Filmmakers, to pay much attention. With Allied, he was planning to go back to the first principles he had initiated at Goldcrest—it would be purely a development financing operation. When news of Sandy Lieberson's imminent departure from Goldcrest came to his attention, Jake immediately proposed to James Lee that Allied take over Goldcrest's development function—and for a fraction of its running cost. Lee was not prepared to consider this; he clearly saw himself as taking over the production reins following Sandy's departure.

By June 1985, the anxiety of the Goldcrest board came out into the open. Committed to financing *Revolution, Absolute Beginners,* and *The Mission* all at the same time, doubts now arose that a European co-financier for *Revolution* would come up with his share of cash for the film, which was already seriously over budget. Goldcrest's worst fear was confirmed; it now had to replace its ex-partner's share of the budget and assume total responsibility for the overruns. The drain on the company's resources began to reach horrendous proportions.

With his offer to help turned down, Jake set about Allied's investment portfolio on his own. *The Emerald Forest* had proved a moderate success when released by Embassy, and Jake eagerly helped John Boorman's new endeavor, *Hope and Glory,* get off the ground. In addition, Jake was involved with seed funding for *The Name of the Rose* and for Richard Attenborough's Biko project, *Asking for Trouble* (later renamed *Cry Freedom*). In a deal similar to David's, Jake's overheads were covered by Warners in return for first refusal. Incredibly, as David had already found, Warners turned down every single project for a hundred percent funding. *Hope and Glory* eventually went to Columbia (very much through David's later good offices), *The Name of the Rose* went to 20th Century-Fox, and *Cry Freedom* ended up at Universal. With his relatively small but crucial seed-money investment in these movies, Jake's cash was refunded on the first day of shooting, and he retained a profit participation in the pictures. Life was beginning to look good for him again after his chastening experience at Embassy.

While he was spending some time at his farm in Quebec, Jake received a call from Michael Stoddart at Goldcrest. "Look, we've got ourselves in a terrible mess. Would you be prepared to come back?" Stoddart asked. Jake replied that he had no wish to be the cause of James Lee's departure, but that if the board had decided to get rid of Lee in any case, they could talk again after that was accomplished. Back in England a few weeks later, Lee was gone from Goldcrest, and the way was clear for Eberts's return.

Knee-deep in problems of his own with the filming of *The Mission* in Colombia, David was not involved in any of Goldcrest's discussions with Jake. Jake agreed by mid-July to take over again, negotiating a contract for his services with Allied Filmmakers. Jake had been led to understand that there was nothing more than an interim financial problem at the company and that it had been brought about basically by having three expensive films made at the same time. Together with the abdication of the outside investment from *Revolution* and the budget overruns on *Revolution* and *Absolute Beginners*, the whole thing had been further exacerbated by the change in the value of the dollar. Even though the company was technically close to bankruptcy, Jake saw that the situation could quickly change if any of the movies turned out to be a hefty revenue-earner. A viewing of the available footage of the three projects was promptly arranged.

Jake felt that *The Mission* had a chance of being a very good film, but he doubted that it would recoup its £17 million cost. Warners had put up only $5 million to acquire it for the United States, since Goldcrest had decided to go for broke, accepting less in advance in return for a bigger slice of the hoped-for U.S. take.

Jake had no idea how *Revolution* would play, and he found *Absolute Beginners* a total disaster. He asked Alan Marshall to supervise the completion of the latter, and he credits Marshall for whatever finally emerged. The budget for this venture ended up at £8.6 million, against an advance from Orion Pictures for the United States of only $2.5 million.

There was tremendous pressure to get *Revolution* out in time for the year end and the Oscar nominations. Jake, too, was in favor of rushing postproduction to make this deadline. "I didn't see much value in hanging around and recutting it," he admits. "There was no way months of postproduction were going to make a change in that film. Those who are being blamed now for the film ending up so terrible in turn blamed me for having pushed so hard to get the picture finished. My answer's pretty simple: it's inherently uncommercial. I actually don't think it was a terrible picture, I think there are some glorious scenes in it, and I think Hugh Hudson's an extremely talented director."

Hugh Hudson had been feeling aggrieved from the beginning of the *Revolution* project. "Sandy Lieberson refused me a scriptwriter at the beginning of the film, then gave me one when the film started, when it was too late. I should have known better than to start it when I did, but I was told the film wouldn't be made unless I was in production by March. Then there was the need to get it out. At that point, to give him his due, Sandy said to wait another three months. He was right—wrong at the beginning, but right at the end. The irony is that when Warners saw the film, Bob Daly and Terry Semel thought it was wonderful. They embraced and kissed me. 'Hugh, this is the best thing you've ever done, it's wonderful,' they told me."

A few weeks after Warners screened the movie, Jake and Hugh Hudson were flown by Concorde to New York to attend the first audience preview. There was a limousine waiting at the Concorde exit, then a helicopter whisked them over to New Jersey and the theater. Everything seemed to go well during the screening, with Semel and Daly in attendance, together with Mike Ovitz, head of the powerful Creative Artists Agency (CAA). After the screening, however, adverse comments came in, and everyone realize that there was a very real and deep-seated problem. Yet with only three weeks remaining before the December 1985 opening, there was time to make only a few cosmetic changes. Most people acknowledged at this stage that the film was not going to be a blockbuster, but few were prepared for the savagery of the reviews and the subsequent public indifference. The £19 million production was taken off after an embarrassingly brief run with just over one third of a million dollars in the U.S. box office. It was a resounding shock. Any hopes that Goldcrest had entertained for a cash bonanza to save the day were well and truly dashed.

Attention was now focused more than ever on *The Mission*. This placed a crushing responsibility on David and his team, who were still deep in the lengthy postproduction process. "If one swallow doesn't make a summer," David asked, "then why should a single flop be held to wreck an industry? Is it really possible that a resurgence of British film has been dealt a mortal blow by the critical and box-office failure of *Revolution*?"

Although David had personally produced *The Mission*, Fernando Ghia (at Warners' and Goldcrest's insistence) asserted that David should retain the executive-producer credit only and that he himself should be listed as the film's sole producer. Robert De Niro, Roland Joffe, and Jeremy Irons supported David. Without David's knowledge, they got together and laid down their own ultimatum—that a co-production credit should be applied for Ghia and David together. "We accept David has to share credit with Ghia," they told Warners. "But if he doesn't get that, we want our own credits taken off the film. The whole thing will be a lie." Terry Semel saw that the billing was promptly altered to "co-produced by Fernando Ghia and David Puttnam"—but only over Ghia's loud protests.

David is philosophical about the affair. "The film industry

has a place for its Ghias as well as its Puttnams." He shrugs. "He's got very good literary taste, but frankly I don't think he could organize a piss-up in a brewery, and I've told him this many times. In British terms, he has no management skills, which in turn breeds a resentment in him. We were getting on with making the picture, and he couldn't stand to see what he regarded as his film being made without him. He knows that, and of course it caused tremendous stress."

A colleague and fellow countryman of Ghia's defends him. "This was to be the film of Fernando's life," he says. "Everybody wanted to buy him out, but he said no, this is mine, they can't buy me out, I've got all the aces. And for a while Goldcrest played along with this. He was a lonely figure, entering into an already constructed team of Puttnam, Joffe, and Smith, who had already worked together on *The Killing Fields*. He didn't mold himself into areas he could have helped in, and there were silly disagreements about where his office was to be in London, which hotel he would stay in, things like that. He played his role wrong, but David does not understand the Italian modus operandi. Try putting an Englishman among Italians! Ghia recommended [Enrico] Sabbatini to do the costumes, which were done in Italy entirely self-sufficiently. And he helped to get [Ennio] Morricone. If Ghia makes a movie on his own, he would make it work. He and David were simply two people at a certain stage demanding space—and there was simply not room enough for both of them. David—being David —prevailed."

Producer Don Boyd was shocked and disappointed at David's distant stand from Goldcrest's difficulties. "He and Dickie Attenborough were, after all, the only experienced filmmakers on the Goldcrest board. How can they avoid responsibility? *Revolution* was started without a completion guarantor in place. On *Absolute Beginners*, the production team simply weren't properly qualified. On his own *he* would never have gone ahead. A large proportion of the blame for Goldcrest's failure must go to David, Dickie Attenborough, and the rest of them. What appalled me also, and appalled Hugh Hudson, was when *Revolution* failed, and all the argy-bargy about Hugh's overspending and wanton behavior, David washed his hands of it all and blamed Hugh and the management of Goldcrest! *This* was a man who was on the board and partly responsible for the company being able to raise money. I couldn't believe it, I thought it was sheer technical hypocrisy. And I didn't just read about his views, I heard him say it privately and publicly. I know that he read *Revolution*'s script, although he denies it. He must have forgotten. And as a director of Goldcrest, if he didn't read it, *why* didn't he? I'll bet there's not a $25 million project that goes forward at Paramount or Universal without proper script approval.

"And at this point there was so much publicity about David's vital role in the renaissance of British cinema—the one big investment opportunity we've had in Britain for twenty-five years. I wonder if David's ever addressed himself to that. I was tearing my hair out watching it happen—from my position of being down and out and having made the same mistakes myself with much more modest funding. It was a complete mess-up.

"When he began to promote *The Mission,* he profited enormously from the high profile he had. He brilliantly manipulated—he's the most brilliant self-publicist I've ever come across. He does it so innocently, but it's so calculated, including the way he appears on television with his slightly self-deprecating manner—it's genius. It's so good, in fact, I occasionally succumb to copying it on occasions."

Had David addressed himself to Goldcrest's predicament? "I didn't let them down," he maintains. "All my films came in on budget. James Lee reckoned there was an American investor coming in. I told him he wouldn't. I met the financier in Los Angeles, had breakfast with him, then phoned James and told him it wouldn't happen. I wrote to James at one point in early 1985, 'You can't afford *Revolution* and *The Mission* in the same year. I am in an impossible position, sitting here with two hats. It's my job to do everything I can to get *The Mission* off the ground, then I have to tell you as a director of Goldcrest that in my opinion you can't afford to make both films. I find it untenable. Then I came back from the States to find not only *The Mission* but *Absolute Beginners* given the go-ahead—and with no tangible change to the cash flow. As late as May 1985, I was still telling James we could pull out of *The Mission*. It would have meant an $800,000 write-off, but it could have been done. And don't forget my remit was not to oppose other filmmakers' films. Dickie and I fought tooth and nail within that constriction."

David was offered a Kennedy Fellowship for the 1986–87 year at Harvard's philosophy school, under Professor Stanley Covell. He was scheduled to give a series of eight lectures as a university visiting artist and spend one afternoon a week with the other six Kennedy Fellows, starting in September 1986. Many skeptics, however, predicted this would never happen, at least in the short term.

Once again, he seemed to be questioning his qualifications to make films responsibly for a worldwide audience. "If filmmakers set the moral agenda, then maybe we aren't clever enough to deal with that," he said. "It does seem to me that as someone who instigates and is at the sharp end of movie production, to expose myself to different forms of philosophy might well influence my work and then might be the beginning of something more. It's literally learning to ask myself the right questions."

In England, meanwhile, David learned that Thorn-EMI's Screen Entertainment Division (TESE) was up for sale. The assets included its film library, Elstree Studios, and the ABC Cinema circuit. David was concerned, but when the U.S. Cannon Group, headed by Menahem Golan and Yoram Globus, emerged with the Rank Organisation as the front-runners, his concern grew. Cannon already owned the Classic and Star circuits, and its acquisition of ABC would mean it would share the vast bulk of cinema exhibition with Rank. David's other objection to Cannon was its determinedly down-market product and its exploitative image—the very opposite of the kind of film-making he stood for.

Golan and Globus were taken aback by the vehemence of the British reaction against their bid. They invited David to a working breakfast in an effort to mend fences. Globus implied after the meeting that David had seen their point of view, but David was not silenced for long. "I make movies that take a position that is essentially humanist," he declared. "It's quite clear to me that the majority of Cannon's work in the past has been work that appealed to the lowest common denominator in the audience."

Despite much behind-the-scenes maneuvering, the Cannon Group prevailed, albeit at a very high price. Golan and Globus were thereby installed as the new heads of the British film industry, controlling 39 percent of all U.K. screens, to Rank's 25 percent. When the possibility of a reference to the Monopolies and Mergers Commission arose, Golan blithely referred to the settlement as 'a done deal.' David was distraught, for his had been almost the sole voice raised against Cannon's ownership.

He had other things on his mind now, however, the most important of which was *The Mission* and the responsibility that now hung on the movie. *Absolute Beginners* had failed at the box office, despite one of the most expensively hyped openings in U.K. cinema history. Goldcrest was now down to its third big throw of the dice. With five more weeks of postproduction remaining, David decided to take an incredible gamble with the film. He accepted an invitation to show it in competition at the Cannes Film Festival in May 1986. An award at Cannes would bring the picture tremendous prestige, David knew, but he was equally aware of the reflection it would be for the picture if it failed to win a prize. And could the film even be ready for showing in Cannes at all in its unfinished state?

The Cannon Group dominated the 1986 Cannes Film Festival. It had entered three films for the coveted Palme d'Or, in direct competition with *The Mission*. "Cannon—the Company of the Future" slogans were splashed everywhere. In view of the immense Cannon presence, the event was dubbed the "Cannon

Film Festival" by many journalists. Its three movies constituted an impressive lineup; Cannon seemed to be making a serious effort to shake off its former schlock image with Franco Zeffirelli's *Otello*, Robert Altman's *Fool for Love*, and Andrei Konchalovsky's *Runaway Train*. The stage was set for a real David-versus-Goliath contest, as Menahem Golan, flush with the success of his "done deal," resumed hostilities.

"I think the British film industry were spitting in their own bowl of soup by trying to keep us out," he declared. "But now they have all changed their minds, except Mr. Puttnam. He stood up at a meeting of the British Film and Television Producers' Association and said everyone should reject us. . . . I think David Puttnam is a very good and talented producer, but he is very stubborn—or maybe he is trying to secure some publicity."

Some of his colleagues attempted to arrange a conciliatory meeting with the Cannon chiefs during the festival, but David resisted, only too aware that the gulf between them was too wide to be bridged by a few platitudes.

Against all odds, what David described as "the unfinished work-in-progress version of *The Mission*" went on to capture the coveted Palme d'Or from under the noses of the Cannon team and the rest of the very considerable competition.

"My heart pounded and I felt full of horror every time we changed a reel of the film in case it went out of synchronization," David told a reporter, and went on to describe the win as a "near-miracle." Some observers would have none of this. One journalist claimed that there was "cynical amusement in film circles over the success of the 'unfinished' film." Another declared, "Everyone knows the Cannes rule is that an uncompleted film is ineligible for the competition. In fact, the film the jury saw *was* the completed picture. Calling it a work-in-progress would have been a get-out excuse if the film had fallen flat on its face."

Bill Rowe (whose last job for David before *The Mission* was as dubbing editor on *The Killing Fields*, but whose association with David goes back to *That'll Be the Day*) was not amused by these inferences, having worked night and day to assemble the Cannes version of the movie.

"We did a preview mix first," Bill recalls, "to sense if they got things right. Based on that, they had to decide, as with every other movie, if they're going to edit, tighten up, or expand, whatever they want to do. Then I got a message, they're going to submit it to Cannes double-headed, which means you have two pieces of film, a piece with the soundtrack and a piece with the picture. And you have a synchronization thing of two machines running separately."

So late was the picture in coming out of the labs that David missed the flight scheduled to take him, Roland, and Jim Clark to Cannes. A chartered flight had to be quickly organized. "We ran the film through at five-thirty A.M. with Jim Clark on the morning of the eleven A.M. press screening," says David, "this being the only picture as far as I know ever to be run double-headed at Cannes. It stayed in sync, but we only did two screenings instead of the usual three. I felt we just couldn't risk a third."

David's critics leveled an even more damaging assertion: that the Cannes jury had been bribed to vote for *The Mission*. "These people are vicious arseholes!" he raged. "They manufacture the truth that's most convenient for them. When people say things like this, do they realize they are seriously stating that Sydney Pollack and an eminent jury are all actually corrupt? These shibboleths need destroying. It was *anything* but a fiddle." The lengths to which the anti-Puttnam brigade would go had once again been dramatically illustrated.

But the controversy surrounding *The Mission*'s victory at Cannes was not yet ended. Still another drama unfolded at the presentation of the Palme d'Or. "I had to *physically* hold Fernando down when Roland went up to collect the prize," says David. "He was screaming that it was *his* Palme d'Or. He had this conviction that he should have collected it. The television cameras were on us, and I was trying to pretend it was an affectionate embrace. In truth, I had to physically prevent Fernando from making the biggest arse of himself of all time in front of a million viewers."

Although he was buoyed by the news of *The Mission*'s triumph at Cannes, Jake Eberts still did not see the movie as a major revenue-earner. Every week he issued a cash-flow report, supervised by an outside director, and often it showed the situation at Goldcrest getting worse. The company began to sell everything off—the rights to films, the television library, office space, anything that would raise cash and reduce the overhead. Gradually, the company staggered to a point where it could just about survive. Then the inevitable search for a new investor began.

"All during that period, David was highly supportive," says Jake. "He made every possible effort to publicly and privately give us the kind of support we needed. *The Mission* was certainly the reason for even continuing with the holding operation at Goldcrest, because it was clear to us that neither *Revolution* nor *Absolute Beginners* had a chance of even recouping their investment, forget about making money. The problem was, the *The Mission* wasn't due to open until later in the year. It was far and away the biggest investment in our portfolio, and we just had to hang in there and see what it was going to do.

"David had a running battle with the press about whether or not the film had gone over budget. That's just the way David is —he's a perfectionist, and he kept on getting exercised, quite rightly, about these comments. After all, his whole reputation and his livelihood as a producer, his financial integrity, were at stake. In pounds sterling, *The Mission* had stayed within its budget; in dollars, of course, it had gone up, purely due to the dollar's fluctuating fortunes. The press picked this up, but that was nothing whatsoever to do with David. The problem with *The Mission* was not any budget overrun on the picture itself, it was the basic cost of the picture. It was a very fine movie, but for £17 million, *any* picture is going to have trouble recouping its production costs."

Alan Parker, for one, could not see why David got so agitated over the budget-overrun stories, reckoning that the vast body of his work spoke for itself. "Supposing he did go over budget," Alan argues. "His reaction was very strange, almost as if his pride were on the line. David's dignity is so important to him, perhaps another legacy from the early days when he didn't feel he was given enough credence. In any case, everyone in the business knew how careful he was with his budgets. In fact, he became famous for always throwing in his own fee to make a point."

Anthony Jones acts as agent for Michael Apted, Iain Smith, Ray Connolly, Colin Welland, Bill Forsyth, and others (which has earned him the nickname of "one-stop shopping" among American filmmakers). He confirms this facet of David with a rueful smile. "There is a classic pattern on deferments of salary," he reveals. "Two weeks before any of David's films are due to start, I'll get the inevitable phone call. He's deferring, everyone's deferring together. I expect it, I *wait* for the call. Of course I agree—David and I find it very easy to negotiate with each other. We recognize the parameters. His word is his bond, it's yes or no in a phone call in any deal we do—*then* there's that inevitable deferment call!

"David should be a shareholder in our agency, the number of clients he's introduced since I first met him and Sandy over lunch to discuss *That'll Be the Day*. He's taken bigger risks over the years than anyone I know, starting films with his own money before getting the official go-ahead. He's a buccaneer, but he's also a masochist. After *Chariots of Fire*, he could have had what he wanted, but consciously he seems to ask himself what project he can put up that the studios will give him a hard time with. 'Right,' he seems to say, 'they all say they want to make pictures with me—let's see how they feel about *this* one!'

"He loves all the agonizing, feels it's not worth it if he doesn't suffer a lot. He's really more of an impresario than a producer, and the best salesman I've ever met. He regards selling these projects as a challenge. His high media profile is totally misunderstood—it's not to get a statue erected to him as many imply, but simply to help him make the films he wants to make the way he wants to make them. The man's a workaholic who never stops, and he's got the most incredibly acute sense of his audience. I remember once he was in my office, and I was arguing about who would want to see the picture he was talking about. He was looking out the window at the time and turned to me, pointing to a window cleaner on a scaffolding across the street. 'That's who I'm making this picture for,' he declared. *'That guy* is my audience. If I didn't honestly think he would come to see the picture, I wouldn't be bothering to produce it!' "

Jones is perhaps only half-correct in summing up David as a masochist. David can probably lay claim to inventing a new condition—pseudo-masochism. Much of his agonizing is in fact done either to make others fall into line with his way of thinking or to issue a signal for the future. As far as the supposedly masochistic act of shunning obviously commercial subjects is concerned, to David this is a nonissue. *Chariots of Fire* provides the perfect refutation.

The reactions of the press to *The Mission* and its win at Cannes was mixed. They found many things to praise, but—based on Puttnam's assertion that it was still a work-in-progress —expressed hope for changes and tighter editing. But despite critical support and the Palme d'Or, the jury—in the broader sense—was clearly still out.

David's sense of isolation within the British film industry began to grow. The Cannon deal became a fait accompli when reference to the Monopolies Commission was overruled at the governmental level. *The Mission* was now expected to save Goldcrest. And there were other factors at work as well, David began to signal. "I don't know whether I can afford to remain a line producer of films," he declared. "If I do a film every two years, I cannot afford to live at the Mill. I'm going to be forty-six next year, I'm self-employed, and I have to think about my pension." And so he did.

Musical chairs is one of Hollywood's favorite pastimes. After a
year of recurring rumors, Guy McElwaine was ousted as chairman and chief executive officer of Columbia Pictures. No successor was announced. Speculation began about the possible
future role of Richard C. Gallop, one of the presidents in
charge of Coca-Cola's Entertainment Business Sector. This um-
brella company included Columbia, under Chairman Francis T.
"Fay" Vincent, Jr. Another consideration on the table, however, was a move taking place between Fay and David's lawyer,
Tom Lewyn. As they lunched together in the spring of 1986,
Fay quickly got to the point of their meeting.

"Tom, would David consider taking over the hot seat at Columbia?"

"No way."

"How can you be so certain?"

"Well, I just happen to have a copy on me of a letter he sent to
Paramount, turning down a similar offer."

"Do you mind if I take a look?"

"Not at all."

Fay Vincent studied the document for a few minutes, sipping
at a glass of Perrier. Tom surveyed his menu with a poker face,
knowing that Fay was taking in David's minimum conditions
and unprecedented autonomy demands. Finally Fay took off his
spectacles and looked Tom straight in the face.

"I think we can live with these," he said quietly. Slow dissolve . . .

In any attempt to relate a "factual" event, no two witnesses
report identical versions. Japanese filmmaker Akira Kurosawa
illustrated in his classic *Rashomon* that truth is always elusive,
even in what purports to be the "definitive" version of an event.
To label any version as "the truth" is to rely heavily, therefore,
on one's attitude toward a witness's credibility. David has allowed the preceding version of Fay's meeting with Tom Lewyn
to pass into Puttnam mythology. But according to Fay
Vincent's version, it is inaccurate in one vitally important and
telling detail. Some would even argue that Fay's version makes

an even better—and a more revealing—tale. Either way, it makes a great story.

Fay confirms that he had a luncheon meeting with Tom Lewyn. *But it was called at Tom Lewyn's request* at Columbia's 711 Fifth Avenue offices—or to be more precise, at the Coca-Cola company's offices. "I've got an interesting idea to talk to you about," Tom had told Fay. Fay knew Tom as a fellow lawyer but was completely unaware that he represented David Puttnam. Tom wasted no time as the lunch proceeded. "How are you doing on the studio job?" he asked. Fay replied that they had a series of names they were working their way through.

"Have you thought of David Puttnam?" Tom asked. Fay replied that the name had never occurred to him, since he had never felt that David would be interested in the job.

"I think he would be," Tom replied. "I know that he likes you, and I think that you like him. He might well be interested." When Fay expressed enthusiasm, Tom pressed on. "There would be three conditions. One is, he would have to have total authority to make whatever movies he'd want to make."

"That goes without saying—that's what the job is," Fay replied. "That wouldn't be a problem as long as there's a budget and he stays within the amount of money we allocate to production."

"Second, he would want to leave the United States with $3 million net capital after taxes to take back to England, because he needs that to support his life-style. He has needs to make major capital."

Fay could see that the lunch was proceeding well beyond a mere exploratory talk. "I'm not negotiating with you now," he told Tom, "but that certainly is possible."

"The third condition is that he would want to do it only for a limited amount of time. He would want to live in Los Angeles and be committed to staying in the States for only three years."

"That's all right, too," Vincent replied, "provided it doesn't mean he'd be leaving the *company* after three years, and that we can talk about where he lives and how he works after that. In other words, that three years doesn't mean he wants to work for that length of time only and then *leave* Coca-Cola? The three years would only be his *residency* in Los Angeles?"

"I think that's correct, but if you want to pursue the matter further, you'll have to talk to David."

"Why don't you tell David I'm interested?"

"What you should do, Fay, is go to England and see David."

"Well, you report back to him on our conversation first."

Within days, Tom was on the phone to Fay. "David is very excited, but he has a lot of questions and would you meet him in London?"

"Sure," Vincent agreed. Second slow dissolve . . .

"When David was approached by Paramount," Tom Lewyn recalls, "the chief executive officer, understandably enough, said, 'I've got to have the final decision on which projects go and which don't. I'll listen to you and I'll probably go with you, but I occasionally won't.' Then, later, David and I were talking and it came up—why not Columbia? That's the *perfect* situation. There isn't a finer gentleman than Fay Vincent. He's a man I have a very, very high regard for, he has always kept his word to me. So it was he and I who concocted the idea of bringing David to Columbia. We bear the responsibility, for the good and bad."

17

Back in 1973, Ray Stark had become extremely concerned about the financial health of Columbia Pictures, from which he expected continuing revenues for his production of *Funny Girl.* He watched with dismay as the price of the stock fell from $9 to $4, and in desperation he turned to Herbert A. Allen, Jr., of Allen & Co., the New York investment bankers. Herbert Allen now approached Geritol tycoon Matty Rosenhaus, and with its banker's promise of a stay of execution until new management could be injected into the ailing company, Allen & Co. gained control of Columbia.

Of the two previous heads of Columbia, Abe Schneider, who had been suffering from ill health, resigned. Leo Jaffe chose to stay on, although the power source was now Herbert Allen, his appointee Alan Hirschfield, and Ray Stark, who had instigated Allen's takeover. Stark was appointed neither an officer nor a director of Columbia, preferring instead to pull the strings from behind the scenes. A $50 million loss for 1973 was reported, confirming their fears that the problems were more deeply rooted than they had seemed—almost as deep rooted, in fact, as the unlikely friendship of Ray Stark and Herbert Allen, Jr.

Raymond Otto Stark had been born in 1914. After failing to graduate from New Jersey's Rutgers University, he had moved to Hollywood in the late 1930s, taking a job first as a florist at Forest Lawn Cemetery, then moving into radio, then to the Warner Bros. publicity department.

The end of World War II had found Stark working with talent agent Charles Feldman, who introduced him to Charlie and Herbert Allen of Allen & Co. Stark and Charlie Allen immediately struck up a friendship. The next decade saw Stark's career as a highly successful literary and talent agent blossom. A short, slightly built man with sandy-colored hair, squinty blue eyes, and blond eyelashes, Stark began to command respect for his ability to hustle on behalf both of himself and of his clients.

When Warner Bros. ran into insuperable difficulties in 1956, Charlie Allen moved in, joining the board and purchasing large blocks of shares. In a fund-raising exercise, the entire pre-1948 Warner Bros. library was sold off to Associated Artists Productions (AA), a company run by Eliot Hyman to license movies for TV. Financing for this purpose was provided by Louis "Uncle Lou" Chesler, AA's chairman, a man with established ties to Mafia boss Meyer Lansky. Nor was this AA's only shady connection. Its vice president, Morris "Mac" Schwebel, would later be convicted of criminal activity. Ray Stark joined AA's board in 1957 through his Charlie Feldman connection.

One year later, Stark left with Eliot Hyman to form their own movie production company, Seven Arts. Stark departed to produce his first movie, *The World of Suzie Wong,* but rejoined Seven Arts two years later, serving under "Uncle Lou" Chesler's chairmanship.

Meanwhile, Charlie Allen and his associates had bought a 25 percent interest in Grand Bahama Port Authority Ltd, 50 percent of which was owned by a convicted stock manipulator, Wallace Groves. A subsidiary, Grand Bahama Development Co., was formed, in which Ray Stark, Eliot Hyman, and Lou Chesler invested, together with Seven Arts itself, to the tune of a 21 percent interest for $5 million. "Uncle Lou" was named president of Grand Bahama Development, thereby teaming up with ex-con Groves. Together they began to pay several hundred thousand dollars to Bahamanian government officials for permission to build a gambling casino on Grand Bahama Island. Following a meeting with Meyer Lansky in Miami, the casino was duly built and staffed by associates of the mobster.

When Jack Warner of Warner Bros. retired in 1967, Seven Arts bought his stock for $32 million and formed Warner Bros./ Seven Arts. Ray Stark left again at this point—with a large chunk of Warner Bros./Seven Arts stock in his pocket. He had a lucrative agreement with Columbia Pictures to produce a film version of his mother-in-law Fanny Brice's life story, *Funny Girl*, which Stark had steered to its triumph on Broadway.

At the end of the 1960s, Warner Bros./Seven Arts was taken over by Steven Ross's Kinney National Services, Inc., and Warner Communications was formed. Allen & Co. was the investment banker involved, and the deal yielded a hefty profit for the shareholders, not least for the Allens and Ray Stark.

Charlie Allen, Ray Stark, and Eliot Hyman had significantly solidifed their financial positions yet remained utterly odor free throughout all these transactions. Although they had formed questionable associations, there was no implication of any illegality or wrongdoing on their part.

Herbert A. Allen, Jr., had graduated in 1962 from Williams College and was appointed president of Allen & Co. in 1967 as his father and uncle were increasingly taking a backseat. Many were skeptical of the young man's ability to run the company, and when allegations of fraud were aired and a Securities and Exchange Commission investigation began, they felt their fears were justified. The fraud and manipulation charges against the company were ultimately dropped, but Allen & Co. was enjoined from violating other laws. Herbert, Jr., smarted under the accusations and was reported by *The New York Times* as having defiantly said, "We trade every day with hustlers, deal-makers, shysters, con men . . . that's the way businesses get started. That's the way this country was built." Although this statement was not disavowed by him at the time, he did so later, when he was four years older and wiser.

Just as Ray Stark had gotten along tremendously well with Charlie Allen over the years, that same friendship now extended to Charlie's urbane nephew. Stark had experienced a terrible tragedy in his life when his twenty-five-year-old son Peter jumped fourteen floors to his death in February 1970. Possibly Stark found a substitute for his own son in Herbert, Jr., although Herbert was in no need of a stand-in father. For whatever reason, the two men overcame the twenty-five-year gap in their ages and formed an alliance that was as close as that Ray had enjoyed with Charlie Allen before him—a relationship that had benefited both men handsomely.

At Columbia, Stark's first string-pulling led to the appointment of his friend ex-agent David Begelman to head motion-picture operations for the studio in Hollywood, under Alan Hirschfield's New York–based presidency. So far so good—except that Hirschfield dared to question the fairly Spartan returns coming to the company from Stark's productions. It was not that Stark's films for Columbia were unsuccessful—they included the 1975 *Funny Girl* sequel, *Funny Lady*, together with Streisand and Redford's 1978 *The Way We Were* and a string of Neil Simon successes. It was simply that the way Ray's deals were structured, Columbia was the last to see any money.

Hirschfield also felt that Ray's overheads, charged as they were under his contract to Columbia, required pruning. This attitude of Hirschfield's was bound to cause a rift, but it was nothing compared to a dispute over marketing methods that Hirschfield was determined to win. Hirschfield objected to Stark's appointment of two "production representatives" to monitor Columbia's marketing campaign for *Funny Lady*—he saw the move as demeaning to the studio. Stark fired back with,

"Friday the 13th would not necessarily seem the likeliest day for you to write me a memo. . . . My support of Columbia in this town has been a helluva lot more important to helping you acquire product than you may realize. . . . I believe the success of a picture, Alan, is contingent upon the whole rather than any individual elements. I welcome Columbia's executive advice as to the creative areas of my production. . . . I know that after you have read this letter, you will agree there is no Frankenstein replacing the lady holding the torch for Columbia Distribution. All we want to do is help make *Funny Lady* the richest lady in the world." Eventually, the two managed to keep their differences from boiling over into outright warfare, although each was increasingly wary of the other.

"Why can't Alan just leave David Begelman in charge?" Ray demanded. For his part Hirschfield retorted, "I can't run Columbia and keep looking over my shoulder at Ray Stark all the time." The stage was set for a split. David Begelman was the catalyst that would bring about the final disagreement.

The Begelman scandal began when actor Cliff Robertson could not recall receiving a check from Columbia Pictures for $10,000 in 1975. Nor could he remember having done any work for Columbia that warranted the payment—yet there it was on his "Statement of Miscellaneous Income" from the U.S. Internal Revenue Service in 1976. After fighting his way through a tissue of lies, evasions, and cover-up attempts, Robertson traced the check. It had been made out to him but had been cashed by someone else who had forged his signature on the reverse. That someone was David Begelman, Columbia Pictures' president.

The next questionable check to surface was one for $35,000 made out to Peter Choate. Choate was allegedly a technician who had been hired to install special sound equipment in theaters for the movie *Tommy*, but he turned out to be an architect who had carried out construction work on Begelman's home. Choate himself was a completely innocent party in the deception. After various other bits and pieces were added in, Begelman's embezzlements and misappropriations totaled $75,000.

Where Alan Hirschfield should have been firm on the issue, however, he vacillated, and he was finally undone when Stark and Herbert Allen excused Begelman's activities as aberrations. Only when the scandal could no longer be contained and exploded across the nation's headlines, rocking first Columbia and then the entire Hollywood community, did Stark and Allen back down and agree that Begelman had to go.

Still, Hirschfield had gone much too far in alienating the formidable trio of Matty Rosenhaus, Stark, and Allen. He tried to override Allen's chief executive role and sought an outside buyer for Columbia without board authority. Although he had presided, with Begelman's help, over Columbia's return to corporate health, his services were now dispensed with. "A disaster and a disgrace" was how Leo Jaffe termed Hirschfield's dismissal, although total concurrence with this is tempered by the question of what was seen as Jaffe's own long-passive role.

The new chairman, Herbert Allen, Jr., brought in Fay Vincent, another graduate of Williams College two years ahead of him, to replace Hirschfield as president of Columbia Pictures Industries. Vincent was counseled by some—*not* by Herbert Allen—to fire Victor Kaufman, who had been Columbia's young general counsel through the Begelman contretemps. It was suggested that he be fired as part of the stable-cleaning exercise, since Kaufman was widely seen as having supported Hirschfield. Fay Vincent declined to do this ("I can't fire somebody I don't know; I have to use my own judgment"), which enabled Kaufman to emerge in the years ahead as a particularly significant player. Frank Price, late of Universal-TV, succeeded Begelman as head of motion-picture production; soon afterward, Vincent appointed him president of Columbia Pictures, in charge of all film activities.

Herbert Allen admitted to Vincent that he had made two mistakes during the Begelman affair. The first mistake had been taking Begelman back, and the second had been not firing Hirschfield sooner. Fay is amused at the frequent press references to Allen as "Herb" or "Herbie." "He hates it. Those who know him least refer to him like that. And the whole issue of the Begelman-Hirschfield era has been wildly oversimplified. It's far more complex than it was made out to be. The company was in worse shape than is generally acknowledged. Hirschfield was simply unwilling to acknowledge Herbert Allen's leadership, and since Herbert's constant theme is loyalty, the end was predictable."

In 1977, Columbia had acquired the rights to the Broadway musical *Annie* for a reported record $9.5 million. Several producers were mooted for the project, which generated stiff competition since the fee for such a big-budget movie would be commensurately lush. One of Frank Price's first acts as head of production at Columbia was to hand over the reins of *Annie* to Raymond Otto Stark.

By 1981, Columbia's management was looking good again. The company was a well-drilled unit under Herbert Allen, Fay Vincent, and Frank Price. Columbia Pictures had returned to financial health. Hits like *California Suite, The Cheap Detective,* and *Midnight Express* in 1978, *Kramer vs. Kramer* and *The China Syndrome* in 1979, *Stir Crazy* and *The Blue Lagoon* in 1980, and *Stripes* and *Absence of Malice* in the current year, 1981, had kept revenues from the film division flowing nicely. Many of the earlier titles were a legacy from the Hirschfield-Begelman era. Columbia had purchased Ray Stark's Rastar Company—with Stark still running it—for 300,000 Columbia shares, each valued at $32.50, for a total of $9,750,000. The stage was set for the entry of the Coca-Cola Company.

Roberto C. Goizueta, Coke's chairman, is a first-generation Cuban immigrant. Born to a wealthy family of aristocrats, he had joined the company in Cuba before fleeing from Castroism in 1961. Once in the United States, he transferred to Coke's technical division in Atlanta as a flavor chemist. Goizueta speaks English as a second language, albeit with a heavy accent. Reporting to him is the president, Donald R. Keough, son of a third-generation Irish cattleman. In 1980, as two of six vice chairmen up for the job of chairman, the duo had agreed over a few drinks that whoever got the title would make the other his

right-hand man. When Goizueta became chairman, he carried
this out.

Goizueta is for the most part well able to keep his emotions
and instincts tightly under control. At times he can be stiff,
patrician, and cold. Only on rare occasions does his composure
slip, and his reserve gives way to a temper that can flare up
quickly under fire. Keough is the perfect buffer for his chairman—smooth, charming, hail-fellow-well-met—the outgoing,
bright salesman personified.

As a team they were resolved from the beginning to make
their mark by leaving no new idea unappraised, no potential
acquisition unexamined, no business opportunity unexplored.
And they regarded as sacred no formula—not even that of their
main product. When Coke's consultants, the firm of Arthur D.
Little, recommended buying into the entertainment business,
Columbia, with its library of 1,800 movies, was a natural target.

The preliminary meeting at New York's 21 Club went well.
Don Keough led the advance Coke party, and Herbert Allen
and Fay Vincent captained the Columbia team. Allen adopted a
soft-sell approach. As he listed Columbia's assets and management strengths, he went out of his way to detail the problems
he could foresee as well.

Coke's board consisted of a large number of elderly, conservative men (and we're talking elderly—average age seventy). How
would Coke feel about any sexy movies Columbia might turn
out? Allen asked. "Just so long as they're not X rated," he was
assured, "that would not be a problem."

Allen next pointed out that Columbia, although only one
tenth the size of Coca-Cola, attracted an inordinate amount of
press attention. "You would think we were AT&T. And if
someone in New York sneezes, somebody in California says,
'Bless you.'"

"We've thought about that aspect," Allen was told, "and we
can live with it."

Allen emphasized that the salaries of Columbia's creative people in Hollywood might be considered out of line by Atlanta

standards. Although Frank Price reported to Fay Vincent in New York, he earned twice as much as Vincent.

"We can handle that," Coke replied. "We don't mind paying, just so long as these creative people deliver. Otherwise there could be a problem."

The litany continued as Allen pointed out that David McClintick's book *Indecent Exposure* would chronicle the Begelman episode. "He [Begelman] was sick," Allen told the Coke team, "which the doctors and the courts concurred with—so we penalized him and then tried to make a deal with him as a human. We tried to rehabilitate him, but that was the wrong decision, given the PR of the day post-Watergate."

"That's in the past," Allen was assured. (Later, when the book was in galley proofs, Allen sent a copy to Goizueta, who claimed he gave up reading it early on, disgusted at McClintick's assertions. Keough has a copy but claims not to have read it at all.)

In any case, Allen pointed out, Columbia had no particular desire to sell to Coke. If a merger were to take place, a hefty premium would be sought. "It will knock your eyes out," he smilingly told Keough.

"Great company," Vincent told Allen as they left the meeting, after a follow-up had been set at Columbia's 711 Fifth Avenue offices. "I bet we make a deal."

"I don't," Allen replied, "because wait until they see the price I'm going to ask."

At the follow-up in Columbia's offices, Goizueta was introduced, a complete listing of the company's assets was made, and further emphasis was laid on how comfortable Columbia felt with its present independence. Allen again zeroed in on the "exorbitant" price he would ask. "I think we are the best in the business," he told the Coke team, "and we have to have a price Columbia can't turn down."

The number-crunchers moved in prior to the final make-or-break meeting in Atlanta. Columbia's stock was bubbling around the $40 mark, a fair way up from the $2.50 Herbert Allen had paid in 1973. (Most of it had been bought by Allen personally rather than through Allen & Co.) Allen and Vincent discussed the "number" they would ask. Vincent was designated to do the talking, and he was convinced that Allen would ask him to go for $100—after all, they had no wish to sell Columbia. Allen came out with an asking price just before the meeting started of a still-hefty $85.

"That's so far off, it isn't even funny" was Coke financial officer Sam Ayoub's immediate reaction before the meeting split up for separate discussions.

When they reconvened, Ayoub declared that the $85 Vincent was asking simply would not fly. Opening his briefcase, Ayoub pulled out a buff-colored envelope. Vincent guessed that Ayoub had a series of envelopes prepared. "Forget that first envelope, Sam," he declared, "and go to the next one." Ayoub chuckled ruefully. "Sixty-eight dollars," he said. Vincent conceded $82. "Seventy-two dollars," said Ayoub. "Seventy-five dollars," said Vincent, "and that's *it.*" Although the Columbia team had been playing it cool, they were stunned when Coke accepted $75. This valued Columbia at nearly $750 million, almost twice the market value of the shares.

A slide in Coca-Cola stock took place when news of the take-over broke. Goizueta was displeased with press reports that he had paid far too much for Columbia. In his defense he claimed he had heard a rumor that Time Inc. was also interested in acquiring Columbia. Within a year, however, he was vindicated by the same analysts who had criticized the takeover; Coca-Cola's stock advanced. What happened next is one of the most astonishing coups in the history of the movies.

If theatrical audiences—people who actually pay to enter movie theaters—were the only source of revenue production companies had, very few of them would be in business. In the old days, the only afterlife of a theatrical release was a theatrical rerelease. Now there's a whole variety of other ancillary uses— network, local, satellite, and pay-television, together with the lucrative home video market. Just as these end uses have grown, so have movie budgets.

All manner of financial arrangements are now worked out in

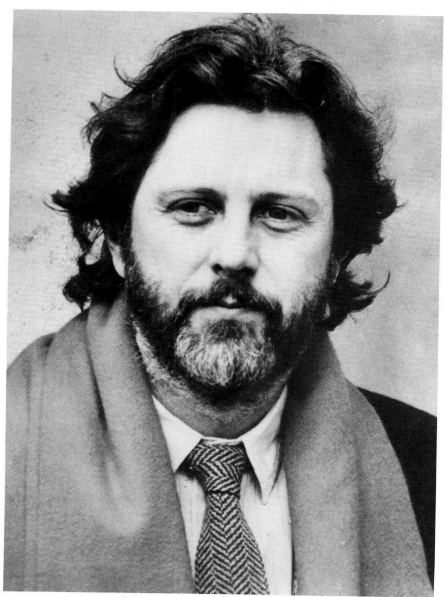

David Puttnam circa 1981 (AP/Wide World Photos)

David's parents, Len and Marie, Isle of Wight, 1933 (Photo credit: David Puttnam)

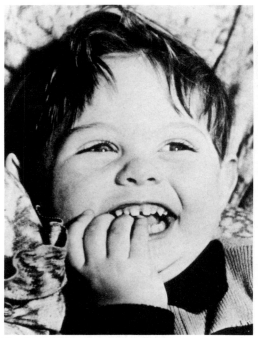

David, 1944 (Photo credit: Jack Esten, *Illustrated Weekly*)

Len, Lesley, Marie, and David
(Photo credit: David Puttnam)

David and Patsy, wedding day
(Photo credit: David Puttnam)

Patsy and Debbie (Photo credit: David Puttnam)

Debbie and Sasha with singer/actor
Donovan on location for THE PIED
PIPER (Photo credit: David Puttnam)

Mark Lester, director Waris Hussein, Jack Wild, and David on MELODY
location (Photo copyright National Film Archive London)

David Essex and Ringo Starr in THAT'LL BE THE DAY (Photo copyright National
Film Archive London)

Scott Baio in BUGSY MALONE (Photo credit: Photofest)

Harvey Keitel, David, and director Ridley Scott on location for THE
DUELLISTS (Photo copyright National Film Archive London)

Brad Davis in MIDNIGHT EXPRESS (Photo copyright National Film Archive London)

Alan Parker and David on location for MIDNIGHT EXPRESS
(Photo credit: Photofest)

Ben Cross and Nigel Havers in CHARIOTS OF FIRE (Photo copyright National Film Archive London)

A jubilant David Puttnam accepting the Academy Award for CHARIOTS OF FIRE from Loretta Young (AP/Wide World Photos)

David and Hugh Hudson, Oscar night 1982 (Photo copyright National Film Archive London)

Director Roland Joffe and David on location for THE KILLING FIELDS
(Photo copyright National Film Archive London)

Haing S. Ngor in THE KILLING FIELDS
(Photo copyright National Film Archive London)

Sam Waterston in
THE KILLING FIELDS
(Photo credit: Photofest)

Burt Lancaster, David, and Patsy on
location for LOCAL HERO (Photo
copyright National Film Archive London)

Robert De Niro in THE MISSION
(Photo copyright National Film Archive London)

Fernando Ghia and David on
location for THE MISSION (Photo
copyright National Film Archive London)

David and Patsy in 1987 at the time of the announcement of his move to Columbia Pictures (AP/Wide World Photos)

Roberto C. Goizueta, chairman of the board
and chief executive officer of Coca-Cola,
with Donald R. Keough, president and chief
operating officer (AP/Wide World Photos)

Francis T. "Fay" Vincent, Jr., the
man to whom David reported
(AP/Wide World Photos)

Ray Stark, in a photo taken in 1964 (AP/Wide World Photos)

Norman Jewison on the set of MOONSTRUCK (AP/Wide World Photos)

Warren Beatty and Dustin Hoffman astride a blind camel in ISHTAR
(Photo credit: Photofest)

Bill Cosby in an unforgettable scene from LEONARD PART VI
(Photo credit: Photofest)

David with Jerry Weintraub, producer of KARATE KID I and II, at the 1987 Cannes Film Festival (AP/Wide World Photos)

David Puttnam today (Photo copyright National Film Archive London)

advance both by major studios and by independent producers. Preselling is one. In preselling, a production company has a script and a star. A theatrical distributor in, say, Thailand guarantees to pay on delivery of the completed movie. Then a bank discounts that guarantee and passes the money on to the production company to make the movie. One percent of the budget is now found. A video company that wants the product must also pledge a guaranteed amount, and so must a pay-TV company, and so must everyone else who wants a piece of the action.

This was the pitch that Time Inc.'s pay-TV division, Home Box Office (HBO), swallowed from Columbia in 1982. Together with CBS, HBO entered a joint-venture deal with Columbia. In return for the license to show Columbia movies exclusively on HBO pay-TV, Time agreed to contribute 25 percent against the production cost of each movie, without a ceiling, *no matter what the movie cost.* If a Columbia picture costing $12 million made no money at all in its theatrical release, $3 million would *still* have to be paid. The killer was the sliding-scale agreement that Time agreed to *on top of this.* If the $12 million movie went on to take in $36 million in rentals, HBO's price tag escalated to 25 percent of $36 million, or a cool $9 million.

On top of this again, Time agreed to finance 25 percent of the costs of the movie as an equity partner, raising its total investment to 50 to 60 percent. Then CBS chipped a further $2 million for free-TV rights into the Columbia vaults.

Another enterprise that sprang from this meeting of minds was a new production entity, Tri-Star Pictures. Conceived in discussions between Fay Vincent and Victor Kaufman, Tri-Star was to be owned one third each by Columbia, Time Inc., and CBS, and it was to be run by the eager, ambitious Kaufman. The same basic terms would apply for all its product, except that Columbia would cream off a *further* 12.5 percent of the films' rentals in return for distributing Tri-Star product.

The inside joke at the conclusion of this deal was that "Coke paid $750 million to *buy* Columbia. Time Inc. will pay the same amount just to *rent* it for three years!" Fay Vincent put it even more succinctly: "We had a pipeline to Time Inc's treasury."

Ghostbusters was the movie that finally caused a renegotiation in the deal, as its rentals soared to an astronomical $144 million. The check that Time Inc. was obliged to write was for $36 million—a cool million more than the entire movie itself had cost to produce.

After this, Time Inc. shouted "Enough!" and requested renegotiation of the deal. Once ceilings were put on production costs and license fees, the deal between the two companies was extended to 1992. "We made an incredible deal the first time," Fay Vincent acknowledges. Who says money can't be made from movies?

As a boy of eighteen in 1956, Fay Vincent had been enrolled at Williams, two years ahead of Herbert Allen, Jr. As captain of the freshman football team, he was following in the footsteps of his illustrious father, who had been an outstanding player at Yale. Fay was first and foremost a serious student and a devout Catholic and was considering becoming a Jesuit after Williams —a prospect that changed one Saturday afternoon when his roommate locked him in their room as a prank. Fay tried in vain to batter the door down, but the fact that it opened inward rendered the task impossible. Resignedly, he decided to make the best of it and take a nap. When he awoke two hours later, there was still no sign of his roommate. Eager to get out, Fay looked at the window. If he could go outside and make his way along the ledge, he figured he could enter another room and be free. But it was December, and he failed to realize in the warmth of his room that the day had turned icy. As he started to edge his way along, he lost his footing on the ice that encrusted the ledge and plunged four floors to the ground below. The railings on a balcony halfway down the building had saved his life by breaking his fall—but they also broke his back: they smashed his vertebrae, breaking his spine before his fall continued. In a later transplant, several inches of shattered backbone were replaced from his hipbone. He was totally paralyzed for weeks and was left with legs that are still semiparalyzed to this day. The plucky youngster made the best of it, however, reckoning he was lucky to be alive, and he spent the time that would normally have been taken up with sports in intensifying his studies. In 1960, when he applied to join the Jesuits, he was rejected because of his limited mobility.

In 1963 he graduated from Yale law school and practiced law in Washington for fifteen years, then spent a few months at the Securities and Exchange Commission in Washington. In July 1978, Herbert Allen called up out of the blue and began discussions that would eventually lead to his being offered the job of running Columbia Pictures. After the Begelman scandal and Hirschfield's departure, they needed a "Mr. Clean," and stocky, square-set, straight-as-a-die Fay Vincent was it. He made an enormous success of running Columbia. He himself was made independently wealthy as the value of his Columbia stock multiplied in the Coca-Cola takeover. "Fay's ability to take Columbia from its lowest period to its peak was vital to the Coke transaction," Herbert Allen gratefully acknowledges.

A warm friendship also grew between Fay Vincent and Don Keough over the years and deals since the Coke transaction. Urged by Vincent, Herbert Allen reluctantly accepted a position on Coke's board in 1982. It was no sinecure; as chairman of the company's compensation committee, he was responsible for awarding to Goizueta a "performance units" bonus worth over $6 million, in the year of the new Coke launch. (Allen's prophetic prelaunch advice to Goizueta had been to bring in the new drink but keep the old one.) He has stayed on the board, Vincent feels, purely because of the close relationship he also developed with Goizueta. Nowhere near as close, however, as with his surrogate father in Hollywood, Ray Stark.

By May 1982, after a reported $40 million had been spent, Stark had *Annie* set for release. The film was directed by John Huston, with whom Stark had earlier made *Night of the Iguana, Reflections in a Golden Eye,* and *Fat City.* It starred Albert Finney, Carol Burnett, and Ann Reinking (soon to become born-again bachelor Herbert Allen's inamorata). "It's the movie I want on my tombstone," the producer declared, unprepared for the withering reviews *Annie* would receive.

In the *Los Angeles Times,* Sheila Benson wrote, "Golly, Annie, how could they have put you in the movies and left out your heart?" *Daily Variety*'s Jim Harwood described Annie as a "lumbering, largely uninvolving exercise," while Pauline Kael attacked the screenplay as "feeble" and "melodramatic." Although the film went on to give Columbia a net return of $37 million, it never went into profit because of its huge production and launch costs. Frank Price tried to take the heat out of the situation by describing the film's $40 million budget as 'the hype sums,' maintaining that $25 million was nearer the correct total. The price for the rights to the Broadway musical was similarly revised downward from $9.5 million to $6.5 million. In fact, Price was referring to "present-value" figures, a common and perfectly legitimate Hollywood numbers game. In Columbia's *Annie* deal, $9.5 million was indeed the purchase price the company was committed to paying—but over a period of years; $6.5 million was the *present-value* amount of money that Columbia was obliged to set aside to provide, with compound interest, the eventual $9.5 million.

Stark's reaction to the adverse criticism his pet project received was truly extraordinary. He vengefully hired ex–*Village Voice* columnist Stuart Byron as "creative affairs executive" in June 1982. "Stark said he wanted to write something about film critics and wondered if I could suggest someone to ghostwrite it for him, or at least to give him some ideas," *New York Times* film critic Vincent Canby recalls. "I suggested Stuart as one who wanted to get into that side of the business." *Newsweek*'s David Ansen maintained that Byron had called him to say he had been hired to pen an article about critics, but Byron insisted that Ansen had misunderstood and described his first task for Stark as "finding a writer who can write a script for a *Sweet Smell of Success*–story about a film critic."

Several were of the opinion that Byron's project was directly inspired by *Time*'s Richard Corliss, who had dared to describe

Annie's tone as "dark, dour, mean-spirited." His review had ended by quoting Stark's tombstone announcement, adding "Funeral services may be held starting this week at a theater near you."

In October 1983, after a year of breathless anticipation as to what Byron would produce, Stark hired Howard J. Koch as head of his Rastar Company. Two months later, Koch dismissed the entire production staff of the company—including creative affairs executive Stuart Byron.

Unpredictable, quixotic, a major player and power broker, Stark had woven an inextricable thread through both the warp and woof of Hollywood legend. Obsessed by a desire for complete confidentiality—many of his telephone calls would begin with a whispered "Are you alone?/Are you sure?/And what we say will go no further?/*Swearzy?*"—few in the community could hope to escape his byzantine influence, especially those incumbent at Columbia. Despite the bottom line on *Annie*, Stark argued that if all the half-price seats given out to children had been doubled up, the film would have ended as a money-maker. When he suggested that a sequel to *Annie* be filmed at Columbia, Fay Vincent was incredulous and turned the notion down.

Stark promptly took the proposal to Victor Kaufman at Tri-Star, who approved the project without consulting Vincent. "We took a loss on the original," Vincent reproached Kaufman. "It makes no sense to make a sequel, especially the price Ray's talking." Stark was infuriated by what he saw as Vincent's high-handed countermanding of Kaufman's decision, and for a while it was open warfare between the two men. Only when Stark resubmitted the project at a much lower cost did Vincent relent and allow Kaufman to okay the deal. "I didn't fight it again," he acknowledges. "I thought, 'What the hell?' "

Then Vincent watched as Stark went ahead with an ill-fated Neil Simon vehicle, *The Slugger's Wife*, that the producer hubristically chose to shoot in Atlanta under the very noses of the Coke bosses. Stark was mortified by the complete failure of the $25 million project and later bitterly regretted the high profile he had maintained during its production. He blamed himself for hiring director Hal Ashby, with whom he had fought constantly. "It embarrassed him so much, he would raise it all the time," Fay recalls. "He said he was going to make it up to the company. It just turned out to be a very bad movie, and he felt very bad about it."

Stark was a proud man who was now into his eighth decade. Time was running short if he were going to go out on a note of triumph.

"Don't give in on any of your demands," Patsy counseled David before his meeting with Fay Vincent and his deputy Dick Gallop at Queens gate Place Mews. As they drove to London, David reflected on a memorable phrase that producer Dan Melnick had used when offering him the job of production head at Columbia in the late 1970s: "Don't forget, this job gives you the right to talk to creative people the world over, not just in Hollywood."

Fay's recollection of the day's events in Queens gate Place Mews is a happy one, although now tinged by the turn events took at Columbia. "We had a very good day and discussed all the issues in question, and really from then on I believed we had an understanding that we were going to move forward. One of the points David raised was over the movie *Ishtar*, when he told us he and Warren Beatty and Dustin Hoffman didn't get along. He told us why. My view was that the picture was already going forward, and I didn't understand the enormity of the hatred. He put it to us very straight. He had had very bad dealings with Dustin during *Agatha*. He had never spoken to Beatty, but they had fought over the Academy Awards and Beatty resented him. He felt that both these people would be very negative about his coming. He was correct. I agreed to deal direct with the *Ishtar* people."

David insisted on a meeting with Goizueta and Keough to further clarify issues before he would sign. But Fay says that by the time that took place, he and David had already reached an agreement. "The meeting with Roberto and Don," says Fay, "was just a case of them getting to know David, since of course they were going to be important to each other, but David and I had already made the deal, and they knew David and I had an agreement. They were a little uneasy because he was a British producer and I'm known as an Anglophile, and I think they worried that I was using my own personal inclination. He was a strange choice to a lot of people."

David's residency was to be for three years in Los Angeles, although Columbia had the right to extend this by another six months. Fay felt secure in the knowledge that this would not be the extent of David's service with the company, for he felt he and David had confirmed their understanding that his tenure would extend *beyond* the three- or three-and-a-half-year point, wherever he was based. David admits he told Fay, "Yes, when the time's up and you want to negotiate a deal—that's fine with me."

He would have complete autonomy for all projects budgeted at under $30 million. He would report directly to Fay Vincent as head of Coke's Entertainment Business Sector, as the company was presently constituted. The one thing Fay was reluctant to immediately concede to David was control of International Marketing and Distribution, since this was tied in with television and video, which were outside David's brief. He was also aware that Patrick Williamson, who had been in charge of International for many years, was unhappy at the prospect of reporting to David. Fay sensed either a dislike or a distrust between the two.

Williamson, who had joined Columbia in England straight from school during the blitz, went so far as to warn Fay that David's appointment was a mistake. His astounding prediction was that David would self-destruct. He would not be able to keep his mouth shut, he had a big antiestablishment chip on his shoulder, and he would cause trouble for the company. "How can you say that?" Fay asked.

"I really know him and you don't," Williamson replied.

18

David solicited "advice" on the Columbia "offer" from everyone he could think of. Almost overwhelmingly, the reaction was "Go for it!"

"Hell's bells!" Robert Bolt declared. "Of course you must take it! You are going to, aren't you?"

"I don't know," David replied, "I don't think so. After all I've said about Hollywood, I don't see that I can. Everyone will think I've just sold out for the money."

"Well," said Robert, "you're a better man than I am if you would turn it down for such a high-falutin' reason."

A few weeks later, Robert and Sarah Miles were visiting Kingsmead Mill as guests for the weekend. "I think I'm going to accept," David told them, "although there's lots of detail to be hammered out."

"Well done," was Robert's wholehearted reaction. Sarah was

not so sure, having herself done some swimming in Hollywood's murky waters during the 1970s.

"David's a fighter," she acknowledges. "He has his enemies, and there's a lot of jealousy attached to his name. The English don't like putting themselves forward—they think it lacks humility or something—but David just goes all out. He's the best PR man for David in the world, and therefore the best producer we have. That's his ace card. One has to question David's taste in the subject he chooses, of course. We'd love it if he would just open up and forget his class consciousness.

"There was a time when he wanted to have his cake and eat it, too, but one has to take one's hat off to Patsy that she hung in through these rough patches. He's past all that now. I think there comes a time when all these energies go into other things. She held back with great dignity, and I think it's all paid off for both of them. They belong together. Many a great man is only great because of his woman, and Putters without his Patsy would be like a ship without a sail. She's the balance for him, in every way a well-earthed woman. There's tremendous toughness—you can see it in her eyes, you can see it in her every move. And there's so much loyalty.

"What's always been between the two of us is table tennis. Putters wants to win more than anybody I know in life. He doesn't see it as sport—it's a life-and-death struggle. You get to such a pitch with him that you think, 'I'd better lose here.' Even if you could win, you don't want to. He's *that* keen to win. I think it's a very healthy attitude, and I'm very envious of that final toughness. Robert Shaw was the same, on the tennis court or any other games you were playing with him. He went white with fury if he wasn't winning. David's got that same quality— for him there's only winning and nothing else. I personally find it very attractive—lots of lovely men have it. I'd love to have seen him and Robert Shaw duel to the death.

"The point about Puttnam is, if suddenly someone said to him, 'Look, English tennis is really down the nick, train this year and enter Wimbledon next year, you've got a good chance of getting into the finals,' he would. You see, he really cares enough about England to do *anything* for it. Something impossible—he'd try to do it for England."

A combination of factors drove David into the arms of the Columbia lady. One was the notion of having a whole slew of projects bubbling at once rather than having to depend on one major project every two or three years. Another was the fact that without financial support from Goldcrest, operations at David's own Enigma had been curtailed.

Still another was the influence of Cannon in Britain. The type of filmmaking The Cannon Group stood for was everything David was against—it was violent, opportunistic, exploitational. Yet he had been forced to stand back and watch as his colleagues bent their knees to the Cannon invasion. Despite its approaches, if it were to be the financial power source in Britain, Cannon was not for him.

And humiliatingly, Warners had once again turned down his latest Enigma project, William Boyd's own adaptation of his comedic novel, *Stars and Bars.* David's associate Susan Richards had kept a flame going in the window for that one, but as David had accompanied co-producer Sandy Lieberson around the Hollywood studios in search of financing, he felt as if he were back at the beginning of his career, as if he had no track record to his name, as if he were a supplicant having to answer a twenty-three-year-old script editor's question, "What makes you think *you* understand American humor?"

Finally, there was the main problem—money to live on. Apart from producer's fees, David had seen no appreciable income since *Chariots of Fire* went through the roof, while Patsy's expenses had soared splendidly and unashamedly into the stratosphere at Kingsmead Mill. The very definite need to replenish the Puttnam coffers would be met spectacularly by the Columbia deal. Kingsmead would be rendered invulnerable, and a little piece of England would forever be the Puttnams'. From the $3 million net guaranteed at the end of his term, there would be enough to maintain Kingsmead and still give David the luxury of making only the projects he really believed in, free at last from any treadmill.

The proposition was beguiling, even against the necessity of having to live above the store at Columbia for three years and wave a temporary good-bye to Kingsmead. And if going back to Hollywood had vague echoes of a defeat of sorts, David swore the community would soon discover he was no lame duck.

The Atlanta meeting with Coca-Cola was organized, and David took Patsy along with him, determined that she see her husband in action against the infidel capitalists. Although he had made the initial approach to Columbia, coquettishly he still wanted to be seen to be seduced on his own terms.

David had all his points ready as he and Patsy were driven to Coke's headquarters, an impressive twenty-six-story concrete, steel, and granite skyscraper on North Avenue, set apart from the Peachtree-laden metropolis. Tom Lewyn had been flown in from New York for support. After being introduced to Goizueta and Keough in Keough's office, David came out with the first of his hypothetical situations—and it was a lulu.

"Suppose," he asked, "I wanted to make a film on the People's Power Revolution in the Philippines, where the San Miguel Brewing Company is both your bottler and a previous Marcos supporter. How would you react?" The Coke executives assured him that the decision would be solely his. David managed to stop short of canvassing Coke's views on a multi-million-dollar epic on the cola wars.

Next, David handed the Cuban-Irish double act his manifesto for Columbia, which they read in reverential silence. "I was brought up on the movies," David had written. "They formed far and away the most powerful cultural, social and ethical impact on my formative years. These were the movies of the fifties, and for the most part, they were American movies. Many of them were made by Columbia Pictures. I was one among millions of young people around the world who basked in the benign, positive and powerful aura of post–Marshall plan, concerned and responsible America. The first day I came to this country was, in many ways, the most exciting of my life. Part of me was coming home. That's how powerful the effect of American cinema had been on me.

"Far more than any other influence, more than school, more even than home, my attitudes, dreams, preconceptions, and preconditions for life had been irreversibly shaped five and a half thousand miles away in a place called Hollywood. I labor over all of this in order to explain exactly where my passion for cinema stems from, exactly why it hurts me that the movies so frequently sell themselves short; unable or unwilling to step up to the creative and ethical standards the audience is entitled to expect of them.

"The medium is too powerful and too important an influence on the way we live, the way we see ourselves, to be left *solely* to the tyranny of the box office or reduced to the sum of the lowest common denominator of public taste; this 'public taste' or appetite being conditioned by a diet capable only of producing mental and emotional malnutrition! Movies are powerful. Good or bad, they tinker around inside your brain. They steal up on you in the darkness of the cinema to form or confirm social attitudes. They can help to create a healthy, informed, concerned, and inquisitive society or, in the alternative, a negative, apathetic, ignorant one—merely a short step away from nihilism. In short, cinema is propaganda. Benign or malign—social or antisocial, the factual nature of its responsibility cannot be avoided. To an almost alarming degree our political and emotional responses rest, for their health, in the quality and integrity of the present and future generation of film and television creators. Accepting this fact, there are only two personal madnesses that filmmakers must guard against. One is the belief that they can do everything and the other is the belief that they can do nothing. The former is arrogant in the extreme. But the latter is plainly irresponsible and unacceptable.

"Without doubt, filmmakers will continue to stagger from real to imagined crises and back again for years to come. The Film Industry is no place for fainthearted 'timeservers.' It needs thoroughgoing professionals with a love for cinema and respect for its audience. There can be no place for heroic posturing or overnight reputations. We have a business to nurture and build and that will require patience and a form of application which allows reputations the opportunity to develop and mature. Only those with a long-term interest in the Film Industry can expect to be rewarded. Speaking from experience, the rewards for that patience and faith are enormous."

Although there was no actual applause when the Coke chiefs finished reading, there was a considerable clearing of throats. Patsy could see that both men seemed moved—or at the very least bemused.

"You're right. You're right," Goizueta volunteered, breaking the silence. "When I came from Cuba, this is what cinema meant to me. I'm ashamed at what we have now."

"Fine," said David, "so you'll understand precisely why I wouldn't make a *Rambo*, no matter what the size of the built-in profit guarantee. If someone wrote me a check for the total box-office gross, I wouldn't take it."

His reason for picking on *Rambo* was not ingenuous. Not only did *Rambo* illustrate the type of film whose values he found abhorrent, perhaps more significantly, it had also been chosen for distribution by Victor Kaufman at Tri-Star. *Rambo* represented a despised genre *and* provided a convenient, close-to-home case in point. ("You don't need to make a *Rambo*," Dick Gallop claims he replied when David raised the same point at an earlier meeting, "but you sure need to make a broader, more commercial slate of pictures than you made heretofore.")

As he elaborated on the way he would address what he saw as Columbia's exorbitantly expensive "housekeeping deals," where producers' overheads were paid in return for first pick of their product, Fay Vincent reflected that David was now talking about subjects in which the Coke bosses were not particularly interested; in any case, a number of these deals had already been terminated. Although the present "housekeeping arrangement" was not dissimilar to what David had enjoyed at Warners, the comparison ended with the richness and scale. David had already been briefed enough to be horrified at the terms on which Columbia had surrendered. Although Warners remained essentially a studio run from the inside, it was clear to him that the "housekeeping system" at Columbia was untenable. The studio was no longer a sovereign state—it was more like a princely state that had to appease and mollify a group of barons.

Close to $10 million was pouring out of Columbia's coffers in retainers to a handful of producers. A massive figure for "general production advances" of several times that sum had accumulated, advances that had been paid out for productions that had never taken place—dead money to all intents and purposes. He was staggered at the breadth and at the loose interpretation of "legitimate costs" that Columbia allowed.

"And you are aware of my conditions of complete autonomy over the product I greenlight," David went on, "up to a ceiling of $30 million on any one film. Talent packages would be out. If I don't have your support in this, then I'm the wrong person for you."

"We hear you, David," Coke responded, "and we like it."

Now the moment of truth had arrived. David asked, "How about the major producers who may well find their situations altered by these policies?"

"Like who?" Keough asked.

"Well, like Ray Stark," said David. "He's certainly going to be one of the producers who'll feel the effect of these changes."

Fay Vincent stared philosophically out the window. He had known this point would come up. Fay's relationship with Ray Stark had for years been strained; the incident of the *Annie* sequel had simply been one of a long line. Following the original *Annie* and the 1985 disaster of *The Slugger's Wife*, many of Stark's other pictures had done poorly; even his ex-protégé Guy McElwaine had refused to give several of Stark's movies the green light, notably *Biloxi Blues* and *Brighton Beach Memoirs*. These Stark had been forced to find a home for at Universal, during Frank Price's reign. What had always made Fay's position especially difficult was Stark's closeness to Herbert Allen, although Allen heroically performed the difficult task of preventing either one from doing the other great harm. At best, it would not take much to upset this balancing act, as Fay was only too painfully aware.

When David had raised the Ray Stark issue with him earlier, Fay had told him he thought Ray was difficult and dangerous. "The trouble with Ray," he summed up, "is that he can't separate a business from a personal judgment. So if you say something to him in a business sense that he doesn't like, he'll say, 'How can you say that? You're not being my *friend*.'" Fay had told David frankly that Stark would indeed be a big problem, but that that was part of the territory. David would have the job and the authority to do what he wanted with Stark. If he got too close to him, the producer would want to run the whole show; yet it would be near impossible to maintain a distance. It was almost a no-win proposition.

"Don't worry about Ray Stark," the Coke bosses assured David, echoing Fay's original comment. "We'll take his calls, we'll be polite, but Ray has no real currency down here. It'll be your show."

Now Patsy had a say. She added her own warning about the support David must be given. "I know my husband," she told them. "He'll give you all the blood, sweat, and tears you could ever want. But if you don't back him to the hilt, he'll walk away. You'll lose him."

"At Coke, we back the people we hire," Patsy was assured.

The heat shimmering on the Atlanta pavement outside was nothing compared with that generated by the outpouring of admiration in Keough's office. One important area had been left for further discussion—the question of David having complete control over International Marketing and Distribution, which Fay had left open. But Goizueta sent Fay a note following the meeting to say how thrilled he was with Puttnam and how tremendous it was that he was joining Columbia—and all because of Vincent's good offices. "I can talk to David and Patsy about movies," Goizueta enthused. "I now have somebody I can talk to in California." The bosses of Coke were elated. Out of the multitude of situations available to David Puttnam, he had chosen *them*.

Patsy and David were both "gob-smacked" by the apparent warmth and sincerity of their reception, although David still felt an advance meeting with Ray Stark was called for. Such a meeting was arranged at Stark's Mapleton Drive mansion in Hollywood's Holmby Hills (once the home of Humphrey Bogart).

During the meeting David divulged that Fay Vincent was reluctant to concede control of International Marketing and Distribution. Ray was all charm. "I'll make a call," he offered. "Leave it to me."

"The great problem for me," David continued, "is the so-called 'special relationship' you seem to enjoy at Columbia. Ray, you really can't continue to be both a customer *and* an adviser. You've got to decide just what you want to be."

There was no immediately discernible chill as the two men sipped their tea in Stark's garden. Only a few seconds elapsed before Stark replied, "Oh, really? That's something I'll have to think about, although all in all I seriously think I'd rather be an adviser. I can get my pictures made at Universal. I've got a good deal there right now, and I've got things at Tri-Star. Yes, I'd enjoy being an adviser."

David felt as if a great weight had been lifted from his shoulders. "Great, Ray, that's terrific." He beamed.

As David was leaving, Stark asked him if he had considered buying a house in Hollywood for his stay. When David replied that he would prefer to rent, Stark insisted it made better sense to buy. If money was a problem, he would lend whatever was necessary. He would help him locate a house, he said. He would help in any way he could. David had a sense that he was being "folded in."

He turned the offer down, but a warning bell was ringing in his head. Back in the 1970s, he recalled, David Begelman had had a three-year lease on a house in Beverly Hills that was owned by a company called Burton Way. Unknown to Columbia, which was paying the bulk of the bill, Burton Way was wholly owned by Ray Stark's lawyer, Gerald Lipsky. It seemed that the house had been purchased by Lipsky specifically at

Begelman's request and leased back to him. While Begelman was being investigated, he was asked if it would not have been more aboveboard to have divulged to Columbia his landlord-tenant arrangement with Lipsky—a man with whom he constantly negotiated over the terms of Ray Stark's pictures. Begelman replied that he saw nothing improper either in the arrangement or in Columbia's ignorance of it. Direct financial ties had been found between Stark and Begelman—a first loan of $15,000 as early as 1964-65 and another of $27,500 in 1976, which Begelman had kept in his desk for use as required. Stark had also guaranteed him a loan of $185,000 from the City National Bank. Although all the loans had been repaid and no impropriety had been inferred, David thought as he drove through Bel Air, "Thanks a lot, Ray, but honestly, no thanks."

David recalls that two days later he was informed that Fay had conceded control of International to him. It looked as if Stark had made the promised phone call. "Ray never spoke to me about this," says Fay, "and David never told me he had raised it with Ray. I had agreed in London that David would ultimately have control of his own films. The main problem was in extricating his product from video and TV and Williamson's reluctance to report to him."

In June 1986 in Beverly Hills, the stage was set for the official announcement of David's appointment as chairman of Columbia Pictures and senior executive vice-president and director of the main Columbia Pictures Industries board, the corporate parent, reporting to Fay Vincent. Although he was not due to officially start at the studio until September 1, David spent the next few summer months immersing himself in matters Columbian, in return for time off later to promote *The Mission.*

David paid a special tribute to the Warner executives, who had agreed to suspend his first-refusal contract with them although it still had twenty months to go. The flip side of this coin—which was not lost upon many in the film community even as David was paying the tribute—was that Warners had refused to pick up in full a single film from Enigma throughout the years the contract had run. "They've simply suspended refusing his films for twenty months," one cynic wrote, reminding everyone it had been Warners' turndown of *Stars and Bars* that had proved one of the last straws. Nonetheless, David went on to declare that Warner's "generosity and understanding" over his contract, together with his working experience with them over the years, was one of the factors that had persuaded him in the end that he might have been too harsh in his earlier criticisms of Hollywood.

The internationalism of Coca-Cola appealed to David. "I came here because of the tenacity of Fay, an old friend," David enthused, "and of Dick, a new one, who frankly wouldn't take no for an answer. I find it incredibly refreshing to be with a company whose outlook by definition is international. When you are a foreigner dealing with the Hollywood system, there is a sense sometimes it is a very parochial society. Coca-Cola is the least parochial company imaginable.

"Roberto understood my Third World mentality, about the responsibility of the American cinema and the job that cinema has to do in the rest of the world. This was something I didn't have to convince him of. He was brought up with it in the same way I was. And Don is this marvelous, enthusiastic entrepreneur who likes the idea of the film industry being given a boot up the bottom. When I went to Atlanta, I was a neutral skeptic, but I came away a positive apostle."

Columbia, too, picked up on Coca-Cola's internationalism. "Wooing the international audience" was the theme Fay Vincent spelled out. Fay's plan was to work to increase Columbia's revenues from abroad. After all, 60 percent of Coca-Cola's business was done outside the United States, his reasoning went; why should only 30 percent of Hollywood's revenues come from abroad? All right, one of the products was brown syrup, the other was celluloid—but why let a little fact like that stand in the way of such unarguable logic? In fact, many other Hollywood studios were discussing increasing revenue from abroad more and more. Fay Vincent's view was that Coke's international strength would be of help in achieving this goal, rather than that Columbia should emulate Coke per se.

Patsy stood by her husband's side. "I encouraged his idea of taking a sabbatical to Harvard and didn't think the Columbia idea was right, but the Coca-Cola people turned me around. The told us they wanted Columbia to be the best film company there is, and I believed what they said. I may look ridiculous in a couple of years, but in any case, I always like the fight better than its resolution."

Back in Britain, disbelief turned in many cases to outrage when the news of David's move was confirmed. Alexander Walker sent a telegram that read simply, "Have you taken leave of your senses?" Hugh Hudson said, "It's everything he said he'd never do." He was dubbed "a defector" by the *Daily Mail.* "So much for Puttnam's patriotism," a *Daily Telegraph* article ran. One of his ex-Goldcrest colleagues said, "Hollywood will chew him up and spit him out."

"I felt like Burgess and Maclean rolled into one," David said, chuckling, then added prophetically, "I may have to eat some of my words, but one thing I'm not is a defector. I see myself in a situation just like an aerospace engineer for Rolls-Royce. Imagine that everybody acknowledges you're producing the best-quality work. Then one day, through no fault of your own, Rolls-Royce closes down and you get a telephone call from Boeing asking you to join them. Honestly, what would you do?"

Warren Beatty, for one, was concerned when he heard the news. He made it clear that as far as he was concerned, there was no question that David would get his hands on *Ishtar.*

"You may have hired a very good person," said Beatty, "but I don't get along with him. I don't want to deal with him. He's going to torpedo my picture, and he'll do everything possible to kill *Ishtar.* I don't know if we can function—there'll have to be lots of safeguards so he doesn't hurt the film." Beatty accused Puttnam of saying a number of terrible things about *Reds* during the fight over the Academy Awards, which Beatty termed "unacceptable chickenshit." Fay Vincent, who holds Beatty in great esteem, describing him as "a clever, sophisticated guy," told him there was no need for concern, that he had already covered that ground with David. "He has no wish to go anywhere near *Ishtar,* " Beatty was assured.

At the same time Fay began to wonder if he had underestimated the strength of feeling of the *Ishtar* participants. It would be neither the first nor the last time he would underestimate the bizarre motivations and rampant paranoia endemic to Hollywood. Both Beatty and Hoffman felt *they* should have been consulted about David's appointment.

19

Hollywood—where the last great movie was *Chinatown* back in 1974, produced by Robert Evans, written by Robert Towne, directed by Roman Polanski, and brought to us by Paramount Pictures, whose highest aspirations today range from *Top Gun* through endless *Beverly Hills Cops*, *Indiana Jones*es and *Friday the 13th*s.

Hollywood—where Elia Kazan once described Harry Cohn, Columbia's founder, as "the biggest bug in the manure pile." Cohn boasted that he had a foolproof device for judging whether a picture was good or bad: "If my fanny squirms, it's bad. If my fanny doesn't squirm, it's good. Just as simple as that." Writer Herman Mankiewicz's response was, "Imagine— the whole world wired to Harry Cohn's ass!"

Hollywood—where a company makes a deal with an artist

for a given project. That's good. But when the starting date arrives, often no contracts have been prepared. That's not so good. When the artist fails to turn up on the first day of shooting, however—contract or not—the studio sues and wins a breach of contract suit. That's bad. That same high-minded studio is in any case planning to deceive the artist with bookkeeping when the eventual profit statement is due. That's really bad. Then the studio expects to be sued, secure in the certain knowledge that the whole affair will be tied up in lawsuits forever, while it has use of the money and is earning interest on it. That's wicked.

Who needs stars in Hollywood?

- David Puttnam (pre–Robert De Niro): "I'd rather go for a nonstar, not someone who's going to bring the baggage of other roles to the part. . . . An awful lot of the pressure the agents rely on to get their stars in these films and get their fees paid is the social pressure that producers or directors feel to be associated with these same people. They love to sit at dinner parties with them. It's the starfucker phenomenon. If someone says a star to me, all I see are the problems—none of the advantages, only the problems. And then explaining why one person gets a trailer and someone else doesn't. I basically despise human beings who feel the necessity to be treated unlike other human beings. I can't be doing with it, can't deal with it."
- David Puttnam (post–Robert De Niro): "Stars aren't stars by accident. By and large they're really quite good actors. You find yourself with a star because actually that is the most talented actor you can find."
- William Goldman (writer): "Stars are a pain in the ass to a director. They have to be coddled. They need to be stroked. Ultimately what they do is waste time, and time is the enemy of all production. As a general rule, I would say if you corner every director in the world and say, 'This is off the record. If you can make your next picture (and you

have the same budget), but in one case you have a star and in one case you don't have a star . . .' there may be *one* director in the history of the world who would rather go with a star, but for the most part none of them would want to."

• Billy Wilder (film genius): "My aunt Lizzie learns her lines, always turns up on time, and does what she is told. But who wants to pay to see my aunt Lizzie?"

Who needs writers in Hollywood—where the moving finger writes and having written moves on, whereupon a rewrite is arranged?

• Stirling Silliphant (writer): "On the set, the writer is very much like a hooker who has been fucked and paid and is there on sufferance."

• Bobbi Thompson (agent): "Being a screenwriter is to my mind the most masochistic thing you can do. They all get treated like shit, and they are raped right and left. It's sad to hear that even the most talented, sought-after writers are subject to the same shitty treatment and lack of respect as the newest beginner who is shafted on the money."

• I.A.L. Diamond (film co-genius): "More directors have ruined their careers by writing their own scripts than by screwing the leading lady. And some of them have done both!"

• Alfred Hitchcock (director): "The three most vital elements in any good film are the script, the script, and the script."

Who needs directors in Hollywood?

• Gore Vidal (writer): "Almost anyone can do what a director does. I've worked on about fifteen movies; I've done 150 live TV plays; I've done eight plays on Broadway—I never yet saw a director who contributed anything. When I went to Cannes for *The Best Man*—there on this banner was the title in French, '*Un film de Franklin Schaffner.*' Well, I just hit the ceiling. I mean, this was my play, my movie. I had helped put the thing together. I had *hired* Frank."

- Steven Spielberg (director): "Directing is 80 percent communication and 20 percent know-how. Because if you can communicate to the people who know how to edit, know how to light, and know how to act—if you can communicate what you want so that what they're doing is giving you your vision and what you feel, that's my definition of a good director."

Who needs sneak previews in Hollywood?

- Rob Reiner (director): "We had a great response to *The Sure Thing* in St. Louis. The research team told us, 'Wow! The only two films that did that well were *E.T.* and *Gable and Lombard.*' I thought, 'That's just it; we're going to be somewhere between *E.T.* and *Gable and Lombard!*'"
- David Brown (producer): "In my experience, a sneak preview can be a triumph and result in no one coming to see the movie."
- Richard Rush (director): "There's an element of self-fulfilling prophecy in research. We keep being told that the audience is teenagers, between twelve and twenty-two, and so we keep making movies that appeal to those people. So in a sense, research is leading the industry down the garden path."
- Brian De Palma (director): "It's appalling that 325 people recruited from shopping malls can shake the confidence of professionals who've been working in the industry for decades."
- Richard Brooks (director): "Today, I hear they bring an audience in to see a picture and ask them to push a little button if they like certain scenes. How the hell are they going to get involved in a movie and push buttons at the

same time? And preview cards—Columbus would still be in Spain if they waited for preview cards."
· David Puttnam: "I believe in previewing absolutely."

Power breakfast, anyone? It's got to be at the Bel-Air Hotel. Power lunch? At Le Dome on Sunset, backrooms are best—or La Serre in the Valley. Power dinner? Morton's in West Hollywood, corner Melrose and Robertson, or Spago overlooking Sunset Strip. (Wolfgang Puck features wonderful food here, but the real reason everyone goes is because it's the in place to be.) Old-time power? Chasen's in Beverly Hills, corner Doheny and Beverly. Can't get a table? Short of change? No problem; most maître d's will take American Express—but for under $100? Forget it.

How about power hotels? The Bel-Air can't be beat for the elite, Chateau Marmont is frequented by the funkies, Sunset Marquis by the rock 'n' roll megas, while Shangri-La on Santa Monica has the best view of Diane Keaton when she's in town. But while nibbling on your Quiche of Sea Bass in Lemon Juice with Cucumber, Tomato, and Cilantro, or on your Sautéed Chicken Paupiettes stuffed with Veal and served with Madeira Mushroom Sauce, consider the words of the bank manager's daughter, Patsy Puttnam: "There's nowt for nowt." Yep, along with that luxurious pad you may have been allocated by the studio, it's all going on the bill of your current movie.

Iain Smith swears that after landing at Los Angeles Airport, palely loitering British filmmakers are courteously guided to an anteroom by bronzed, smiling Californians with perfect white teeth and are tendered a swift injection of a powerful inadequacy drug, the size of the dosage varying only with the proposed length of stay.

Once upon a time, it was whispered, the lunatics were taking over the asylum; the actors were trying to run the studios. Way, way back, Cagney tried it. Then Bogey. Then Alan Ladd and his "over-the-hill gang" at Warners. Then big John Wayne himself, followed in more recent times by Dustin Hoffman, Barbra Streisand, Sidney Poitier, and Steve McQueen in their First

Artists venture. The keepers were laughing up their sleeves. Poor loonies! They had forgotten about the small matter of distribution, which was forever securely retained in the studios' clutches.

After the end of the studio contract system, the era of the agents arrived: MCA, William Morris, CMA, ICM. Hugh French broke the bank with the first-ever $1 million contract for a star on a single picture, Elizabeth Taylor in *Cleopatra*. B. O. (Before Ovitz), each star had one basic contact with whomever they dealt. This agent would have little or no dialogue with his counterparts in the business. But at Creative Artists Agency (CAA), President Michael Ovitz and his team of Ron Meyer, Bill Haber, Rowland Perkins, and Martin Baum not only represented specific clients, they constantly cross-collateralized their career moves. The era of "the package" arrived, allowing studios to abdicate responsibility for stitching together the various elements in any given project. Run like a military operation, CAA's day starts at the crack of dawn and ends when it ends—which can be at dawn the following day. Considered by many to be the most powerful man in Hollywood, Ovitz is today's Talleyrand, a modern Metternich, able to whisper in the ears of kings.

David's ballroom-dancing experience as a young boy would come in handy in the next year. He would soon be engaged in a constant series of danses macabres with some of Hollywood's toughest acts: Ray Stark and his Stomp, Bill Cosby's Can-Can, Victor Kaufman's Carioca, Warren Beatty's Blackbottom, Barry Diller's Dirty Dancing, Marty Ransohoff's Rock 'N' Roll—and Mike Ovitz's Entrechat, for which there is no known remedy.

For the six months before David's arrival at the studio, Columbia had been slipping badly in the box-office stakes. The total for the period was still reasonable—$291 million; however, *Karate Kid II* accounted for $110 million of that, leaving the balance, $181 million, split between thirteen other features: *White Nights* ($42 million), *Stand By Me* ($31 million), *Murphy's Romance* ($31 million), *Jo-Jo Dancer* ($18 million), *Armed and Dangerous*

($15 million), *A Chorus Line* ($11 million), *Care Bears II* ($8 million), *Quicksilver* ($7 million), *A Fine Mess* ($5 million), *Violets Are Blue* ($4 million), *Out of Bounds* ($4 million), *American Anthem* ($4 million), and *That's Life* ($1 million).

Paramount was making everyone else look sick with its $412 million, far above 1985's champion, Warners, which trailed behind in second place with $307 million. Columbia was at number three, but thanks to only one film, and it was being challenged by 20th Century-Fox with $236 million and by Disney/Touchstone with $235 million. Responsibility for restoring the Columbia lady's somewhat down-at-heel fortunes rested heavily on David's fairly slender shoulders.

The Puttnams' plan was that David would stay on his own at the Bel-Air for a month until the house Patsy had selected was ready. She had picked a furnished bungalow in Coldwater Canyon that Dudley Moore was due to vacate for a house in Malibu. But his Malibu house ran behind schedule, and Dudley inconveniently opted to stay an extra month. This extended David's booking at the Bel-Air and delayed Patsy's arrival from Kingsmead Mill.

To David, the first few days at the eleven-acre oasis of the Bel-Air was like a time-out from the real world. On Saturday, in a scene reminiscent of *The Godfather*, an Italian wedding reception was held outdoors beneath the exotic palms that lined the hotel's swan lake. Serenaded by a bank of violins that were sheltered in a shady balcony overlooking the celebrants, David was regaled by a medley of "Romantica," "That's Amore," "Love Letters," "Fascination," and the inevitable "Tie a Yellow Ribbon (Round the Old Oak Tree)," as he tried to concentrate on the scripts that had been left for his attention.

By contrast, the atmosphere at Columbia's Burbank came as a rude awakening. Balefully overlooked by a huge water-tower, flanked by administrative offices at Columbia Plaza South, and opposite the Producers' Building (housing Ray Stark) stood the barracklike Columbia Plaza East. The second floor was David's destination.

"Who are you here to see?" the doorman inquired politely.

"Nobody. I'm David Puttnam, the new start."

"Are you sure you have the correct building? There's no one here by that name, sir."

"I'll be in Mr. McElwaine's old office."

"Oh, that's through the doors, turn left, up the stairs, then the far end of the corridor."

Huge black and white blowups of scenes from Columbia hits lined the corridor walls, among them *It Happened One Night, Mr. Deeds Goes to Town, Gilda,* and *Guess Who's Coming to Dinner.* But up and down the executive corridors, the doors were shut tight. The company seemed to have been running on fear and uncertainty for so long that a conviction that the new broom would sweep instantly clean had become embedded. The whole building appeared to be in a state of siege.

Valerie, David's secretary, was already installed and busy typing a list of the thirteen hundred script submissions that had poured into the studio since the announcement of David's appointment. Earlier, she had opened the door of David's office, unprepared for the eyeball-assault of Guy McElwaine's deep maroon period. The color was wall-to-wall and floor-to-ceiling. The furniture consisted of four gigantic settees, festooned with what resembled skunk throws. A single naked light bulb hung guiltily from the ceiling. Smoked glass covering the two corner walls ensured that not a single mote of sunlight penetrated the stygian gloom. Valerie sighed and closed the door on the apparition. "David, you'll need to move somewhere else while that nightmare-on-wheels is sorted out," she told him when he arrived.

"Fine," he replied. "Now, first things first. I'd like to speak to everyone, from the executives down to the janitor."

When all the personnel were congregated in the largest screening room, David gave an inspired and inspiring speech to the bemused, demoralized gathering. They would work as a team. They were going to make great movies. There would be problems. They would be overcome. He did not have all the answers. He was prepared to listen to those who thought they had. There would be an open door to his office at all times.

There would be monthly seminars ("The Reel Truth") to which they would all be invited.

The reaction was astonishing. "I've been here ten years," said one studio publicist, "and I've never even met the head of the studio. It was like the mountain coming to Mohammed."

By early evening, even the normally tireless Valerie was flagging. "It's been nonstop," she told David. "As fast as I'm logging the scripts, more pour in." She smiled. "Doesn't look as if you'll be short of subjects, David." After dinner at the Bel-Air, their business resumed again as the two went through the day's calls and David dictated letters of reply and filled his diary with appointments for the week.

In the next few days, in between systematic individual meetings with every member of his executive staff, David acquired Ridley Scott's thriller, *Someone to Watch Over Me*, in turnaround from MGM. He had bluntly told Michael Nathanson, a twenty-nine-year-old production executive, "You're earning far too much money for what you do. You stand out like a sore thumb." Out of David Begelman's stable via the Guy McElwaine regime, Nathanson replied he had negotiated his salary. "Fine," said David. "I'm putting you in charge of Ridley Scott's new picture. We'll see how you do." (Three months later, David told Nathanson, "You're on my team.")

As the week progressed, David saw that his plan to make the best of his inherited team was going to be impractical in some cases. These individuals had never pulled together—they had fallen together—and certain members were going to have to be removed from the mix. He was horrified at the backstabbing he had to listen to, the naked animosity that was rife in many of the conversations.

"How has it been?" Patsy asked when he called.

"Ask me again in a couple of days," David replied. "If I told you now, you wouldn't believe it. Morale is so low, it's off the chart."

Within days of his arrival at Columbia, David received a script from director Norman Jewison. In Jewison's checkered career, he had traipsed from the wilder shores of *Jesus Christ Superstar* and *Rollerball* through to the relatively modest, well-received *A Soldier's Story* and *Agnes of God*. The present submission was an update of the only script ever written by H. G. Wells, *The Man Who Could Work Miracles*. It was intended as a Richard Pryor vehicle with a projected budget of $19 million. "I said I wanted to start shooting in three months' time," Jewison recalls, "and must have an answer. I'd spent all that time, and at my age— sixty-one—you've only got so many films left in you. A week goes by, no answer. So I called my agent and asked him to get in touch with David and have him call me. He never called. Finally, a month goes by and I get a letter from David saying he didn't wish to do the film." David maintains that he passed the script on to colleagues within days with a "not for me" comment, to be relayed to Jewison's agent.

Jewison phoned David, incensed that it had taken a month to be turned down. "How dare you keep me waiting!" he raged down the phone. "Then you didn't even have the courtesy to call me personally!"

David says that he both likes and respects Jewison, although he found both *A Soldier's Story* and *Agnes of God* dull. Although Jewison's contract was not as rich as some, David did not feel inclined to extend it after the abuse the director gave him over the phone following the *Miracles* turndown.

"It was clear," says Jewison, "that David Puttnam had no interest in my future at Columbia, so I announced I was leaving." He took with him a property that was eventually entitled *Moonstruck* and promptly placed it with Alan Ladd, Jr., at MGM. With Cher and Nicolas Cage cast, the film would go on to garner Oscars and to win Jewison greater critical and commercial success than he had enjoyed for years. Could it have been a Columbia picture? "It was never offered to me," David declared, an answer that would come back to haunt him.

David's relationship with Dan Melnick went back to *Midnight Express*—the suspension over the shower scene—then the 1978 offer to take over as production head at Columbia. Melnick was now back at Columbia with his Indieprod company after a stopover at 20th Century-Fox—and a series of worthy, but expensive flops. Melnick's contract was up after two more films.

David heartily endorsed Melnick's new Steve Martin vehicle, *Roxanne*, and he supported the casting of Daryl Hannah. He was equally keen on Melnick's offbeat comedy-drama *Punchline* with Sally Field and Tom Hanks and talked of an Oscar-qualifying run for this in late 1987. There was only one problem with Melnick's pictures, which he neatly summarized: "They were good for everybody except Columbia, the goose laying the golden eggs for other people. Dan's 7.5 percent of the gross was the killer. It meant a film like *Roxanne* would have to take a fortune before Columbia would see a penny."

When it was clear there was no deal, Melnick exited in a huff and joined the *Rambo* team at Carolco Pictures. A year later he gave his version of events to *Variety*: "I had a contractual commitment that was running out. David indicated a strong desire to continue the relationship. It was unique. I funded my own development and then made a distribution deal which was advantageous. He said he wanted to take over the development costs. We struck a deal over the phone. Later, he called back and said, 'This is embarrassing, but Fay doesn't want to make any rich production deals.'"

Fay Vincent denies he was ever informed. "David was using me," he maintains. "I didn't veto Melnick's deal. I didn't know of it until after the decision was made."

"I wouldn't want it to be implied that it was Fay's decision," David later admitted. "I may have told Fay, but it was my decision. It was not personal. I admire Dan Melnick. I just felt that the terms of the deal were too high to live with."

Fay had now been exposed to an aspect of David he had not anticipated. "We all have our foibles," says Fay, "but one of David's problems is, he's capable of lying. They're not serious, but he does have a problem with the truth and it gets in the way."

Another instance of this involved David's hiring at Columbia. The question was who had approached whom, David or

Fay. "I'm telling everyone *you* made the approach," David told Fay afterward. "It sounds better."

"That's up to you," Fay replied, "but I'm not going to lie for you, David. I simply won't say how it happened. I'll say we had lunch, that's all."

In an effort to straighten out this particular point of difference and hopefully to lay it finally to rest, the author had a further conversation with Puttnam in August 1988, the text of which follows:

AY: Fay says you somewhat bent the facts about who made the approach.

DP: No. *I* didn't make it. Tom Lewyn did.

AY: Well, he's your lawyer, after all, isn't he?

DP: You'll have to talk to Tom about it.

AY: Tom says you both more or less cooked it up.

DP: *No, no, no.* Tom approached me about Paramount out of the blue. I'd never had any thoughts at all about going to that studio. When the whole thing at Paramount didn't work out, he's the one who said to Fay I might be interested. My understanding clearly is that Fay had lunch with Tom.

AY: I can only tell you what Fay told me.

DP: Maybe they're changing their minds; they told me they had lunch. I wasn't *unaware* they were having lunch—perfectly true. Tom speaks to me once a week. He's one of those people—he's a what's-happening guy—he's an information collector. No, I don't think so, I don't think the facts bear that out. I wanted the job. Fuck me, we didn't half play hardball. Did I mind him and Dick coming over and spending a day in telling me what they could offer?

AY: Fay's not denying that as soon as he heard you were available, he was interested, but he hadn't actually thought of you originally.

DP: Tom, I think maybe as a result of the Paramount thing, having tried to broker that deal, saw there was a deal to be brokered, so maybe he saw that my turndown at Paramount was a specific one, not an absolute one, and—yes —he *did* tell me he was having lunch with Fay.

AY: What Fay said specifically was that you said to him "I'm telling everyone *you* made the approach," and Fay wasn't enthralled with that idea.

DP: I really don't remember. *I said that?* Well, again, all of my early conversations with Fay, maybe I wanted to make it clear, to make it unambiguous—that's the only thing I can think, to avoid any ambiguity. I tell you what I *might* have said was, because the question's going to be asked, we did a rehearsal of a press conference, and what I *may* have said to Fay is that if the question gets asked "who approached who?" I want to make it unambiguously clear that you approached me, rather than say it was a conversation with our lawyers, etc., etc. I can imagine that.

One night in 1983, while Bill Forsyth was in New York with actor Peter Riegert, they and some friends went to see Preston Sturges's *Sullivan's Travels* at the Regency Theater. Afterward, while strolling through Columbus Circle, one of the women in their party enthused about a marvelous novel she had just read entitled *Housekeeping.* Bill asked to see a copy, and after reading it, he became fascinated by the book. Several months later, when he began to envision the movie that could be made from it, he took an option on *Housekeeping.* The author, Marilynne Robinson, visited Bill in Scotland with her family while he was shooting *Comfort and Joy;* then at the end of 1984, he began working seriously on the book. By this time, he was in correspondence with Diane Keaton, who had expressed interest in working with him. She was enthusiastic about *Housekeeping,* and an informal understanding was arrived at that she would be in it. The script was written by the spring of 1985, and the hope was to start shooting that autumn. Unfortunately, Bill found little interest in the project from the majors, even with Keaton's name attached to it.

The script had its champions everywhere—at Disney, at Columbia, and at Fox—but everywhere the champions were in the minority. Jake Eberts thought it too depressing and worried about the suicide in it. "But it's at the beginning, not the end," Bill argued. Some Norwegian oil money that was fleetingly available would have seen half the film shot in Norway and the balance in Canada. Months of fruitless negotiation took place in New York with Al Clark and Robert Devereux of Virgin. John Daly at Hemdale professed to love the project, but he was hard to pin down.

At last, in January 1986, Bill found a home for the film, albeit an unlikely one—at Cannon. With Diane Keaton on board and a budget of $5 million, they were happy. Filming was set to begin in Canada in September, and preproduction offices were set up. Then a call came for Bill to meet Diane at her home. He took along the script, prepared to hold an impromptu rehearsal session. Instead, over the course of an hour Keaton indicated that she had changed her mind and had decided not to do the movie after all.

Bill put through a call to Anthony Jones in London, who said he would try to set something else up before the news leaked to Cannon. But as soon as it did, Cannon immediately dispatched an accountant to shut down preproduction. David, soon to take the reins at Columbia, was contacted, and the situation was explained to him. Yes, he would pick it up, providing a budget and an alternative star could be agreed on, and Bill would make his next film for Columbia. ("A *commercial* subject this time, if you don't mind," David said, laughing.)

There was some doubt that Cannon would let the project go because of its bumpy relationship with David, but following the refund of its $300,000 preproduction costs, it did. The name Christine Lahti kept cropping up as a replacement actress. Lahti was flown to Vancouver to talk to Bill, and to his delight she loved the script. This rescue operation complete, *Housekeeping* started shooting for Columbia Pictures on its original starting date, just six weeks after Diane Keaton walked out. It was David's first acquisition for Columbia, and it represented a wel-

come reunion with the Scottish director he admired so much—
all before he had officially started at the studio.

Only weeks after his first meeting with Ray Stark, David was
startled to receive a script from the producer. "There's just this
one I want you to check out," Ray explained. Despite the fact
that this maneuver flew in the face of their "agreement," David
was the soul of tact. "I'll get back to you quickly," he promised.
"I'm leaving tonight, but I'll read it on the plane."

The script turned out to be based on the life of another rela-
tive of Ray's, singer Libby Holman. (Stark's wife was the
daughter of Fanny Brice, the subject of *Funny Girl.*) David
phoned Ray two days later with his verdict on *Sweet Libby:* "I've
read it, Ray, and it's not for me."

"What's wrong with it?"

"I just didn't like it. I didn't like the subject matter."

A pause, then: "Admittedly it needs more work, David. It
needs another rewrite."

"No, Ray, I don't think so. It's got nothing to do with a
rewrite—that would be a waste of time, as far as I'm concerned.
It's the subject matter. I've seen this backstage drama half a
dozen times. It's *Funny Lady* all over again. I think it's out of its
time."

Another pause, this one longer. Finally: "Well, fair enough. I
don't agree with you, but at least you got back to me quickly."

Now, just two weeks into David's Columbia stint, Stark was
on the line to him again.

"Why haven't you called me? You've been here two weeks. I
thought you wanted me to help."

"Christ," said David, "I've only been at the studio for thirty
seconds! Give me a break, Ray. I haven't even had time to work
out what my problems *are* yet. I'm living like a displaced person
at the Bel-Air, reading scripts all night and working all day.
Sure there'll be a lot to ask you about, but right now I'm up to
my ears in it."

"Well," said Ray sulkily, "I thought I'd see you every day. So
what do I get instead? All you've done since our meeting is to

turn down *Sweet Libby*. It's not good enough. Get over here for breakfast tomorrow morning—we've got things to talk about."

After a restless night at the Bel-Air, David squealed his Audi to a halt in Stark's driveway, ready for the scrap he knew was before him. To hell with it, he thought; if I give in now, I'm finished. We'll soon find out if Coke meant what it said about supporting me. Stark's massive home, with its Henry Moore sculpture garden and its enormous collection of paintings by the likes of Braque, Magritte, and Léger, reminded David of a small private museum. Breakfast was served by the "keeper" before the "curator" came down to join him.

Stark launched straight into the attack. "Am I going to make pictures at Columbia, or am I not?"

David set down his orange juice. "If you're asking me on principle, because you're Ray Stark, would I say yes to you, the answer is no, I won't. It depends on the script. My mandate from Coke is to go with scripts I think will work. That does not extend to anything and everything you care to send me."

Stark got up and threw his napkin down on the breakfast table. "Well, fuck you, then," he hissed. "Think I need you?"

David got up to face him. "I don't know whether you need me. You're acting like you do need me, but you're telling me you don't. I don't understand you—there's no logic in your position."

"I need to know where I *am* with you."

"I'm telling you—if you've got something you want to do at Columbia and you send it in and it's terrific, I'll be the first person on the phone saying, please make it. Otherwise, no."

"Are these the rules?"

"Yes, these are the rules."

"Well, that's not what I had in mind at all."

"Well, it's exactly what I had in mind when we had our conversation about your being helpful and advising."

Later, Stark invited David to a private view, with himself and Mike Ovitz, of the new Museum of Contemporary Art, but David refused. "I'm too busy reading scripts," he said tersely.

"You'd better get your priorities right," Stark snapped, oblivious of the irony in his remark. Then the breakfast meeting broke up, amid recriminatory remarks about Stark's access to friends in high places.

David clearly had no idea of the depth of feeling between Stark and Herbert Allen and unwisely remarked, "Your relationship with Herbert Allen bothers me." The advantage now went to Stark. The many shared years and secrets had bred staunch allies.

"I can fight my own battles," Stark haughtily informed David. "I don't need Herbert, I don't need anyone."

That very afternoon, a second packet marked "Ray Stark Productions" landed on David's desk. Inside were a novella and two scripts for a project called *Revenge*, an item owned by Columbia that Stark had decided to develop. Over the next few days, David dutifully read through the material before he departed for Europe and a meeting of filmmakers. Although he was unimpressed by the existing scripts—one each by Walter Hill and John Huston—he could see that the novella could be made into something interesting, but only at the right price. The grapevine had it that Walter Hill himself and his producer David Giler wanted a crack at it, but not with Ray Stark aboard. David decided to flex his Columbia muscles and wrote to Stark.

September 16, 1986

Dear Ray,

REVENGE

I'm just off to Europe for a couple of weeks and I thought I should set down my thoughts regarding the above property.

During the past ten days I have painstakingly picked my way through the novella, the Walter Hill and the John Huston screenplays. I came to the conclusion last night that this wasn't a property that we'll be in a position to move on in the coming months. With this in mind I suggest the following.

We arrange either formally or informally for you to have a 90-day period in which to set the film up at another studio.

Failing this, it will return to Columbia without any further lien and we'll be free to offer it elsewhere.

I say this because in reviewing the film it transpired that the material had been of interest some while ago to a team of filmmakers whom I rate highly. There is always a chance that I can interest them in picking up the pieces and turn out a good film at a price that makes it attractive. I'm eager not to close us out of the possibility of being able to reinterest them on terms that we could live with.

The reason for all the neuroses regarding this property is that we have over $600,000 tied up in it and most of all I'd like the use of the money!

See you when I get back,
Warmest regards,
David

This time there was no holding back Stark's fury. He even disliked what he saw as David's prissy way of dotting every "i" and crossing every "t" in a welter of correspondence, but the contents of this particular missive, as well as the style, enraged him. Moreover, he had heard a rumor—apparently unfounded —that the team of Alan Parker and Alan Marshall was interested in the property.

"Who are these jerks who want to make *Revenge* without me?" he roared into the phone.

"They specifically asked me not to say who they are," David replied.

"What do you mean? You can't treat me like this. Who *are* they?"

"I'm not going to tell you."

The final meeting between the two men during David's entire Columbia reign came only weeks later, during the first week of November 1986, when Stark brushed past David's startled secretaries and barged into his office.

"I never see you—" Stark opened the conversation, which was to be brief and icy.

David had no answer. For him, the breakfast confrontation, followed by the *Revenge* farrago, had killed off any question of a "deal" or "special understanding" between himself and Stark.

"—and it's wrong of you not to tell me who the people are who want to make *Revenge*. Why can't I take it elsewhere?"

"You can," said David. "I've already covered that in my letter, but I want it back here after the ninety-day period is up so the company's got a chance to get its money out."

As he watched Stark turn on his heel and march out of his office, David knew that he had made a mortal enemy of one of the most influential players in Hollywood. Still, he underestimated the truly apocalyptic nature of Stark's wrath. To David, Stark seemed most like the Wizard of Oz after Toto has pulled away the side curtain. But to many others he was nothing less than Godzilla, capable of raining down hellfire and damnation on the selected denizens of his own personal Tokyo. "If you cross Ray Stark, you'd better make sure he's dead first," ran the legend.

So who needs Ray Stark in Hollywood?

- Bobby Littman (agent): "He's a brilliant film producer, like he was an agent before that, a showman in the true old-fashioned sense. He's made some darned good movies, and he's been good to his friends."
- James Bridges (director): "My two experiences with him were quite crazed. We had such a fight over *Houdini* that I thought I could never work with him again. But I'm tempted because he gets his hands on the best material, and he's a superb producer."
- Ex-employee: "No one who has ever worked with him has escaped his generosity."
- Raymond Chandler (author, commenting on Stark the agent): "Ray Stark seems to me like a flickering light on a wall."
- Peter Guber (producer): "I was the Columbia baby. I was twenty-six years old, a punk kid from the East the first day I walked into Columbia. My pictures—*The Deep, Midnight*

Express, and *Thank God It's Friday*—did $130 million in revenue for Columbia. I had never lost a penny for the studio. I enjoyed a good relationship with the management. I thought Ray was my papa. He can be the sweetest man, the most charming to be with. But his involvement with Columbia at the time of my departure was so all-encompassing that it caused one of the most incredible, bizarre episodes of my life. I was run out."

- Dan Melnick (producer): "Like Richelieu, Ray doesn't like change. . . . Ray never forgave me for leaving the presidency [of Columbia]. He turned on me for a complex variety of reasons. Leaving was a betrayal of him, of Herbert Allen, of Columbia—since all three are merged in his mind. Ray loves Herbie. His affection for Herbie is genuine. He sees him as a son."

- Alan Hirschfield (ex-chairman, Columbia): "He's the kind of person who does take delight in playing with people's lives. This is like a game to him; he gets his kicks from it."

David, with his four most successful U.S. releases totaling $68.2 million in net rentals—*Chariots of Fire* ($30.6 million), the disowned *Midnight Express* ($15 million), *The Killing Fields* ($14.3 million), and *The Mission* (which would go on to make $8.3 million)—had just locked horns with a producer whose top seventeen films had netted $468 million—well over a billion dollars in box-office gross.

David had no illusions that the tremor would reach Fay Vincent, Herbert Allen, and the Coke duo in short order. So be it, was his attitude. Fuck it! Apart from his refusal of Stark's friendship, he knew that the worst insult he had dealt Stark was his refusal to be part of the community the mogul had spent his life cultivating. How *dare* David not see what a magical world this was, this Hollywood that had driven Stark and his friends all their lives! Some observers felt David had taken Stark's dignity away from him. David's feeling was that the producer had done that to himself years before. As far as Ray was concerned,

David was no longer David but forever "that little prick, Puttnam."

Before he could wholly immerse himself in Columbia, David still had some unfinished business to attend to—the launch of *The Mission* in key territories. ("I think it makes me a natural for a *Trivial Pursuit* question," David says, laughing. "What head of a major motion-picture studio simultaneously promoted a film for a rival studio?") The film opened to tremendous initial figures, first in Spain, then in Paris. *The Hollywood Reporter* gave the film a glowing review after its Cannes showing, but *Variety* saw it as a questionable commercial prospect. It forecast the film would open well on the strength of De Niro's name, but thereafter all bets were off. It looked as if Goldcrest would not necessarily get the overage in the United States that it so desperately needed, although the figures from Latin America and further European openings continued to be encouraging.

On the eve of *The Mission*'s première in Britain, David declared himself confident that the film would be a hit and would garner Oscar nominations. Eventually, he estimated, the movie would end up with a worldwide box-office gross of between $90 and $100 million. He was erring, he added, on the cautious side and making the major assumption that the film would be a hit in the vital American market. Fernando Ghia was more sanguine. "It's been proved over and over again," he said, "that some films have a different life in Europe than in America."

"With the state it's in, the industry cannot afford *The Mission* to be an elegant failure, or even an honorable failure or a glittering failure. It *has* to be a success!" David stated, clearly willing the film through to his predicted figures. "What is criminal is that *The Mission* is now having to do the very thing I always said it shouldn't have to do, and that is salvage Goldcrest. No one film should ever have to do that."

Jake Eberts agreed that if *The Mission* did well, it would help pay off some of Goldcrest's debt. If it failed, however, he still reckoned that Goldcrest would survive. "The running of the company is covered by existing cash flow from contracts already signed or committed to," he pointed out. "We are currently negotiating with several companies for additional capital, and that does *not* depend on the success of *The Mission.*"

Still, the media insisted that *The Mission*'s success was absolutely crucial, if not to Goldcrest then to that old media turkey, Britain's entire future as a maker of mass-audience films.

The Mission's initial openings in the United States were in New York and Los Angeles only. Underpinned by a costly and beautifully organized Warners ad campaign, the film brought in good but unspectacular returns. No box-office records were broken, but the hope was that good word-of-mouth would propel the film through to the February 1987 Oscar nominations.

The film opened in London to what is euphemistically referred to as "mixed" reviews. "Beautiful, roaring, stupendous froth," the *Independent* summarized. "Carry on up the waterfall," echoed the *New Statesman.* "So worked up has this country become about British cinema," it continued, "that any Puttnam/Goldcrest production appears not as a mere film, but as the trailer grandly puts it, 'Destined to become the motion picture of the year.' " The movie was likened to a spiritual *Top Gun*, with Jesuit priests Irons and De Niro "up there with the best of the best."

Critic Iain Johnstone in the *Sunday Times* remained the film's undisputed champion, as he had from the beginning at Cannes. *"The Mission,"* he wrote this time, "may not be beyond criticism, but it is certainly beyond compare with the vast majority of modern movies. Visionally and viscerally, it is the most powerful film of the year."

In general, the critics varied in their reactions in what may be termed "honest differences of opinion." Some, however, were more savage in their "honesty" than others.

David's meeting with Stark had taken place just weeks after a resignation that took the outside world by surprise. While Dick Gallop had appeared to be one of the key figures behind David's decision to join Columbia, Fay Vincent had in fact hinted to David from the beginning that Gallop might soon be taking up

a different role within the organization. Even with this knowledge, David was taken aback to learn of his destination—Allen
& Co., Inc. Did *all* roads lead to Herbert Allen? (In fact, Gallop
would still report to 711 Fifth Avenue, where Allen had now
moved his company. Different floor, though.)

The whole episode seemed at sinister variance with the bland
harmony the double act of "Roberto and Don" had presented.
Or was the fruit simply falling close to the tree?

20

In the few weeks he was in office, David was already sucker-punched. The dealer of the blow was producer Martin ("Don't walk on me with your 'fuck-you' shoes") Ransohoff, flush from his runaway *Jagged Edge* success. Ransohoff had a three-picture pickup deal with Columbia. The first was *The Big Town*, starring Matt Dillon (in his umpteenth try for stardom), Diane Lane, and Tommy Lee Jones. That film was already in production, greenlighted before David's appointment.

"David, I need your advice," Marty began ingratiatingly. After the welter of administrative details that had been flooding him ever since his arrival, David was frankly flattered and a little relieved that his advice was being sought by an actual producer.

"If I can help, I will, Marty. What's the problem?"

"Okay. We've been shooting *The Big Town* for a couple of

days. I think we've got a pretty good script, David, but the director and I are just not working out. I'm gonna have to replace the guy. You're a whiz with directors—how about it? Could you suggest someone who's available and help me out of this hole?"

David agreed to think about it, and he took the script home to the Bel-Air with him that night for another look. After an hour's reappraisal of the script—which he had never liked in the first place—he became convinced that it was there that the main problem lay. It could probably be sharpened up. Robert Bolt's son Ben was around, in between directing *Hill Street Blues* segments—he could replace the present director.

Next day, he mentioned his name to Ransohoff, who promptly clasped David's hands in his bearlike paws. "You've got a friend for life, David," bold Marty declared, then marched off to contact young Bolt and ultimately hire him to take over *The Big Town.*

Later, when David related the story to a colleague, the colleague put the affair into focus. "Marty does this sort of thing," David was told. "If the picture's a hit, the credit's all down to him. If it's a flop, he'll blame you for foisting Ben Bolt on him. Either way, you can't win. And he can't lose."

Marty already had a go-ahead for a second project at Columbia, a thriller called *Smoke,* to star Burt Reynolds and Theresa Russell. The third project he put to Columbia—and to David this time—was *Switching Channels.* It was an updated version of the classic *Front Page* remake, *His Girl Friday,* only set in a television station instead of in a newspaper office. Marty had been hawking the property around for over a year, having unsuccessfully touted Debra Winger, Bill Murray, and Dan Aykroyd for the leads in an attempt to get their agency, Mike Ovitz's CAA, interested. CAA had not bitten, probably recalling the fate of their last endeavor together, the 1986 *Legal Eagles,* which had surrounded the unfortunate production company, Universal, in a $38 million sea of red ink.

Legal Eagles was a textbook example of the kind of "package" of mismatched talents that David was absolutely set against. It starred Robert Redford, Debra Winger, and Daryl Hannah. Allegedly a comedy and written by those well-known *Top Gun* wits Jack Epps, Jr., and Jim Cash, the enterprise had been well and truly run into the ground by the further lightsome touch of director Ivan *(Ghostbusters)* Reitman. Despite the film's failure, it made a fortune in commissions for CAA, which had supplied all the major talent in the picture. It had also brought CAA a deluge of bad publicity and ultimately the loss of Debra Winger as a client.

Marty's ploy to get CAA on his side failed, as Winger, Murray, and Aykroyd in turn all passed on the project—as David now did when it was presented to him. His idea of a movie stamped with the logo of the Columbia lady did not include *Switching Channels*, with or without the new cast Marty had assembled: Michael Caine, Kathleen Turner, and Christopher Reeve. Infuriated, Marty arranged to have lunch with the outgoing Dick Gallop, on the eve of his joining Allen & Co.

In one of the labyrinthine moves that characterizes buying and selling in the entertainment business, Coca-Cola purchased Embassy from Jerry Perenchio and Norman Lear, Jake Eberts's erstwhile employers. Roberto Goizueta described it to Fay Vincent as "the best acquisition in the history of Coca-Cola." Then Columbia split Embassy in two. It sold Embassy Pictures off to Dino De Laurentiis and parceled off Embassy Home Entertainment separately to Nelson Entertainment. Part of the latter deal was that Coke would co-finance twelve pictures with Nelson over a three-year period.

Marty proposed *Switching Channels* to Gallop as an ideal first project for Nelson. He had a truly wonderful script, he assured Gallop. Despite the fact that that jerk Puttnam had turned it down (he neglected to mention that the rest of Hollywood had too), it was still a brilliant property.

Gallop agreed to refer it to Frank Biondi, Jr., head of Coke's Entertainment Business Sector's TV Operations, who was also responsible for any Nelson co-productions undertaken. Although Biondi may be seen as having swallowed Marty's bait, as far as he was concerned he genuinely liked the project. When

Biondi agreed to fund *Switching Channels*, Marty's end run around David was complete. A project that Columbia, Coke's main movie company, had turned down would still be financed by Coca-Cola!

Thrown out the front door, Marty had sneaked in the back. It seemed that his appetite for being walked over by anyone's "fuck-you" shoes had not increased over the years. Glee over Marty's triumph was widespread. But what everyone missed in all the glee was the only pertinent issue—the validity of David's rejection. Instead of Rosalind Russell, Cary Grant, and Ralph Bellamy being directed by Howard Hawks in one of the most brilliant, scintillating comedies ever made, Ransohoff was offering a cast ultimately comprising Burt Reynolds (Michael Caine having defected for greater things in *Jaws 4*), Kathleen Turner, and Christopher Reeve, directed by Ted (*First Blood*) Kotcheff. The embarrassment for David would have been compounded if Columbia had been forced to release *Switching Channels*. But at least he was spared this, as Victor Kaufman at Tri-Star, anxious to develop a professional ongoing relationship with Kathleen Turner, agreed to release the picture. David and the Columbia lady would yet have the last laugh.

Although much was made of this in the press, Fay Vincent took a cooler view of the development. "The whole strategy, after all, behind Tri-Star, was that we would have a number of places making product. When David took the job at Columbia, he saw himself as Coca-Cola's filmmaker. Although it was explained to him, I think he chose not to understand that there were going to be three or four Coke film people, of which he was one. There was Victor at Tri-Star, there was the Nelson link, which to David was a pain in the ass he never understood, then there was our involvement in the Weintraub [Entertainment] Group. David resented all that, but that was his problem, not mine."

Then it was Vincent's turn to get directly involved in the Ransohoff wrangle. "Ransohoff called me early on and said David didn't want to make a sequel to *Jagged Edge*. He wanted to use it only as a sort of '*Jagged Edge* presents' label. I said, why didn't he put the idea of *Jagged Edge II* to Victor Kaufman or one of the other companies we were involved with. It turned out that Victor at Tri-Star was interested, although it was more complicated than that, since there was an expensive deal between Ransohoff and Columbia that he didn't like, and if they took *Jagged Edge II* they'd have to live with what they thought was a bad deal."

Views of Marty Ransohoff vary widely in the Hollywood community.

- Take One (Bobby Littman, agent): "Marty's an extremely clever man and a brilliant businessman, who caters to the popular market. Unlike some, he puts his money where his mouth is, often part-financing, sometimes paying for prints and ads. Marty knows what he's doing."
- Take Two (former Columbia female executive): "He's a foul-mouthed bully. One day, in the middle of a business meeting, he called me a fucking cunt. My boss told him to watch his mouth, not to use that expression about one of his staff. 'Oh, it's nothing personal,' Marty protested."
- Take Three (another agent): "I'd rather do business with Marty than a lot of others. I know exactly where I stand with him. Even if I don't like what he's got to say, I know he's telling the truth."
- Take Four (a Hollywood reporter): "The *Big Town* story's balls. If Ben Bolt had made a better film, Marty Ransohoff would have given credit to David. I think that part of David's problem—and it's a major flaw—is his constant self-justification. He thinks things through in a somewhat paranoid way, not even 'someone's following me,' but 'what *if* someone were following me?' He can always find some justification for himself in something that has gone wrong."

The Cannon Group's takeover of Britain's Thorn-EMI Screen Entertainment Division in May 1986 had been made before shares in Cannon reached their highest peak of $44. When the stock market crash in July brought them back down to $35, most companies quickly began to claw back lost ground. Not Cannon. Just when it should have been advancing again, with another ostensibly excellent quarter's results announced, it still languished. The slide continued after the announcement of a Securities and Exchange Committee investigation into the company's accounting procedures. "They keep reporting higher earnings on pictures that nobody goes to see," said Gordon Crawford, a senior vice-president of Capital Guardian Research in Los Angeles. Cannon's shares later dropped to under $3.

In October, David was asked for his views on the prospects of the company he had fought to keep out of Britain. First he emphasized that for the sake of the British film industry he would rather be wrong. Then he stated, "I don't for one second believe that the Cannon organization as presently constituted will still exist this time next year." Replying to what they referred to as Puttnam's "bizarre commentary," Menahem Golan and Yoram Globus declared, "We were amused, and decided to invite you to a gracious dinner in a year's time to review where we *both* are (meaning you and us). However, in our generosity, we are prepared to extend the date to twenty-four months from now." The assumption seemed to be that they would be able to afford a "gracious dinner" two years hence.

Hollywood was rapidly splitting into two camps, the pro-Puttnamites and the anti-Puttnamites. The pros largely belonged to the creative community of writers and directors; they saw an opportunity during Puttnam's term to produce some worthwhile movies, a departure from the juvenilia that had largely overtaken Hollywood. The antis were the deal-makers and fat cats, the ones with the most to lose from his espousal of rich contracts and packages. Each camp had its own view of David's appointees.

When David appointed his old friend David Picker to the Columbia team as his deputy, for example, it met with a mixed reception. Picker's appointment flung both camps into confusion, since he was widely seen as one of the fat cats David had been trying to starve. Picker was also viewed as a creative dinosaur, who had been out of the Hollywood mainstream for many years. David was relying on his close friendship with Picker over the years, but would Picker really guide him through the Hollywood jungle and protect him from the pygmies' blow-pipes? "He wouldn't shoot Puttnam himself," was the widespread consensus, "but he might not deflect the arrows."

"He asked me to share the mandate he had from Coke, which I found irresistible," said Picker. "I'd determined that I never wanted to be an executive again, but what David offered me was so seductive, so intelligent, and so unique, I had to take it." Picker's predecessor, Steve Sohmer, was to move into the nebulous "creative areas of movie and TV production," areas that would turn out to be located in Bill Cosby's back pocket.

David also got Greg Coote for his team. Coote had been a successful producer-exhibitor-distributor in Australia. His appointment as Columbia's bicontinental creative executive was questioned by some ("Okay, he knows the Aussie market—so what?") and praised by others. Columbia domestic marketing executive Bob Dingilian quickly discovered Coote's strengths. "Talent, knack, panache—*that's* international," he gravels in a voice that seems to emanate from an underground cavern. "What can I tell you? Coote's a smart man, real smart."

David continued to build up his Columbia team. From Public Broadcasting, Catherine Wyler (daughter of director William Wyler) stepped in to handle Columbia's new nonfiction unit, a brainchild of David's. Lynda Myles was appointed head of European Creative Affairs as a liaison with local filmmakers. ("A postmistress," one British producer grumbled. "You send her the script, and she posts it on to David in L.A.") Jim Clark, who had been David's eyes and ears on *The Killing Fields* and had won the Academy Award for his editing on that movie, was reluctantly coaxed to L.A. as a senior production editor on a one-year contract. ("A fixer of projects in trouble," he later called himself.)

Former Ray Stark protégé John Fiedler, who had moved to Columbia from Tri-Star, moved again, at his own request, into independent production for the studio. What was not announced was the main reason for his request to move: he was unlikely to be able to work with David's new appointee, David Picker. The immediate friction between the two at staff meetings rapidly made Fiedler's position untenable.

As a gesture from the Hollywood establishment, David was invited by Mike Ovitz to address a meeting of CAA's agents in early October. Although David claims that his comments at the event were heavily distorted, what he is rumored to have said sounds like a virtual rerun of what he had said to the Coke bosses—that agency packages, big stars, and exorbitant salaries were a thing of the past at Columbia Pictures. Well, the news had gone down well in Atlanta, after all—why should the reaction at CAA have been any different? The speech caused a furor. A story also circulated about David's response to a remark from the floor about a "young" forty-four-year-old director: "That's indicative of the age bias built in here," he reportedly snapped.

Shock waves reverberated from the CAA event. Herbert Allen met with David and gave him the advice that he should attempt to build a better personal rapport with Ovitz. David felt his hackles rise. Was he being *lectured?*

Other actions of David's were also controversial among the film community. He disclosed that South African exhibitors had been warned that no Columbia pictures would be available to any segregated theaters after May 1, 1987. He pointed out that Coke's decision to pull out of the country and turn its franchise over to black businessmen had preceded his action. "What they did showed real class," he declared. "They were ahead of me, and they've done it. I thought that was terrific." A somewhat tight-lipped Jack Valenti, Motion Picture Association of America president, described David's move as "a responsible position, quite responsible," even as he reflected that the deadline was still a full seven months away. Valenti's view was that feature films and TV programming were different from other sanctioned areas, such as investments, automobiles, and construction steel, because they advanced the cause of opposition to apartheid in South Africa by exposing the South African population to the example of a multiracial society. In any event, 85 percent of South Africa's four hundred theaters had been desegregated already, Valenti pointed out, compared with a figure of 8 percent a year earlier. "If we withdrew our pictures," he maintained, "the only people who would be hurt would be the black majority. The affluent white South Africans have VCRs. Pirates would move in quickly, and they would have all the movies to see, but the blacks would be denied."

David's castigation of irresponsible filmmakers—using the name Coke—was also controversial. "If Coca-Cola accidentally created one hundred million cans of faulty Coke, you know for sure the entire one hundred million cans would be dropped in the Atlantic or Pacific Ocean without a second thought and irrespective of what that did to the year's profits. What do we do with a crappy movie? We double its advertising budget and hope for a big opening weekend. What has been done for the audience as they walk out of the cinema? We've alienated them. We've sold the audience a piece of junk. We took twelve dollars away from a couple and think we've done ourselves no long-term damage." He conjured up visions of disillusioned couples walking around in a daze, their lives diminished, twelve dollars lighter, and vowing never to go near a cinema again.

In November 1986, with most of his team in place and himself an object of intense debate, David felt the time was right for a statement of policy to the outside world. Stinging from the series of encounters he had had with the likes of Ray Stark, Marty Ransohoff, and the CAA team, he decided to serve notice on others who doubted the strength of his policy commitment. He chose a showing of *The Mission* at Glen Glenn's Hollywood screening room, just twenty-four hours after his last meeting with Stark, to make his point. Although the audience had been aware of his reputation for outspokenness, they had arrived expecting merely a mild question-and-answer session after the movie. They were thus taken aback at the vehemence with which David lashed the community.

"I'm appalled," David began, "by the mind-set I've met everywhere in the last few weeks. In Hollywood now, you're not shooting movies anymore, you're shooting deals. At Columbia we're going to shift radically from prepackaged products to in-house development. The reason we want to develop in house is because everything starts with material. Unfortunately, what I've witnessed is that the film here starts with a book, let's say, and a star—not necessarily the right star, but a book and a star. They are brought in by an agent, and that becomes what's referred to as the package.

"You're already in trouble because it's difficult to get a screenplay out of that book. It's twice as difficult when you've got a star who doesn't really want the book. What he or she wants is the role they like inside the book that would be good for them. This kind of game-playing, I promise you, will be *out* under me at Columbia.

"You start from the point of view of material and a producer. You get a screenplay and bring in a director who loves that screenplay—not someone out of work who needs a job, not someone who will do it because you offer him two-and-a-half million dollars and ten percent of the rolling gross, but someone who actually loves the screenplay for the same reason you do. *Then* you develop the screenplay to the point where you and the director are happy. *Then* you cast the film.

"When you do this, it is not to a set of preconceived ideas, for how or why you might get the picture off the ground, but the right cast and right movie. These are the things we're doing, I promise you. The reason there are so many lousy films around is because of the corruption of the role of producer. Only independent producers actually prepared to *produce* will find a welcome here at Columbia.

"In the few weeks I've been here, I've had several conversations with people about the making of a movie. Among the first questions they ask is, 'Who shall we get to actually produce it?' I'm absolutely *furious*. This is why you see these ludicrous three-producer, four-producer credits. The one poor soul who knows how to produce the film isn't even included. The three people are the agents or the friends of the writer, or the writer's mother, who *claim* to be producer. I find it grossly offensive and really very, very upsetting.

"We can't get away any longer with shortchanging audiences. We at Columbia are going to be far more demanding of those who work for us. We will challenge directors to direct better. We'll challenge actors and actresses to act better. We'll challenge technicians to be better. Frankly—and I include myself—I think we're all a little bit lazy, we've gotten away with not giving the audience enough. If there's been a breach of faith in the last five years between the audience and the filmmaker, I have to say it's been on the side of the filmmaker. Audiences have been unbelievably patient, while there's been too much carping and moaning on the part of filmmakers. Audiences will turn out when a film delivers and absent themselves when it does not. On the occasions—all too many—when I've known in my heart that the film didn't really deliver, sure enough, they smelled it out and didn't come.

"We're going to make an all-out effort to woo intelligent adult audiences," David concluded. "Our new credo at Columbia goes like this: We're saying that audiences are people, too."

After a few seconds of stunned silence, a hearty round of applause came from the room. If there had been any doubts before, there were none now. What had just been declared was nothing less than total war on the existing Hollywood system.

In early November 1986 Patsy arrived to find David still in temporary office quarters at Columbia. For two months she had been worried by the increasingly negative phone calls from David and Valerie. On one occasion she had never heard her husband sound so defeated. "This place is rotten through and through," he had told her. "I honestly don't know if I'm going to make a go of it." Valerie's lowest point had come when she told Patsy, "Don't send my trunks on just yet!"

Now in Hollywood, Patsy found workmen finally lifting the maroon carpet in David's office and beginning to lay a wood flooring. "Excuse me, but isn't that concrete under there?" she inquired.

"Sure is."

Patsy turned disbelievingly to David. "They're laying a wooden floor on top of concrete? The moisture will warp the wood! This is where they make *movies*? Who's in charge around here?"

Set designer Tom McCarthy was duly located and his help enlisted. "These clowns have had two months to sort David's office out!" she raged to him. "Now *I'm* having a go—and I need your help, Tom. Let's talk materials."

Three weeks later, David was installed in Patsy's designated style of homely substantial comfort, perfectly represented by the office furniture that took its name from Papa Biedermeier. It sat serenely on parquet flooring that was down to stay. Patsy had found speckled glass for the corner walls, which made the room look sunny even on dull days. All David's favorite pictures and mementos were carefully in position. *Now* David could work.

The domestic side was taken care of as well when the couple moved into their furnished home high up in Coldwater Canyon. Twin orange trees flanked the swimming pool and outdoor Jacuzzi that Greta Garbo and Gaylord Hauser had installed in the 1950s. When Columbia offered to install a screening room in the house, they would not hear of it. "It would be a terrible waste of money," Patsy said. "We're ten minutes from the studio, where there are lots of perfectly good screening rooms. We'll go down the hill any hour of the day or night to see a movie if a projectionist is happy to do it."

Her first glimpse of the screening rooms at Columbia changed her mind—not about having a screen installed in Coldwater Canyon, but about the conditions under which films were viewed at one of Hollywood's major studios. "It's unbelievable!" she told Alan Parker. "They're all pokey little rooms, full of small, uncomfortable chairs—and using sound and projection equipment that's been out of date for years." When Alan asked her why she didn't do something about it, Patsy determined that she would. Armed with a budget, she was given one screening room to convert to state-of-the-art perfection and comfort. On the triumphant completion of her project, she declared, "Now we're even happier to go down the hill."

Fay Vincent could not escape a feeling of concern. "One of the problems is, David had set himself up as this low-cost individual, then all of a sudden he spent a fortune on his office and a variety of other things. His office was elegant, if not downright opulent. He spent a *lot* of money. It was inconsistent. Not with his position, necessarily, but I'm not sure I'd have expected it from David.

"Then he gave an interview in which he said I'd encouraged him to get a Rolls-Royce instead of the Audi he'd chosen. 'David, why did you say that?' I asked him. 'Well, it's better,' he told me. 'You can't *do* that,' I replied, 'you can't *lie* to the public about me. Nobody in the world is going to believe that I'd encourage you to spend money—it's just not in my nature.' Then he said it was someone else who had put out the Rolls-Royce story, not him. He should have said, 'Well, I shouldn't have done that'—but that's not David's way, as I was discovering." (David steadfastly maintains one of the staff circulated the story.)

By mid-November 1986, *with the meter now running,* David had completed a review of every item in Columbia's inventory. Of the 121 projects that had been in various stages of development at the studio, 57 were to be axed. Every new script submission had been gone through, marked A for "definite," B for "further development required," C for "I need to be convinced," and D for "dross." With only a thin release schedule in prospect for the first half of 1987, David was open for any "pickups" available. The most controversial upcoming item was *Ishtar*, which had been greenlighted by David's predecessor and former Righteous Brothers agent Guy McElwaine. (Coke had lost that lovin' feeling after taking one look at the soaring costs on the movie.)

According to one school of thought, the writing was on the wall then for Dick Gallop for his failure to control the excesses on *Ishtar*. Another had it that even Fay Vincent had been lucky to survive. Director Elaine May had exposed 108 hours of film on the project ("kinda long for a comedy," Robert Osborne of *The Hollywood Reporter* cracked), and the impending turkey had so far swallowed up $40 million. Postproduction was still going on, as David could hardly fail to notice since he was the recipient of the weekly bills. "Since I'd been told the worst was over with *Ishtar,*" he says, "I was staggered by the postproduction costs that kept coming in. The theory had been that Columbia was out of the woods when shooting had finished, but financially we weren't. The whole thing ballooned even further out of proportion in postproduction, both in cash terms and in delivery terms."

"Who gives a shit what Puttnam thinks?" Warren Beatty asked one Columbia executive. "I certainly don't. Just tell the asshole to keep paying the bills."

Despite David's arrangement with Fay Vincent that he would have nothing to do with *Ishtar,* Beatty and Dustin Hoffman were still concerned that David would somehow or other foster a negative attitude toward the movie. A former Columbia executive commented, "Beatty in effect took it out on us for hiring Puttnam. How? Just by being more difficult. He believed he couldn't trust the studio. Everybody worked for Puttnam, and Puttnam was against the picture, so every decision that came from the studio he saw Puttnam influencing or controlling. I think in some respects he was right."

Beatty now turned down some of the marketing team at Columbia that he had known and trusted in the past. "I can't use you," he told one furious executive. "You're a Puttnam man, and I think you'll always be loyal to David and not to me."

The reaction of the Hollywood community to David's first slate of movies ranged from cool to lukewarm. "You don't feel the heat that's in Touchstone's program," said one reporter. Many detected a distinct element of the cerebral; it seemed that catering to audiences' erogenous zones would continue to be the province only of Warners, Universal, Paramount, et al. In some cases the drama of getting a Columbia movie on the screen would be at least as interesting as the movie itself:

- *Housekeeping.* Featuring the return of David's association with Bill Forsyth; canceled by Cannon with six weeks to go, rescued by David.
- *Someone to Watch Over Me.* An attempt at a mainstream thriller. Nail-biting suspense as the question is posed: can Ridley Scott tell a straightforward, gripping story without reliance on flashy effects?
- *Vice Versa.* A simple tale of a father and son changing places, adapted by Dick Clement and Ian La Frenais from the 1940s British original, which starred Roger Livesey and Anthony Newley. After almost forty years, surely there was no other studio planning virtually the same remake, especially a sister company?
- *Little Nikita.* A surefire heartwarmer with thrills and excitement, but could director Richard Benjamin focus on the winning elements?
- *Punchline.* Dan Melnick's last throw of the dice under his Columbia housekeeping deal; would it be ready in time for an end-of-December 1987 Oscar-nomination run?
- *Vibes.* Dan Aykroyd and Cyndi Lauper—or was it? Dan didn't consider Cyndi a big enough name. An ultimatum for David!
- *The Big Town.* Would this one do it for Marty Ransohoff? Or Ben Bolt? Or Matt Dillon? Or Diane Lane? Or Tommy Lee Jones? Or *anybody*?

David would like to have had Alan Parker work with him at Columbia, but the idea failed to take off when Alan reluctantly turned down David's offer. "He's my best pal," Alan explains. "I value our friendship so much, I didn't want to risk it in making films with him. The reason I came out here was because he's here, Patsy's here, Patsy's a good friend of my wife, Annie, and everybody seemed to be here. David wanted me to come and be like the old-fashioned staff director, to do as many films as I could while he was at Columbia. I quite liked the idea of that, taking away the preciousness of what we do, because it does become more and more difficult each time deciding which

film to make, but I chickened out. The first four things he sent
me I didn't want to do, so it was obviously not going to work.
And I thought it was better we remained friends.

"I stayed at Coldwater Canyon with him and Patsy for weeks
while Annie got the kids organized back home, and we'd never
discuss the proposition. People would ask me, 'Well, did you
talk about it?' And I'd say, 'No, we don't like to mention it to
one another. We talk about everything else under the sun, except the fact I'm supposed to be doing films with him.' "

A friend of both men reckons there were reasons for Alan's
decision other than the ones Alan gives and other than the
rather frugal terms that David was offering. "It's really hard for
Alan to swallow that after his two biggest successes, *Bugsy Malone* and *Midnight Express*, both made with David, he's never had
a major box-office hit on his own. Even critical acclaim has
often been grudging, except in France, where he's idolized.
Alan really wants to be considered an artist—'An Alan Parker
Film' and all that. David's often told him he's not entitled to
that credit unless he's both written and directed the film, which
he does do occasionally. None of his films—*Fame, Pink Floyd—
The Wall, Shoot the Moon, Birdy,* or *Angel Heart*—have really taken
off where it matters most, in the U.S. market. So if Alan went
back to David and the film they made together was a hit, quite
honestly it might destroy him."

Anyone who knows the extent of David's involvement in
Bugsy Malone and *Midnight Express* would take issue with this
argument. The much more likely explanation for Alan continuing to plow his own furrow is his singleminded view of auteur-
ship.

"What will I achieve here?" David rhetorically asked one journalist, only weeks after his arrival in Hollywood, in an interview that would come back to haunt him. "Jarvis Astaire once
told me that I have a tendency to bite the hand that feeds me.
There's something in that. I like a scrap. It's a working-class
thing. Screw you, I don't need any of you. I leave here in March
1990. I have the date ringed in my calendar. If I make good

movies and they don't work, I will go with my head held high.
I'll still be a producer. I can always go back to my day job."

Fay Vincent was surprised and dismayed at David's decision
to go public about the length of his Hollywood tenure—and
with no mention of staying with the company thereafter.
"That's not our understanding," Fay told him. "You've made
me look silly, David."

"The truth of the matter," David explained to another journalist, compounding the felony, "is that the day I signed on, at
least half of me was still wondering if I'd done the right thing.
Which means my attitude toward losing my job, or having it
taken away from me, is very different from that of the normal
studio executive."

Vincent cringed yet again when David pointed out that his
deals with Coca-Cola did not involve bonuses tied to grosses.
"What I earn will be exactly the same, whether I deliver five
more *Ghostbusters* or fall flat on my face. In other words, I'm
allowed to fail." David was beginning to remind Fay of the
biblical fool, uttering all of his mind. "You're a Coke executive,
David," Fay reminded him. "Don't maintain such a high profile. You don't have to spell out all the options and fallbacks
you've got. That's not what Roberto and Don want to hear."

David's attitude was that he had to be his own man. He had
to show that he could not be bought and sold. He had always
shot from the hip—why should he change now? Did Coke or
anyone else think he was overawed either by the Hollywood
climate or by Coke's corridors of power? In David's view, being
upfront about his term would allow him to make deals without
hidden agendas. And his self-esteem would not allow him to
appear "affected" by Hollywood; he must never be seen to have
changed his views because of the "role" he now played. There
would be no hedging of bets, no favors to return, and no egos to
stroke. There were other reasons, too, but these he would
scarcely admit even to himself.

The feedback to Fay Vincent was horrendous, both from
Coke in Atlanta and from Herbert Allen in New York. "He's
made himself a lame duck by spelling out the three years and

reporting it as if he's then leaving the company" was the message. Universal's elder statesman Lew Wasserman phoned Coke from Hollywood. "Puttnam was a great choice," he told them, "but the three-year provision is self-defeating."

The reaction from Coke was, What on earth was Puttnam playing at? The way David told the tale, it was three and a half years, then good-bye, Columbia. What about the rest of it, the understanding Fay had reached with him that their relationship would be ongoing? Why was Puttnam telling only half the story? In any case, surely the details of his contract were between David and Coke alone? They had assumed that Puttnam understood about corporate responsibility. Other executives did not shoot their mouths off to the press like this.

"David's single problem," as Fay spells it out, "was, his private agenda became his public agenda, and that ultimately caused Coke and Herbert Allen to turn negative on him, because he either missed or miscast the subtleties of what we were trying to do. My recollection is that the difficulties related to things David *said* rather than the things David *did*. All of that press comment—he's so public and open-mouthed, he just talked too much. He wasn't careful, and I don't think he really understood the significance of being part of Coca-Cola. He understood the benefit, but he never understood that when he spoke, he spoke as Coke. Every time he spoke, the press all over the world would pick it up and call me, saying, What is he doing, why is he saying this? Some of the remarks were innocent, some were misquoted, but there was just so much of it. I think everyone agreed with his principal points, but saying it publicly was like announcing we were going to land at Normandy. Costs were too high, we were paying people too much, there was too much control by agents—it was a great strategy, but why talk about it?

"I said to him, 'The problem is, you talk about Hollywood this and Hollywood that—it's not subtle, it doesn't reflect a high quality of intellect, because there's no such thing. You and I know that's bullshit. Who are we talking about? We're not talking about Disney. You admire them, and so do I. You're not talking about Bob Daly and Terry Semel at Warners. You're not talking about us. You're not talking about Paramount.' We went through the list, and I said 'Who *are* you talking about? All these generalizations aren't helpful, either about the studios *or* agents.' I argued with him that he got a lot of attention and people knew what he meant, but when you really got specific, what he was saying didn't hold up." Perhaps Fay had in mind Ezra Pound's homily that any general statement is like a check drawn on a bank: Its value depends absolutely on what is there to meet it. It was beginning to look as if David's misfortune was having an ability to speak but insufficient judgment as to when to keep silent.

Fay was not the only one to resent David's blanket condemnations, reminiscent as they were to some of Joe McCarthy and his infinitely variable number of "card-carrying Commies in the White House." The difference was that Fay shared his dismay only with David. Others were not so subtle and hid under a blanket of anonymity.

"Of course he didn't save the British film industry," said one American director. "His trick was to make it look as if he did by taking the moral high ground. He's on the right side of all the issues in this town now, like whether to tint the movie classics and the apartheid issues in South African cinemas. But there are a lot of people who would forget the miracle and call him Sammy Glick. David knows how to *get* the best of his films, but he doesn't necessarily *make* the best. In England he is a coffee-table filmmaker. He is a fixer. He buys a country house in Wiltshire, and it doesn't look old enough, so he gets in the makeup department to have it antiquated. In Hollywood, even the fact he knows the word *antiquated* makes him into an intellectual."

One scriptwriter reckoned he could see beyond David's provocative public statements. "Publicity is his acknowledged forte. But he'll tell you things he doesn't necessarily mean. It doesn't always matter, as long as you make things happen. Producers *should* lie and bullshit and do all they can to make movies."

Another scriptwriter agreed. "He says he is going to be a

professor at Harvard, and he ends up working for a soft-drinks company. He says he'll ignore the youth market that everyone else is playing to, but he won't ignore it—he'll just not talk about it. The great thing about Puttnam is, he says things people want to hear."

A rival studio head joked, "No one knows what they are doing right now—except for David Puttnam, who's talking as if he knows what everybody should be doing."

"He shoots from the lip," a columnist sniped.

"Take all his pictures," said a rival executive, "and between the lot, they didn't take as much as *Sixteen Candles*" (an esoteric reference to Universal's 1984 teen success).

David marched on regardless. When he suggested to the creative community that they take less money upfront in return for a bigger profit share, he blithely anticipated the inevitable reaction, for many had been suckered already by similar promises. "I have to say," he admitted, "the onus is on the studios to provide the burden of proof there'll be a fair count. If you enter into a partnership, you have an obligation to ensure that if things work out well for you, they work out for them too. It's up to us to spend the next twelve months proving they'll get a straight count here. Will we be all things to all men? No. Will there be calls that don't get returned and movies people think we were crazy not to make? For sure. But basically, Columbia will be a polite, decent place to work for those who do work here, and when we make a profit, that profit will be shared."

David was asked, "Can we expect a massive invasion of British talent now that you are ensconced here?" He laughed and replied, "I'd be surprised if that happened. This is only one studio, and even if I completely swamped the place with British talent, that would still be a very small blob on the overall horizon. I can't be blamed, though, if in the first few months, when staring at a pretty empty production slate, that I turn to people I know and trust. I'd be foolish not to. I'll probably get a bit of stick for what seems to be a slightly disproportionate amount—maybe a third of the material—being with people I know."

Despite this, Jake Eberts doubted that he could do business

with David, lest the charge of "cronyism" be leveled. But he could not have been more wrong. In October, David was shown the footage of the new John Boorman film *Hope and Glory*. It had initially been funded by Jake's Allied Filmmakers, but it was nonetheless enthusiastically adopted by David, who described the movie as "an English *Amarcord*." Jake had completed his caretaker role at Goldcrest, although Brent Walker's Masterman company would not have been his ideal choice as a buyer for the ailing company. With a loss to the shareholders of £16 million, the inglorious demise of Goldcrest had been a low-key, mournful affair, as the lowering of a coffin into the ground tends to be.

Jake knew that David admired the work of German director Doris Dorrie and successfully interested him in her proposed new comedy *Me and Him*. A third property, sent by Jake in script form to Columbia in December, was a little $23.5 million item that was to be Terry Gilliam's new opus, *The Adventures of Baron Munchausen*. Agreement would be reached with David on this one too. A bit further down the line, David rescued Simon Perry's *White Mischief* when the original backer withdrew—again with Jake.

At the end of 1986, David was able to look back on four months of momentous change at Columbia, albeit wrought at considerable personal cost. His "no exceptions" philosophy of cutting out producers' "housekeeping deals" had made him powerful enemies. Brandon Tartikoff, whom Fay Vincent had approached for the Columbia job before David's appointment, confided to David, "You did what I knew I couldn't do. You stood up to the 'barons.' "

One day while sorting through the studio files, Valerie came across a 1979 Columbia interoffice memo which caused much amusement. It ran: "Return herewith *Chariots of Fire. I am sorry to tell you this has no viability at all in the American market-place because of style and tone as well as subject matter.*"

"Make me a copy and have it framed," David, smiling, instructed Valerie. "That's definitely one for the office wall."

As Christmas approached, David discovered that Columbia

dished out $45,000 worth of gifts each year. "I want to stop this," he told the Christmas gift committee. "Let's spend $1,000 on Christmas cards and give the other $44,000 to charity instead." Despite the turmoil the suggestion caused, the idea was taken up. David's director friend Roy Battersby was one recipient of the card, which ran:

Christmas is surely one of the most evocative words in our language. For most of us it conjures up childhood, gifts, family, friends, and a general sense of security and well-being. Sadly, not everyone is so fortunate, which is why we at Columbia Pictures have given, in your name, our entire Christmas gift allocation to three organizations. *One for the young, one for the old, and one for the homeless.

Enjoy a very happy Christmas knowing that your generosity has made it possible for many less privileged to feel cared for at this very special time of the year.

*United Friends of the Children
The Los Angeles City Department of Aging
The Salvation Army Harbor Light Center

Underneath David had scribbled self-deprecatingly to Roy, "This card represents my *first* small victory. Love as ever— David." At least his sense of humor was still intact. Pointedly, a year later many other studios had followed his lead.

David's Christmas gift to Mike Ovitz was not so generous. To one interviewer, discussing the subject of agents' fees in Hollywood, David asked, "Where do they get off asking for that much? Is it just because there's some schmuck in a large tower in Century City that's got the balls to ask for it?" Ovitz's Tower of Babel in Century City somehow managed to remain standing.

21

A Christmas respite at Kingsmead Mill reminded David and Patsy of what life could be like away from the machinations and intrigues that are the daily stuff of life in Hollywood. Afterward, their return to Los Angeles was a low point. A minor domestic argument that flared into an angry scene brought home to David how much his job was getting to him. "I'm the wrong person for it," he told Patsy as they sat up half the night talking. "You're damned well not," she replied, "and if you pack it in now, you'll be sorry for the rest of your life."

Ironically, the zenith of David's year at Columbia arrived two weeks later. The occasion was Coke's Entertainment Business Sector summit dinner, held at Santa Barbara in January 1987. Coke executives Goizueta and Keough vied with each other to praise the start David had made at the studio. "David Puttnam had the guts, sheer guts, to say, okay, I'll do it, I'll do it my way," Keough's panegyric began, "and it is courageous for him and his wife to leave a wonderfully comfortable cocoon and come out here, where you know every agent in town is out to get you."

Goizueta was not to be outdone. "David Puttnam, David Picker, and the team they have assembled have taken the first steps down the road that we believe will lead to an unprecedented era of creativity at Columbia Pictures. This leadership is going to give the studio a personality, a character, a style such as the studios had during the Golden Age of motion pictures."

David's speech, no less resounding, was received with extraordinary enthusiasm. If progress were measured by speeches alone, David was on a roll. Unfortunately, he seemed to have ignored that he had to get along with the personalities within the community as well as lecture them.

Vibes, which was to star Dan Aykroyd, had been set before David's arrival at Columbia. David saw the tests of pop songstress Cyndi Lauper and determined that she was perfect for the co-starring role of the ditsy psychic. Aykroyd took a look at the package, which now consisted of an untried co-star and an unknown director, Ken Kwapis, and concluded that it was all too much. Mike Ovitz, Aykroyd's agent, conveyed his sentiments to David: "Drop Cyndi Lauper." But David Picker put his oar in too. "We've got the best combination," he told David. "If Dan Aykroyd doesn't agree, he has the right to withdraw."

David decided to write to Aykroyd. This infuriated Ovitz, who felt that all overtures to his client should be made through him. A lot of David's letters are mere acknowledgments, a legacy of the English middle-class "thank you for having us to tea" variety. But others are filibusters, and such was the one Dan Aykroyd was sent. Although the sentiments are admirable, David clearly does not believe in writing a paragraph where a page will do.

11 January 1987

Dear Dan,

Although we have never met, I have watched, admired and envied your talent for a number of years. As a producer I always hoped that I might find myself with a piece of material so tempting that you would drop everything else to do it. For good or ill I was promoted (or demoted) before ever coming up with the definitive Dan Aykroyd project.

This is by way of background to the fact that one of the attractions of the Columbia job was the opportunity to work with you and your colleagues and become familiar with an area of the entertainment business which has thus far simply been a distant fascination. It's also true to say that of the dozen or so scripts that I read before I joined the company *Vibes* represented one of the two or three home runs. For this reason I have monitored its progress and taken it particularly seriously.

I won't bore you with a litany of my impressions of the way things have gone during the past three or four months. It certainly occurred to me that they weren't proceeding in a particularly orderly manner, but I accepted the fact that the way in which I've worked as a producer and the type of material I've worked on was so at variance to this type of situation that it was impossible to draw any day to day analogy.

The important points which have now come back to haunt us are the following:

1. At his urging I was shown the test that Ron Howard did with Cyndi Lauper and I must say, despite initial scepticism, I was won over by her and fully understand the enthusiasm that Ron and, for that matter, everyone else seemed to express.

2. I gathered that there were problems in bringing you and Cyndi together, but my clear understanding was that these, for the most part, related to geography and the fact that she was travelling whilst you were preparing your present film, they were exacerbated by the fact that you were filming by the time she came "off the road."

3. Although you may well have expressed reservations early on, please believe me when I tell you that these only reached me in early December. Subsequent to this we all felt that the manner in which you met with David Picker, and subsequently with Cyndi herself, reflected highly on

your attitude to the Studio, a fellow artist and the cause of professionalism in general.

4. As Mike Ovitz and I discussed on Friday the present situation has been typified to me as being some form of "arm wrestle" between Columbia Pictures and your agency. This is not true.

5. Columbia Pictures will make a significant loss this year, as indeed it has in several of the years preceding. I have to assume that I've been brought in to alter the company's thinking and the manner in which it operates rather than ape the mistakes of the past.

Now the issue at hand!

Since arriving in my present position I have, in addition to attempting to restructure the company, only taken about half a dozen decisions which could honestly be regarded as being relevant to the onscreen quality of the material that will emerge in the fall of next year. Most of these came about as a result of my believing in the *quality* of the individual screenplays and the fact that casting opportunities existed which could embellish the strengths of those screenplays.

The downside of all of this is the fact that I have had to swallow hard and accept that the ["insurance factor"] has been diminished in some cases by going *with* the movie as opposed to the more obviously appealing "package."

At the end of the day my performance at Columbia will be judged on the basis of these decisions and I'm perfectly prepared to be flung out on my ear in the event that I'm wrong more often than I'm right.

A few examples of what I'm attempting to describe above are the preference for Tom Berenger over Richard Gere for the lead in Ridley Scott's picture. Our decision to make Bill Forsyth's film with Christine Lahti in the lead rather than wait and hope for Diane Keaton; fighting for Sidney Poitier to take on a role in *Little Nikita* originally written for Jack Nicholson and, as you may know, holding out for Tom Hanks to play the lead in *Punchline* in the face of concerns expressed by a number of thoughtful people.

In all of this I believe I have shown a general consistency. I have no idea if I'm right, but I have at least trusted my instincts, the same instincts which have brought me rightly or wrongly into my present situation. It's not a question of a lack of admiration for the talents of Richard, Diane, Jack, or any number of others, it's merely fighting for who's *right* as against who's "bankable."

The issue involving Cyndi is admittedly rather different. Is she right for the film? Off the page the answer for me is unquestionably "yes." Can she act? Again for me the answer is also a conclusive yes. I thought her timing was superb and the only video test I've ever seen which similarly excited me was the one for Haing Ngor when we were seeking a lead for *The Killing Fields*. I'm also immensely comforted by the fact that David Picker and all the rest of my colleagues at Columbia, as well as the producers and director of *Vibes* enthusiastically feel the same way.

Everyone involved very much wants you to play opposite her and all of us in our different ways believe that you're right to have reservations. In fact I would be concerned if you *didn't* have reservations. Any artist, director or producer going into a movie without qualms is an idiot. Most of us feel as though we put our careers on the line every time we make a significant creative decision—that's both the nightmare and the challenge of the job. Personally I wouldn't have it any other way.

I've told Mike that I would very much like to get together with you, but he feels that a meeting in the present climate would probably be fruitless. I have to trust his instinct.

What's important is for you to know how much every one of us would like you to be in *Vibes* and for you to understand our reasoning. At the end of the day we've decided to cast Cyndi and are left hoping that you'll climb into the bath with us and take your best shot based on our tortuously considered judgment.

I'm sorry this letter is so long, but I hope that it goes some way towards encouraging you to understand how truly important every film and every decision such as this is to us. I can only reiterate what David Picker has already told you; we'll go to any reasonable lengths to make you feel comfortable and confident enough to go along with our instincts. All of us believe there's a wonderful film to be made and, without doubt, it will be a better film if you're in it.

I very much look forward to meeting you.

Warmest personal regards,
David Puttnam

Dan Aykroyd's reaction to this missive is unrecorded; he had probably read shorter scripts. In the absence of a reply, David promptly signed Jeff Goldblum for *Vibes* instead. (And, indeed, the film did eventually star Goldblum and Lauper. It was slaughtered by the critics and ignored by the public. So much for "home runs.")

David dined with Michael Ovitz at Spago in a further attempt to find a way forward. But once again there was no meeting of minds, for to each, the other man represented the complete opposite of his values. On the face of it, they should have had at least one shared purpose—the making of *Ghostbusters II*. But David suspected that Ovitz was having trouble putting the package together, since Bill Murray was said to have no desire to goof around again with his particular role, at least for the time being. If Ovitz needed to cover that embarrassment, David would soon oblige in spades.

While giving a speech at a British-American Chamber of Commerce lunch, David cited Robert Redford as a shining example of an actor who gave back to the community in the form of his Sundance Institute work. According to the New York *Post* "Page six" gossip column, he then said, "Bill Murray exemplifies an actor who makes millions off movies, but gives nothing back to his art. He's a taker."

David denies ever having mentioned Bill Murray: "Bill's lawyer was supposedly at the lunch. This phantom figure apparently left in disgust. He never came forward and identified himself."

An infuriated Bill Murray was reported to have snapped, "What the hell's it got to do with him how I spend my money?" Concern over what he saw as a blatant fabrication, David wrote to several lawyers who were present at the luncheon and asked them to testify that the Bill Murray reference had never been made. One of those, contacted later by the *Los Angeles Times*, stated that the *Post*'s comments on the luncheon had been "misconstrued" rather than "fabricated." The host at the affair, Nigel Sinclair, was less equivocal and described the *Post* item as "absolute balderdash." Other columnists contrived to report the remark as a fact and even had Bill Murray informing Michael Ovitz that he would no longer be involved in *Ghostbusters II*. "Wow, there goes $200 million for Columbia," ran the gossip mill; "Puttnam sure made an expensive crack!" Ovitz was well and truly off the hook—now no one could blame him for failing to put the package together!

David was sufficiently concerned to write to Bill Murray personally, assuring him that he had been misreported. Murray replied through David Picker that he had never believed it in the first place. David also wrote to Mike Ovitz; "Sadly, I gather that even you are tempted to give credibility to this shoddy gossip. Michael, please understand that to do so characterizes the writers of these letters, as well as myself, as liars." No reply was received from Ovitz.

Were they liars? Or were they mistaken? A few of David's colleagues are convinced that he did in fact make the remark. According to one: "There are times, when he's nervous, that he's not a particularly good speaker. Then he often rushes his words and occasionally departs from his text and makes impromptu remarks. Of course I'm sure he doesn't remember saying it and I'm certain he thinks he didn't. I'm equally sure he *did*, and that it was a fatal mistake."

One amused agent reckoned that if David had said it, he had in any case gotten it wrong. He cited a movie that Murray had forced on Columbia as part of his *Ghostbusters* deal—a remake of

Somerset Maugham's *The Razor's Edge*, with Murray cast in the leading role first played by Tyrone Power. "Bill Murray *does* give back," he said, "not only to the industry, but to Columbia specifically. They may not have wanted it, but in return for playing the fool in *Ghostbusters*, for only a few more million he gave them one of the year's biggest turkeys in *The Razor's Edge*!"

Over a year later, *Variety* finally tracked down a witness to the lunch who was prepared to speak out. "There was a Q and A at the end," Tom Hansen, a Los Angeles attorney recalled, "and someone stood up and said, 'You've been very outspoken in your criticism of how highly paid many Hollywood stars are. Could you comment on that?' "

According to Hansen, Puttnam praised Robert Redford for his Sundance Institute work, before adding, "You don't see people, for example Bill Murray, putting back any dollars from *Ghostbusters*." Hansen confirmed that he had related the incident to Mike Ovitz while emphasizing that it was an impromptu statement rather than part of David's prepared text.

"I wasn't there," says Fay Vincent, "but I've had people who were there tell me without question he said it. I phoned him about it when I saw it in one of the papers here. He hadn't seen it and was upset and surprised. Tough as it is, because I have affection and regard for David, he didn't deny saying it, but he said the reaction was ridiculous. He called me back an hour later and said he'd talked to people who said he *hadn't* said it. I told him, 'If you tell me you didn't say it, then I believe you and I'll take that position. However, there are people who say you said it.' He may not have remembered, although I think he knew he'd mentioned Murray.

"My initial advice was that the report would cause trouble and he should call Murray. When he called me back to say it was all a misunderstanding, I said he should still call Murray. I believed him, but the issue with Murray was important. We talked about what the damage control should be."

David had already looked at the *Ghostbusters II* package and was considering hiring new cast members and cutting the costs down to a more manageable size so that more would be left for the studio. There was also the possibility of signing up bright new talent for a whole new series—*Ghostbusters II, III, IV* and *V*. The suggestion was enough to infuriate Ovitz. "He saw the very idea as a slap in the face to himself and the system," said one observer. "To Ovitz, this was David really throwing the gauntlet down."

There was no containing the storm over the *Ghostbusters* sequel dispute. David inferred that the barrage of publicity over the Bill Murray remark suited Ovitz's book. Pressure mounted on Fay Vincent from all sides.

"The sequel was a huge asset of the Coca-Cola Company," he explains. "David was seen as hurting the company by causing a principal asset to be affected when it wasn't necessary. So ultimately I had to get into that. Ovitz wouldn't deal with Puttnam, and we had to get negotiations going. Almost every single cast member and director Ivan Reitman said the movie would never be made with Puttnam, as did Ovitz. They would deal only with me. When I told David that, his initial stand was that to give in to Ovitz was ridiculous and that his authority was being violated. How could he be the head of Columbia and have nothing to do with its biggest picture? I pointed out that that made it two, counting *Ishtar.* Later he calmed down and phoned me and said of course I was right, it was wrong of him to stand in the way of the film getting made. I hadn't wanted to go over Puttnam's head, but I couldn't let the project die in the water. It got to be a nightmare and caused an awful lot of trouble, because to Coke it was very simple: it was our duty to get *Ghostbusters II* made.

"That was when Herbert Allen got into it, because while he didn't care what David did in terms of making movies, he thought it was wrong to hurt the company that David would be leaving anyway. After David got pushed out of *Ghostbusters* and I started dealing directly with the participants, the agreement was, they'd make it for no up-front salaries. We'd all be going in on a partnership share—Ovitz's suggestion. He got everybody to agree to that. Everyone recognized it couldn't be made costing $40 to $50 million."

There were differing views over the *Ghostbusters* fracas and even the notion that Ovitz was ever having difficulty putting it together. "That's an interesting theory," said a rival agent, "and it's also a pile of shit. Believe me, in Hollywood greed will conquer all. It'll be put together, though David might not be around to see it."

By February it was clear that *The Mission* was grinding to a halt in the United States with net rentals of just $8.3 million, adding up to a major disappointment. When Fernando Ghia went on record with his view that the U.S. reaction was a backlash to its victory at Cannes, David reacted—some would say overreacted —furiously. "That was probably the most asinine interview I have ever read in my entire life," he railed. "I can't believe it, it's absolute madness. It's also extremely dangerous, because if people are stupid enough to believe what he says, then that attitude could be the death, not just of Cannes, but of every festival around the world."

What had crazed David, it seemed, was the possibility that he was responsible for *The Mission*'s U.S. failure. Nonetheless, there was at least some measure of artistic reward—the film went on to be nominated for no fewer than seven Oscars: Best Picture, Best Director, Best Cinematography, Best Art Direction, Best Editing, Best Costume Design, and Best Original Score. Ultimately, however, only one award was given to the film, to Chris Menges for Best Cinematography.

The creative community was next to feel David's wrath: he gave them to understand that it was not only producers and deal-makers who had inflated ideas of their own worth. "If you have a dream to make a particular film," he told one reporter, "and someone is prepared to invest $20 million or even $10 million in it, there's something wrong in saying 'I wish to earn $2 million to fulfill my dream'—I mean, the canon of human experience doesn't allow for that. If someone's dream is about to be realized, there is an energy and commitment that should be much more important than sitting holding the bridge of your nose and demanding $2 million. If someone came to me and said, 'This is the film I've always wanted to make, but this (naming some silly figure) is the minimum fee I'll make it for,' I would say, 'There are five other excellent studios, here are their addresses and telephone numbers. I suggest you go and talk to them.' If, in America, I come across a director who has made a film as good as Ingmar Bergman's *Fanny and Alexander*, I'm going to take him very, very seriously. But if he has never made a film half as good as that, I'd like him to accept that as a starting point in our relationship. It doesn't mean he's a diminished human being, it means that in his own eyes he's a man with a lot to learn and a long road to travel. With any luck, we as a studio can help. Sadly, an awful lot of directors don't see it that way. They see themselves as having traveled the road and now they're getting their revenge. Well, I'm not in the revenge business.

"This picture of me as some kind of St. George come to slay the Hollywood dragon is extremely embarrassing. I'm no St. George. I'm not an intellectual. I think I'm a reasonably thoughtful person. I read and I think, and Hollywood is probably not an environment in which a lot of people do read, and frankly, not a lot of people do think.

"I was naïve. It took me a month to realize I was the kid in charge of the candy store. And what came out of recognizing that was the realization of what extreme abuse there had been in the past. If I do succeed here, other studios will follow suit and the American industry will benefit. If I fail, the industry will still survive. It's a win-win situation for them."

In David's mind the reason for the renewed media blitz was quite clear—to let everyone know yet again exactly where he stood. Terry Semel at Warners advised him that what he was doing was self-defeating, as did his friend Jeff Berg at ICM. "Do your good work, but keep a low profile" was the advice from one supporter. "But for Christ's sake, David, lighten up, it's only rock 'n' roll, after all!"

"David's problem," said one rival studio executive, "is that he regards the press here as he did when he was an independent producer in England. There he was lionized by the press, he was quoted ad nauseam, he was the guru of the industry, and no one dared to disagree with him, because he was too important. When he got here, he didn't realize the depth of antipathy toward him—nothing personal, he's a likable guy—but the antipathy that would have been felt for anyone coming in. He was not an ex-agent, not an ex-lawyer, not an ex–TV producer who had come up through the ranks. He was an outsider whose commercial record in the eyes of Hollywood was insignificant. *Chariots* was a major success, but *The Killing Fields* was not, nor *Cal,* nor *Local Hero.* And *The Mission* was bombing. So, number one, he talked to the press too much, and number two, his track record was bordering on zilch. And he tries to take on Ray Stark, who's made more hit movies than David's had climaxes?

"I know people who told him he would have to get used to working with people he didn't like, because in this business you've got to do fifteen to twenty pictures a year. If you're lucky enough to work with four or five people you actually like, that's about it. The others you may neither admire nor like, but they are filmmakers of consequence and turn out commercial hits. I have to slog my way through a dozen pieces of crap to get to the stuff I really want to do—but I do it. I'm highly paid to turn out a certain amount of product, and let's face it, you can't feel appassionato about everything. The trouble with David is, he can't seem to separate his personal feelings from the studio interests."

David was the recipient of the Jean Renoir Humanitarian Award on February 13, 1987, at a ceremony held in the Sportsman's Lodge in Studio City, close to his Coldwater Canyon Drive home. The award was presented by the Los Angeles Film Teachers Association—an organization clearly distanced from sordid financial considerations—who went on to cite him as "the best last hope we have." After the battering he had taken since his arrival at Columbia, David was delighted to receive the honor and pointedly stated, "There may well be, in this room, more legitimate love of cinema than exists on all the lots in Hollywood."

Robert Radnitz spoke for most of those present as he declared, "David is someone who understands picture making. There are many who feel he can't succeed, but many of us feel he can. His outlook appears to say that art and entertainment are not separate."

Frank Biondi, Jr., executive vice-president of Coke's Entertainment Business Sector and greenlighter of Marty Ransohoff's *Switching Channels*, caused a ripple with his announcement that a feature-film entity *separate from Columbia Pictures* was being set up by Coca-Cola. He went out of his way to deny there was any particular strategy. "It's just the other side of the Nelson joint venture," he claimed, "a deal done essentially by the Entertainment Business Sector as opposed to Columbia Pictures." Although basically designed for this purpose, Biondi stated that feature production by the new entity on its own, although *not intended* at present, *could not be precluded* in the future.

Fay Vincent knew that David felt the move was "aimed" at him. "But it wasn't," he says. "It had nothing to do with David. It was to do with a fact he found difficult to swallow—that he was only one star in Coke's film constellation, *not* the whole constellation."

By April, David had soldiered on, producing with his team a $269 million package of twenty-five features with an average budget of under $11 million each, about $4 million less than the average cost before his arrival. Several were "pickups":

- *Stars and Bars* was to be produced by his former partner Sandy Lieberson ostensibly as an independent movie, with Susan Richards aboard as co-producer. Pat *(Cal)* O'Connor was to direct William Boyd's screenplay. Daniel Day Lewis and Harry Dean Stanton were starring.
- Director Gregory *(El Norte)* Nava had completed *A Time of Destiny*, another leftover from Coke's Embassy deal; William Hurt, Timothy Hutton, and Stockard Channing were featured.
- After viewing Jim McBride's thriller *The Big Easy*, starring Dennis Quaid and Ellen Barkin, David bought it for Co-

lumbia release. "It's a great asset to have creative people like Puttnam, who is a moviemaker, in charge at Columbia," said McBride, "and not a bunch of lawyers and accountants. We just hope he survives."

· Island Pictures gave up the rights to Spike *(She's Gotta Have It)* Lee's *School Daze* when the budget soared past $4 million. Columbia stepped in, this time at David Picker's instigation, guaranteeing a negative pickup on a $6 million budget. Other executives were upset at the total control Picker gave Lee. "You just don't hand someone who's only made a little home movie $6 million to spend" was one comment. "Look," Picker said, "we're paying for a Spike Lee movie. If you do that, you have to run with the guy. There's no point in turning it into something else. Either you believe in him or you don't."

· John Boorman's World War II memoir *Hope and Glory* was due for release in the autumn.

· Apart from *Ghostbusters II* (for which any hope of glory was by now extinguished), the only rock-solid commercial success Columbia had in its locker was *Karate Kid III*. The series producer, Jerry Weintraub, had formed his own Columbia-supported Weintraub Entertainment Group (president: Guy McElwaine). If only Columbia didn't have contractual rights to the sequel, Jerry must have pondered, he could have made it entirely independently. Ah, well. Although it was "set to start filming in October," for some reason it never did.

· *The Beast* was to be produced by A&M Films, starring Steven Bauer. David described it as *"Das Boot* in a tank in Afghanistan." One of his associates, Uberto Pasolini, misunderstood David's enthusiasm for the picture after reading its simplistic but crudely effective script. Surely David could see this was not a serious comment on war? "Every picture doesn't have to be," David explained. "What we have here is a classic exploitation picture in the vein of *Midnight Express.*" Uberto had discovered the commercial side of David—there *was* a mogul in there after all!

- *Little Nikita* had been in development for three years at Columbia and was Sidney Poitier's comeback picture after a long absence from the screen. His co-star was River Phoenix, a standout in *Stand By Me*. *Nikita* had almost completed filming, but already there were glum expressions every time the film was mentioned. Why? One theory: "It was originally conceived for Jack Nicholson as a relationship adventure. He's an agent who discovers the kid's parents are Russian moles. What happened was, director Richard Benjamin and the writer fell in love with the thriller aspect of the picture and overplotted it. It became a mishmash."
- In the fall, Jane Fonda's own production company was due to make a "comic adventure," *Flawless*, under a preexisting four-year arrangement at Columbia. This was subsequently dropped and another project, *The Old Gringo*, was put into production in January 1988.

Then there was the strange, convoluted case of *Vice Versa*.

David was on the panel that had granted Brian Gilbert entry into the National Film and Television School in 1979. Brian recalls saying at the interview that British films are often misunderstood in the United States because British obsessions tend to be easily misunderstood. David immediately pounced on the comment. "How do we remedy this?" he asked Brian, who replied, "I don't know—that's what I'm here to find out."

Three years later, when David went over to BAFTA with Alan Parker and Alan Marshall to view Brian's graduation film, *The Devotee*, David met Brian again. Brian was dumbfounded when David greeted him afterward with, "I want you to write and direct a movie for me."

David wanted Brian to take the character he had created in *The Devotee* and transfer her to another screenplay. Brian went away ecstatic—a former actor, he had just been handed a movie after only three years of film school study. He had to pinch himself to make sure it wasn't a dream.

The script for *Sharma and Beyond* was written in late 1982 and filmed a year later. Brian had a great deal of input from David at the script stage—long, detailed handwritten notes kept arriving. Then he found himself left entirely on his own to shoot the movie.

As the editing on *Sharma* was ending, David approached Brian about another script he wanted him to direct, *The Frog Prince*. With Iain Smith as producer, *The Frog Prince* was shot in Paris with a little help in the translation department from the multilingual Uberto Pasolini.

After David's departure for Columbia, Brian was trying to develop a project independently. He heard David had something in mind for him—a remake of the 1950s British comedy *Vice Versa*. Brian read the script by Dick Clement and Ian La Frenais and was highly enthusiastic. When David asked him to come out and meet the writers, Brian thought he was being invited to Los Angeles for the weekend and took a small overnight bag. He remained in Hollywood for a year.

Everyone was psychologically committed to the film by November 1986, but then rumors began to circulate that another movie was in development that had a virtually identical storyline. This was confirmed when Dudley Moore (now transplanted from Coldwater Canyon to Malibu) announced that his new picture, *Like Father, Like Son*, was soon to start shooting. Could it be? Yes, it could. But the biggest shock was *where* the development was taking place—at Victor Kaufman's Tri-Star, Columbia's sister company!

David went to see Kaufman and discovered Hollywood hardball in action. "Why don't we put all our resources behind the one picture?" he suggested. "There's no need," Kaufman maintained. "You've got a terrific script there, David. You've got nothing to worry about. Our script still has problems and we haven't even got a director lined up. Furthermore, our treatment's different—more of a madcap romp. Yours has style, texture. But no, we can't cancel, we're committed. We even have a release date."

David knew he could win the race by rushing *Vice Versa* through, for he had a head start of several weeks on Kaufman's film. But he decided not to do that and instead to make the best of a bad job by negotiating with Kaufman to divide up first domestic and foreign release. Kaufman cannily snagged first U.S. domestic release, somewhat hoisting David on his own international petard. The only comfort was that everyone knew the Tri-Star version was inferior. And that Dudley Moore hadn't had a hit for over a hundred years. And that quality would win through in the end—wouldn't it?

As the *Vice Versa* crew began shooting, with Judge Reinhold top-cast, further rumors started. Still another version was about to go into production—this one called *18 Again,* with veteran George Burns. Unbelievably, yet another appeared with a similar theme—*Big,* with Tom Hanks. Suddenly *everyone* was making teenage-adult role-reversal comedies. All that was now required was a rerelease of the original *Vice Versa,* and there would be five versions with the same premise floating around!

One of the projects that David was most excited about was a Barry Levinson/Valerie Curtin script that Levinson was keen to direct called *Toys.* The project had been at 20th Century-Fox for years, but there was no problem, David was assured—Columbia could have it on turnaround. Levinson's agents, CAA, would deal with Fox directly on the matter. David saw that *Toys* would not only make an intriguing film, with its plot about a military man left a toy factory, but also had far-reaching merchandising possibilities. Coke was alerted and enthusiastically agreed to contribute $4 million to a joint merchandising program intended to coincide with the film's release. Iain Smith was summoned. "I have a task for you," David told him, "to executive-produce *Toys.*"

Barry Diller, head of 20th Century-Fox, got wind of the excitement being generated at Burbank over the project. Was Fox letting something go that it should hold on to? Had he missed out?

Diller's relationship with David went back to when he ran ABC's Movie of the Week from a tiny office in New York. At first, the two men had gotten along reasonably well; then when Diller surfaced as head of Paramount Pictures, there were a couple of minor altercations over *Bugsy Malone*. A big contretemps between the two, however, had arisen over Warren Beatty's *Reds*, when Diller—and Warren Beatty—had felt that David had deliberately depicted the Oscar competition as a David-versus-Goliath struggle between *Chariots of Fire* and *Reds*, with David delivering a V-sign with his victory. ("And I did," David admits. "I went out of my way to get it seen in those terms. I played up the cost of *Reds*, which at the time Beatty and Diller were desperately trying to play down. I crazed both of them.")

Somewhere during the negotiations between CAA and Fox, *Toys* slipped through the cracks. Suddenly, Leonard Goldberg at Fox was said to be hot for the project. If there was an easier way to embarrass David than for Fox to hold on to *Toys*, it was not readily apparent. Diller knew David had been to Atlanta and had millions from Coke. He could not help but savor the situation—the egg on David's face would be especially thick.

"Fox has decided not to let *Toys* go" was the brief, unthinkable message relayed to David. Infuriated, he contacted Levinson. "I'm going to fight this," he told him. "Will you get your head down with us if it comes to a showdown?" When Levinson equivocated, David was forced to go it alone. The thing left to do was to explain the situation to Coke as best he could—and let Iain Smith know the project was a nonstarter.

David was impressed with Bill Cosby at their first meeting. He watched as America's biggest TV star put himself across as a professional who had more money than Croesus—and a dream to make a movie, *Leonard Part VI*, a spoof on spy pictures. Cosby had outlined his basic plot idea to screenwriter Jonathan Reynolds; it involved a supercool special agent, who echoed Cosby's own original television *I Spy* success. *Leonard*'s antagonist was certainly one of the most original creations of all times: a malignant female animal-rights fanatic who discovers a way to control the brains of animals by using a secret chemical and urges them on to commit terrorist acts. Cosby was convinced it would be a wow. "They'll be lining up around the block for it," he informed everyone who would listen.

He boasted to David of his terrific relationship with his audience. He was prepared to work his butt off, he said, and talk through any problems like the professional he was. There would be no requirement to pal up to him. He would not need to be stroked, schmoozed, or have his hand held. For David, it was a dream on a plate. Here was America's top-rated TV star, eager and ready to turn in the family blockbuster that would be Columbia's big Christmas picture for 1987.

Or was it a dream? David was highly critical of the first two drafts of the screenplay, and in the end he grew ambivalent about the whole notion of the movie, despite the built-in insurance that Cosby represented. Temporary president Steve Sohmer had stitched together the extraordinary Cosby deal, which gave the comedian virtual control over everything on the picture, including approval of script, casting, costume, music, sets, and final cut. For $5 million, he was the star. For another $750,000, he was the producer. In return, Cosby awarded Sohmer one of the most meaningless and demeaning titles in movie history, "executive producer for Mr. Cosby."

David decided he would give the $24 million project the go-ahead only if Coke itself agreed to underwrite the movie's release. At least then, he reasoned, Columbia's liability would be limited to the film's cost, although it would remain by far the biggest item on the studio's slate. Unfortunately, his action also signaled to Cosby that David's faith in his vision was insufficient and that David was not prepared to back him unequivocally.

When a director for the project was discussed, Cosby indicated his liking of English humor and plumped for a British director; he reckoned that an American would be full of preconceived ideas of the image he wanted put across. Indeed, he wanted to get as far away as possible from his TV persona— this was to be a *new* Bill Cosby. When David put forward several suggestions, Cosby selected an award-winning young commercial director, thirty-four-year-old Paul Weiland, after viewing his tapes and meeting with him in Cosby's New York brownstone.

Paul Weiland and David Puttnam had been neighbors for
about five minutes in 1958, when five-year-old Paul and his family had moved into the same small street in Southgate where the
Puttnams had lived, in the very week that the Puttnams crossed
town. Paul's life and career had followed the track of a pinball,
hitting David Puttnam buttons at various stops. He had worked
as a copywriter at Collet, Dickinson, and Pearce. He had met
David socially when he was working for the Alan Parker Film
Company and had observed Alan's strong but often schizoid
relationship with David. He had set up his own commercial-
producing firm in the 1980s and had had a brief early romance
with Debbie Puttnam.

An unexpected chemistry developed between Cosby, the
black American superstar, and Weiland, the Jewish directing
candidate. But, Paul wondered, who was this guy Sohmer,
schlepping around and slapping everyone on the back and repeating Cosby's slightest utterances as if they were holy gospel?
Paul felt he had passed the acid test of getting along with Cosby
—but would that be the high point of the deal? The script
drafts he had seen were terrible. "Cosby's shtick will make it
work," he was told. "He's the funniest guy in the business. It'll
be magic time." Paul was allowed to see a live show that the
comedian was recording, and he recalls that he wanted to like
him so much, his own hands were sweating. But he found the
show bland, and Cosby did not strike him as at all funny. He
remembers stumbling into a New York street close to tears after
viewing Cosby's performance in an earlier movie, *Mother, Jugs
and Speed.* Had Cosby *ever* been funny? He figured out that on
each week's television show, Cosby wandered in and out, aver-
aging ten or fifteen minutes of screen time. In a feature movie
like *Leonard Part VI,* he would be onscreen for at least ninety
minutes. Paul felt like the odd man out. He must be wrong—or
was he? His best hope was that David would have the sense to
call the whole thing off. His dearest wish was to board a plane
back to London and get the hell out of it.

Instead, he was sent on a tour of Columbia executives. David

Picker was welcoming for two minutes; he reverted to his brusque big-shot act for another two, then cut out. Michael Nathanson, who had assumed the role of David's blue-eyed boy, was all over Paul. But Paul found hardly a single enthusiast for the *Leonard* project outside of Nathanson and one marketing executive. Was David aware of this? Paul wondered. Was he all that *interested*? Having shown himself willing, and having gone along with all the ballyhoo, Paul now felt he was sinking into a hideous quagmire. It was the most expensive first film any director had yet been handed. The marketing man told Paul that the project would be their biggest film ever—Cosby was a commodity millions would turn out to see; it was simply a matter of pushing all the right buttons.

In January, at Coke's Santa Barbara dinner David had missed his last chance to get out from under the movie. He had been riding high with all the lavish compliments that were flying. With "Roberto and Don" present (and he referred to them as such publicly, to the annoyance of Fay Vincent and possibly of "Roberto and Don" themselves), he could have taken advantage of the situation, bitten the bullet, and said, "That's all the good news. The bad news is that Cosby's script is dreadful, and we just shouldn't make the picture."

The impact would have been horrendous to Coke's "relationship" with Cosby. ("Christ, he [Cosby] was their toy boy," said one Columbia executive. "He owns half of a Coke bottling plant and has been one of their main advertisers over the years." But David thinks he might have walked away alive at that point. Instead, he missed his opportunity.

"I didn't want to have an argument," he says now. "And I'd got up to $8 million from Coke to promote the movie—but $8 million worth of *advertising*. That was a mistake, the biggest mistake I made all the time I was at Columbia. *Never* make a film with a script you don't believe in on the assumption it will somehow play. It was Ken Russell and *Lisztomania* all over again, putting your life and fate in someone else's hands. I made a fundamental error. It was a fundamentally lousy idea that

Cosby brought us. It was no good. It just wasn't funny. It was the same old thing—you want to believe that the 'star' knows what he's doing. The truth of the matter is, he didn't.

"Under other circumstances I wouldn't be so rough with myself, but that week in Santa Barbara I had every card in my hand, and with hindsight, I *could* have gotten away with stopping the picture. It would have been a bit of a shock, but that would have been it."

Patsy could see why David shirked biting the bullet. "He'd just been through the most horrendous four months of his life. It's the old thing of 'It'll be all right on the night,' same as *Trick or Treat* or *Agatha*—and it's *never* all right. History should have taught David that it wouldn't work, but he was still stinging from all the attacks on him. He was really pleased with some of the things he'd managed to develop in spite of everything, and I imagine he was thinking, 'Do I really need another terrible problem at the moment?' He didn't want any more wars. His eye was off the ball."

Despite David's agonizing, there did exist one simple and pain-free alternative both to proceeding *and* to cancellation that he chose not to pursue: the wholesale transfer of the project into the eager arms of Tri-Star, where Kaufman and his film chief David Matalon were ready to pick up the baton. "I would have been happy to make *Leonard Part VI*," Matalon confirmed. Was the fear that he might be handing Tri-Star a potential blockbuster the real reason David decided to allow it to proceed at Columbia? "I don't doubt that he could have transferred it, but he chose not to," says Fay Vincent.

With shooting due to start in San Francisco in April, the ill-fated vehicle lurched along. Cosby smarted at the slight delivered when David sought insurance funding at Coke.

David installed his blunt cockney pal Alan Marshall—with Cosby's approval—as line producer of the project. This gave him some peace of mind that Columbia's most expensive undertaking ever would at least move along in a workmanlike manner.

In a rash moment David said, "The budget is completely justified for *Leonard Part VI*. The film could really work." Whether he was trying to convince Paul Weiland, Alan Marshall, Bill Cosby, or himself is unclear.

22

One of the first disputes that arose was between Paul Weiland and Cosby over Cosby's choice of Diahnne Abbott to play his wife in the film. Paul took his courage in his hands and turned her down as unsuitable. Sohmer was alarmed, but he said he would smooth it out with the star. Alan Marshall's first fight with Cosby was over the money he wanted to pay Gloria Foster, a black stage actress who had been cast as the evil, crazed Medusa, head of the International Tuna terrorist gang. Ultimately, her salary was cut. Hackles high in inverse proportion, Cosby indicated that he wanted to appoint his own black makeup assistant at a "special salary." Marshall calculated that the special salary would add $30,000 to the normal fees over the course of the film. Noting in any case that Cosby used hardly any makeup—a fact Marshall felt was possibly germane

—the special salary was resisted. Again Cosby backed down and came up with another choice at standard salary.

Since Cosby had clearly promised jobs to serried ranks of his friends, each turndown was a mortal blow to his pride. Paul and Alan were putting up more suitable choices purely for the good of the film and relying on Sohmer to smooth the star's feelings. After all, they had a $24 million film on their hands with a tight shooting schedule; Cosby had indicated from the outset that he was off to the south of France in July come hell or high water. They needed professionals to see the film through, not a bunch of "pals" or first-timers. The feedback from Cosby, with the liaison problems apparently being swept under the carpet by Sohmer, was that he was becoming good and mad.

He wanted 90 percent of the cast to be black, even down to his English butler. With difficulty, he was persuaded that this was not appropriate casting, and he reluctantly allowed Tom Courtenay to be brought in. He decided to take a stand, however, over a character named Giorgio, a senior-citizen Italian theater director that his teenage daughter falls for in one of the movie's convoluted subplots. The perfect casting for the role, Cosby felt, was sixty-six-year-old black veteran actor Moses Gunn. This time David got involved. The alarm bells were ringing loud and clear from the San Francisco preproduction offices. In a letter to Cosby, he questioned the casting of Gunn. Cosby replied that it was important that his daughter's Italian suitor be black. If he was white, he explained, it would look as if Giorgio's antagonism toward him in the film were based on racism. The message David got from Steve Sohmer was "For Christ's sake, don't rock the boat." David asked Paul what he thought. With Sohmer's warning ringing in his ears—*"Don't upset the biggest star in the world, he's a phenomenon"*—Paul replied, "Oh, it'll be all right. We can't expect to win every battle." And the ship sailed on.

As filming began, the pellucid logic of Gloria Foster's casting as Medusa was made clear as she proceeded, with Cosby's full support, to demand that her role be dramatically extended. She said many of the costumes that had been especially designed for her, would work only on "approved" floor surfaces, and insisted on spending endless hours in makeup each morning. If her role had given her the opportunity to bring one balancing ounce of humor to the production, there would have been some compensation, but of humor there was none. As far as Paul was concerned, she ruled the roost and became, as Paul put it, "the biggest pain in the ass on the film."

He found Cosby himself professional and courteous, never hogging scenes and encouraging everyone else to give of their best—except Gloria Foster, who was a law unto herself. Relations between Paul and Cosby were still cordial, despite the crossed lines Sohmer seemed to allow. The actual victim of these was Alan Marshall, for whom Cosby cultivated a deep and terrible loathing.

For his part, the laconic producer was concerned to steward the film through to its completion under the brief David had given him. "The problem with *Leonard*," he says now, "quite apart from the awful script, was that Cosby never allowed any part of it to be changed. He was like a god and was treated as one by jerks like Sohmer. But not by me. All his pals thought he could walk on water, but I wasn't impressed. A producer that doesn't even watch his own rushes? To me that's no producer at all. You can't stroll through a movie like you can a TV show. All we got was stupid talk about how they'd be lining up for the movie. The man was interested only in dollars."

(David confirms Cosby's intractability with regard to script alterations. "I wrote a lot of comments down for Steve Sohmer," he said, "and I got an embarrassed note back from him: 'Mr. Cosby has made it clear that he wants to have no further amendment to his vision.' And he used the word, *vision* instead of *script*.") According to some reports, David received a call from Cosby in late April to the effect that he could no longer work with Marshall, whom he considered a racist. He wanted him fired. I asked David, *Was* he asked to fire Marshall? Well— yes and no, came the answer, take your pick. "No. Never. The problem is, people like Cosby—and when I say people like Cosby, 99.99 percent of people reading this book are not like

Cosby, therefore they're going to find this very hard to understand. He is used not just to having what he says operated on, but to being interpreted and anticipated. There's an old story they used to tell about when I was working on Albert Speer's story, about Eva Braun, that she was very dangerous. Without ever knowing it, she would come back from a dinner party saying, 'I think that the mayor of Hamburg is incompetent'— and he would be fired; or, 'I don't trust that man'—and he might end up dead. She never knew what she was doing. Other people, probably Hitlers, know exactly what they are doing, and they don't have to say things like, 'Do me a favor, bump off Andrew Yule, will you?' It's the old 'tiresome priest' syndrome. So it may well be that Cosby was saying things to Sohmer, possibly, then Sohmer was couching them to me in terms that I was supposed to pick up."

Concerned, David flew to San Francisco to pour oil on the troubled bay waters, but he found Cosby away at his daughter's graduation, obviously expecting David to attend to matters. Dinner was spent with Paul and Alan, listening to their tales of woe. If the atmosphere had been chilly before Cosby left, it turned to ice after he returned to find Marshall still around, his head perversely attached to his body. "He thought," says David, "that Marshall would either have been fired or at the very least publicly—and that is his word, not mine—*publicly* humiliated. I'm not in the business of public humiliation, so he was asking for someone to be fired who'd done nothing wrong, or to be humiliated in a way I would never do to anybody, black, white, green, or yellow. If I'm going to fire somebody or tell somebody off, I'll do it privately. So I think what we may be talking about here is a vast culture gap."

Cosby put up Stu Gardner, musical director of his TV show, to score the movie. After asking about his qualifications for the job, Alan contacted David. "Let him do a couple of tracks and see how he does" was the suggestion. When this was relayed to Cosby, the sparks flew. "I'm telling you, Stu's going to score the movie," he raged, "and you're not going to do anything about it, Marshall!"

Two short sequences were chosen for Gardner to score. When Gardner was finished, Marshall, Cosby, Gardner, and Weiland assembled in the small viewing theater to hear the results. When it was over, Alan knew it was bad, but he was ready to counsel Gardner, "Okay, you haven't got it this time, but have another shot." But even as the thought was passing through his mind, Cosby was dismissing Gardner from the movie. There was no chance even to say good-bye to the musician, so fast was he loaded onto a plane for New York. Cosby turned to Paul Weiland and said, "Okay, do what you like with the music," and walked out. Paul looked at Alan, who just shook his head. "I'll get Elmer Bernstein," he said.

Alan was never fired, but following a visit from David Picker and Michael Nathanson, he diplomatically seemed to make himself scarce for the last month of the production. He only returned full time after the shooting was over, for the final dubbing sessions.

"Racist?" Alan laughs. "Coming from him, that's a good one —someone who's totally antiwhite. Have a butchers at *Fame*—I couldn't care less what color of skin someone's got. All we wanted was the best for Columbia to make the bloody thing work. Paul worked his backside off. I just wish David had told me at the time that Cosby wanted me fired. I'd have walked out —I don't believe in staying where I'm not wanted. But he didn't, he kept it from me. I'd have gone—but I'd have told Cosby a few home truths first—and that asshole Sohmer, who stabbed everybody in the back." (Fay Vincent has a very different view of Sohmer: "He was very complimentary of Marshall all the way through. He said Marshall and Cosby just didn't get along. There were very bad feelings. Sohmer was trying to bridge a gap that was not bridgeable.")

David decided at the end of shooting that a little present for Cosby would be in order, which not unusual when a film wraps. But certainly on this occasion it would be more in the nature of a peace offering than anything else. David himself collects photographic prints, and he selected a magnificent study of blues singer Muddy Waters for Cosby's gift, which he had beautifully framed. The package was returned to David in the next mail, opened and resealed.

The word to Coca-Cola was incredibly damaging. "He's a great producer," Cosby told them, "but he can't run Columbia. He's killing the studio."

Ever since Ray Stark had stormed out of David's office in late 1986, nary a whisper had been heard directly from that quarter. It took several months and a meeting of Coke executives in Atlanta before Herbert Allen felt that an initial foray was called for. David detected from the animated flicker of expression on Allen's face as soon as he entered the room that a jousting session was on the agenda.

David had felt a disquiet toward Allen ever since an early meeting, when he had observed the New Yorker peel off a £20 note and hand it to Claridges bellman. It had not diminished at their subsequent meetings. Although he found Allen a basically cold personality, he had to concede that the man had an original mind and that nothing he did was obvious. Still class conscious; still resistant, despite his own enhanced circumstances, to the idea of gentlemen and players, David's theory was that the rich are different and march to a different drum. As far as he was concerned, Allen and Ray Stark were bound together by their overwhelming cynicism, which David had always interpreted as a form of despair dressed up as sophistication. To certain types he felt instinctively attracted, and to certain types he did not—both Allen and Stark belonged firmly in the latter category. ("The difficulty with Herbert is that he's much more complicated than is apparent," says Fay Vincent. "The stereotype of remoteness is not accurate. He's a man who's that powerful and that wealthy. . . . The stereotype would be that he was a very conservative traditional. He's not. He's been a liberal democrat all his life and very, very liberal. The people who are closest to him and know him the best are very loyal to him. He's a terrific friend.")

At this meeting, Allen asked, "David, why are you alienating so many people—like, for example, Mike Ovitz? I hear that CAA has stopped sending scripts to the studio."

David detected a follow-up to Allen's original lecture. He asserted that CAA's billings to Columbia were still running at an annual rate of $8 million. This was alienation? "And we've plenty of scripts without worrying about CAA," he told Allen.

"You put the making of *Ghostbusters II* in jeopardy," Allen persisted. "You're supposed to be running the studio for Fay, but he's got to handle this picture himself now—or it'll never get made. Ovitz won't deal with you. Dan Aykroyd won't deal with you. Bill Murray won't deal with you. Ivan Reitman won't deal with you—"

"Why don't you just stop at Ovitz? Doesn't that say it all?"

"No, it doesn't, David. These people have minds of their own."

"Do they? And does anybody else in Hollywood, when they'd rather believe a gossip columnist's version of the truth than a dozen lawyers'?"

"Whatever, David. The Murray remark, true or otherwise, accurately reflects your attitude. We're not dealing with puppets—we're dealing with real people, with talent, with egos."

In an effort to defuse the situation, Fay Vincent interjected, "Look, the main thing is, the project is going to go ahead."

By this time David had his second wind. "You've known all along," he addressed the board, "that what I'm mandated to do is to get Columbia back to being a sovereign state. I've always made it clear that that couldn't be a painless process."

"Fine," Herbert Allen agreed, "but have some regard for prime assets of the Coca-Cola Company, like the right to do *Ghostbusters II*. You have every right to make whatever pictures you want, but you announced your retirement in three years, so you have no right to tamper with the franchises of Columbia, which includes our library, people we want to do business with in the future, sequels, and the infrastructure of the company that will extend after your three years are up. Had you not announced your retirement, this would have been an entirely different subject."

Fay was in one of the most difficult positions he had ever been in. Of all those present, he knew as well as any that Herbert Allen was absolutely correct in his judgment. The crux of the whole affair was David's three-year declaration, which had made Fay look foolish in the eyes of Coca-Cola and had made Coca-Cola look foolish in the eyes of the film community. And the reason David had given for his announcement had only increased rather than diminished Fay's concern.

After the meeting ended in agreement, David sought Keough out. "What was that all about?" he asked.

"Oh, he's been grumbling a bit," Keough replied, "and I felt it was better for him to come out with it at a face-to-face meeting. You handled it very well, David."

Although it was not mentioned at this meeting, an intriguing rumor was now sweeping Hollywood: that David had gone to CAA's main rival, the William Morris Agency, and offered it a blanket deal. However, the ruse had blown up in David's face, the story ran; his offer was turned down flat, and the iron door of the Hollywood establishment had clanged shut. Although there was not a shred of truth in the story, it produced many a smirk of satisfaction at cocktail hours all over Hollywood. David was being squeezed out between William Morris (where Bill Cosby paid the overhead) and Mike Ovitz's CAA!

A few days later, one of David's secretaries confronted him with some unusual news. According to the grapevine, he was being "tailed." Sure enough, a black limousine seemed to be forever behind his car wherever he went. A colleague with whom he was traveling independently came out with the same thought. David grew anxious. Finally, he sought out David Picker. "If you're really worried about it, go see Lew Wasserman and ask for his advice," Picker said. "He's dealt with this sort of thing before."

The idea of consulting elder statesman Wasserman appealed to David on several levels. First, it would be as if the British godfather were consulting the senior American version. Second, Wasserman was Wasserman—who knew what might come out of the conversation. Third, despite the monklike existence

David led, every passing day further convinced him that some-one had hired a private detective to monitor his movements.

David met with Wasserman. His advice boiled down to, "Forget it. If it's true, there's nothing you can do about it; if it isn't, you're only going to drive yourself crazy." As David drew away from Universal's Black Tower, he felt let down, but he decided to follow Wasserman's advice and let it fizzle out, reckoning that in any event the "tail" would die of boredom fairly soon. And if by any chance one of the powerful enemies he had crossed was responsible—so much the better.

In May, David flew to Europe to attend the Cannes Film Festival—and made a speech there that plunged him straight into yet another storm of controversy. The occasion could scarcely have been less appropriate: it was a gala dinner to honor Sir Alec Guinness, and the Prince and Princess of Wales were in attendance. From the podium, David bemoaned the pessimism that he felt still plagued the British film industry, and he beseeched the four hundred diners "not to give up" on British films. Late that night in Cannes bars, one reporter found that criticism of his remarks was "heartfelt and loudly expressed."

Producer Don Boyd was present, flanked by his *Aria* directors. He had been annoyed months earlier by David's apparent distancing of himself from the Goldcrest debacle; now he listened with embarrassment and rage to the man who had helped reestablish him on the British film scene. "I have to say it was the most diabolically bad speech I'd heard from a public speaker in a long time," he says. "First, he hardly mentioned Alec Guinness. Then the whole attitude and atmosphere of what he had to say was patronizing. How it came over was, '*I* am the most powerful film executive in the world. What *I* have to say you have to take on board, whether you like it or not, and if you don't, you're stupid and unrealistic.' He was saying this in France, not Britain, as head of an American company—lecturing us at an international meeting about British parochialism!

"Then he announced his contribution to the British film

scene—a film Lynda Myles had developed, *To Kill a Priest*—to be made in France, with a Polish director! With a roomful of British directors sitting around, it was a ridiculous political gaffe. 'We've started casting,' he went on, 'and I'm trying to get the director to *consider* British actors.' Not a word of any direct British film investment.

"It was a rambling, ill-thought-out disaster that angered everybody there. Of the seven directors I had with me, every single one of them left *enraged.*

"Next day, however, rather in the way things are, nobody would say anything. And I thought, Fuck this, I know David well enough to let him know. I chose my moment—a round-table press conference for *Aria.* What I didn't know was that there was a reporter present and that my remarks would go around the world. I never intended that to happen. He must *so* regret that speech. He wrote a huge letter to me later explaining why he thought it was justified."

Although he admits that he has given better speeches, David says he had intended to aim many of his comments at Geoffrey Pattie, the British government's film minister in an attempt to get more funding pumped into the National Film School. (The attempt was successful.) Then he had cited *To Kill a Priest* as an example of internationalism. It is perhaps ironic in view of the Hollywood accusations that he overused British talent that at Cannes he was pilloried for its nonuse.

David's speeches had become a way of life for him and a way of elucidating his thoughts; they had also become, for observers, a reliable guide to his current state of mind. He was going through the roughest period of his entire life and felt beset on all sides. He had a suspicion that the low-key Herbert Allen assault was but the tip of the iceberg.

Unrepentantly, David underlined his views at Cannes to Iain Johnstone: "Yes, we are in danger of having what I would call 'over-the-garden-wall' movies. That's to say, movies of riveting interest to the next-door neighbors, maybe to the street, but of less than passing interest to anybody in the town. There's a smugness creeping into British films which is worrying."

He admitted all was not sweetness and light back in Los Angeles either. "I have to accept that I'm relatively unpopular there. It's the most important thing I had to come to terms with. It became clear within two weeks of starting the job last September that there were only two options—either to assimilate and be popular, or not."

Ishtar opened—and quickly closed, clobbered by incredulous reviews and complete public apàthy. The Columbia marketing campaign had been exemplary, and Warren Beatty himself had handpicked the marketing people responsible—the ones who passed the "say-Puttnam-is-a-perfect-prick-twenty-times" test. Yet he still tried to pin some of the blame for the film's failure on David. "Warren will never forgive David for bad-mouthing *Reds,*" said one marketing specialist who had been overlooked. "Never, never, *never.* And I don't see David and Dustin ever wandering off into the sunset together either—no way. David never even saw *Ishtar* and says he never will, which I think is a little stiff-assed. It's all ego. Could David have gotten involved and tried to make peace with the two of them? I guess he could have tried, but I honestly don't think he gives a shit. It's possible to live a fairly complete life without Warren or Dustin."

Fay Vincent has his own view of the distance David kept from *Ishtar.* "In some respects Warren was right," he says. "He complained that Puttnam never helped the picture, never said he liked it, never said anything good about it. In fact, he never even saw it. Beatty was very upset by that. David didn't try to hurt the picture in any way, but after it was finished and available, they were very resentful that he hadn't taken the time to see it. How could the head of the company be distributing a huge picture that he hadn't seen? Personally, I liked the movie, I liked it a lot. The problem is, you get conditioned. When a picture gets that expensive, you almost want to hate it before you see it, because it's portrayed as being this sort of bloated extravagance."

David had planned an eleven-hundred screen opening for Dan Melnick's Steve Martin and Daryl Hannah comedy, *Rox-*

anne. But after studying the results of previews held across the United States, he changed his mind. "You pays your money and you takes your choice," he said at the June 1988 première party for the movie. The number of screens had been drastically cut back to just over eight hundred. "Basically, we looked at the sneaks all last weekend. It played very strongly in all the areas we thought it would, and where they extended it outside into downtown locations, we were having our problems."

In Fay Vincent's view, the relatively lighthearted announcement about *Roxanne* covered up a major faux pas. "There were two reasons *Roxanne* lost money," he tersely explains. "First, it cost too much to produce. Second, there was substantial overspending on its marketing. Here Dan Melnick influenced David. David made a mistake. He was new at the job. When he didn't get the result from the previews he was looking for, he panicked and decided to cut back to fewer screens. It was a *terrible* mistake. Picker, who knew more about such things, was away at the time. It wouldn't have happened if Picker had been there. The cutback in screens hurt Columbia and hurt David's relations with theaters. The owners were furious at the lateness of the cutback—they went crazy."

David defends his action nonetheless. According to David, the person who most stood to be affected was Garth Drabinsky of Cineplex Odeon, yet Drabinsky was unperturbed. "I spent the weekend with him when we opened *Roxanne*. He couldn't have cared less. The research figures we got indicated we had a big-city urban film that wasn't going to work outside the big cities. We wanted to wait for word of mouth to get out. It was *unquestionably* the right thing to do, and I'd do it again tomorrow."

Yet Fay insists that real damage was done. "The telegram from Puttnam to the cutback theaters was almost amateurish, and it really hurt him. He let himself down badly in the eyes of his main customers. It was a bad episode."

The Ritchie Valens biopic *La Bamba* produced a happier result. It was released with both Spanish and English soundtracks, a sensible nod to the growing Hispanic movie market.

With grosses just above the $50 million mark, Columbia turned an extremely healthy profit on *La Bamba*. Although the movie had been left over from Guy McElwaine's regime, David had nonetheless enthusiastically supported it, reminding him as it did of his own *That'll Be the Day*.

After seeing only forty minutes of footage from Bernardo Bertolucci's *The Last Emperor*, David was immediately captivated by the film and determined to purchase it for the United States and as many other territories as were available. For producer Jeremy Thomas, the film was the fruit of four remarkable years of labor. It was the first Western production ever allowed to be filmed inside Beijing's Forbidden City.

John Daly at Hemdale had guaranteed Thomas a U.S. release for the film through a major studio. Through Daly, Thomas chose to steer the film to David at Columbia. Thomas had first met David while *Melody* was being filmed; then he had worked as an editor on *Brother, Can You Spare a Dime?* before branching into production himself. Over the years, his eclectic slate of notable movie successes ranged from Jerzy Skolimowski's *The Shout* through a Nicolas Roeg series that began with the remarkable *Bad Timing*, Julian Temple's *The Great Rock 'n' Roll Swindle*, and Nagisa Oshima's *Merry Christmas, Mr. Lawrence* (with Hara San, David's great friend from his *Melody* days, on board as executive producer).

David appeared on CBS-TV's *West 57th Street* to discuss the impact of U.S. movies abroad. (He found himself sharing airtime with his old arch-enemies, Menahem Golan and Yoram Globus of The Cannon Group.) The questions were angled toward the hostility he had encountered in Hollywood. In a departure from his brief, David gave yet another uninhibited summary of his views.

The first Goizueta had heard of David's appearance was when he switched his television on. "All of a sudden, Roberto's watching television," says Fay Vincent, "and here's David on. Nobody had told him. Roberto called me, very concerned, because he thought anytime one of our major people was going to be on national television, we should know so everyone could see it. He just stumbled on it. He was very upset with me because he thought I wasn't keeping track of what was going on. David hadn't told anybody here that he was going to be on, although he maintained he did. Six months before, we'd talked about it, he said.

"It wasn't the subject matter that bothered Roberto; it just looked again as if here he was on national television and doing something very prominent and I didn't know about it. That made me very vulnerable, because the guys in Atlanta were critical of me for not knowing what was going on in my own shop. David saw it as a nonevent, but I think that was just his failure to realize that he wasn't just David Puttnam, producer, he was David Puttnam, Coca-Cola. When you're on national television and you're Coca-Cola, a lot of things happen. They send out notices so that everybody in the company can watch. They treat it as a big deal."

"Look," David defended himself, "I'm a free agent. I've appeared on network TV so many times both here and back in Britain, I don't even think about it anymore."

"Maybe you *should* think about it," Fay countered. "I've told you before that you're not an independent producer anymore—you're working for the Coca-Cola Company."

During this period, it became clear to Fay that the difficulties with David were growing in size and dimension. A steady procession of complaints had found their way to Coca-Cola. The heat was such that Fay could no longer shrug it off. The three-year public announcement had been a terrible error (the real reason for which David had confided only to Fay). Moreover, CAA's script submissions to Columbia *had* dried up, regardless of what David said; to Coke, this meant that the cream of CAA's talent was being offered elsewhere, to its distinct disadvantage. Coke's relationship with Bill Cosby, a Coke shareholder and a valuable spokesman for the company, was in jeopardy. Although *Ishtar* had not been David's responsibility, the perception was that he could have shown more magnanimity to the principals. Hadn't he fluffed a rare chance to bury the hatchet with all concerned? And Coke had not failed to note the *Toys* debacle; for whatever reason it had slipped from their grasp, David was viewed as having been premature in his judgment that the project was Columbia's.

Then there was Stark, Raymond Otto Stark. He had had many hits in the past, but were his biggest successes behind him? Coke wondered. Damned if they were! He had taken *The Secret of My Success* from Touchstone (who had turned it down) over to Universal, and the Michael J. Fox starrer had brought in over $60 million at the box office. Could Stark *ever* be counted out?

David's appointment of Greg Coote months earlier had been specifically made to replace Patrick Williamson and to grant David access to Columbia's International Marketing and Distribution setup. In July, David was at last able to announce a revamp of Columbia's marketing with an international rather than domestic perspective. Greg Coote and Bob Dingilian were the key players in charge of the new Burbank-based Worldwide Marketing Group, which was set to become fully operational in time for Columbia's autumn 1987 release schedule. First on the list would come John Boorman's *Hope and Glory*, then Ridley Scott's *Someone to Watch Over Me*. Global campaigns were to be the order of the day, but the new concept was built on the premise that the worldwide push would not come at the expense of domestic marketing. In fact, David insisted, domestic would be enhanced by the move, although it would now be just one part of the process rather than the priority it had been before. As for Patrick Williamson, he was being sent upstairs— "promoted," in corporatespeak, to "special assistant to Francis T. Vincent."

Although it seemed that David now had what he wanted, he was still not content. The International concept had been a bone of contention for so long that even after the announcement was made, he still had the feeling that Fay Vincent was not truly behind it. Fay maintains that by then David had figured out the folly of separating international theatrical from

international video and TV. "Once he got into the job," says
Fay, "he realized he had been wrong and that you couldn't keep
the theatrical side separate. He changed his mind and recommended we keep it together, but the problem was that when
that happened, it wouldn't work for him, since he had no responsibility for video or television. He didn't like the solution,
because although it was the right answer, it was the wrong
situation—one that denied him full control. He went along
with it, though. Part of it was the need to get a different structure and different people involved. Patrick Williamson was unwilling to be in a position where he was part of Puttnam. He
had no use for Puttnam, and Puttnam had no use for him."

Fay discussed all his concerns with David. He also pointed
out that anything David put in motion during the second year
and a half of his tenure would scarcely be at the release stage
before he left. Some form of succession had to be thought of—
and quickly. "What are you going to do at the end of the three
years?" Fay asked. "Because I can't let it go on into the third
year, the way you've portrayed it. We have to solve this problem. Because if you're really going home and leaving the company, if that's what you now think, *there's no point in staying the
whole three years.* You've got to go sooner. At Christmas we
should really sit down and decide what you're going to do."

Relations between Fay and David gradually deteriorated in
their subsequent meetings, for David had begun to feel he was
walking on constantly shifting sands. For that matter, so had
Fay. Fay sensed that David was planning to resign; the feeling
was reinforced when a colleague at 711 Fifth Avenue told him,
"David really wants to leave the company. He's tired and home-
sick and really wants out."

"I wish he'd told me," was Fay's heartfelt reply. Since David
was en route to Europe, Fay's first opportunity to talk to him
was on the phone. They spent two hours on the transatlantic
line.

"If you really want to go, you only have to tell me, David, but
you can't play around," Fay told him. "But if you're going to
go, it has ramifications in financial terms. I can't pay you as if

you'd stayed. It would have to be a different economic arrangement."

Fay was well aware that from David's legal point of view, it made no sense to quit. If he did, he would wave good-bye to his $3 million golden parachute. The following night David returned from Europe, and they met in Atlanta. A lengthy discussion took place between the two. "You misunderstood me," David now told Fay. "I never had any intention of resigning." As far as Fay was concerned, two things had happened. David had talked to Tom Lewyn, who had told him that if he quit, he'd get nothing. Then David had thought more about it and had seen that his gesture would be seen as full of defeat.

"You never give me a straight answer," David told Fay. "You turn jesuitical on me, answering my every question with another question. If there's something cooking on International or anything else that I ought to know about, just tell me. I'm a good soldier, Fay. If you've got bad news, tell me what it is, and I'll deal with it. What I hate is your 'now-you-see-it, now-you-don't' act."

"Why don't you go through the issues, David," Fay suggested, "and I'll tell you the things that are really causing trouble."

"Take your pick," David replied, "Stark, Ovitz, Murray—"

"Your problem is, you just talk too much. I don't think you understand the complexity of Coke. You have misunderstood Goizueta and Keough's role. You tend to go to them [instead of me], and they keep saying to me, 'He works for you, not us. What's he coming here for?' "

Fay was becoming alarmed at the prospect of open dissension, but there was worse to come. David decided to lay on the line his disillusionment with the whole setup. "Maybe you've realized now," he said, "that I no longer feel the same way about competitiveness. Oh, I'm competitive with myself in that I want to do what I set out to do. But I don't honestly care if another studio does better than ours"—Fay's jaw dropped—"or if another film opens the same day and out-grosses us. It honestly doesn't bother me."

Fay had already reported in detail to Goizueta and Keough all of the previous conversations he had had with David, and he had set up a pre–board meeting the following morning with the Coke bosses. But now that David had changed his mind about resigning, Fay told him, "I can go on my own to Roberto and Don and bring them up to date, but it's much better if you come with me. Tell them you're unhappy. Let's get the air cleared. And Herbert will be there too."

This threw David. "Why Herbert? He's never been part of any informal meetings before."

"We feel he should be present at this one," Fay replied.

"Well, I don't think it's appropriate."

The next morning, when the meeting convened, David saw Herbert Allen's sphinxlike face.

"Fay tells me you've got a few things on your mind," Goizueta opened to David.

"I have," David replied. "I need a lot of the issues made much clearer. People seem to keep shifting their positions on certain aspects of the company, particularly International. What's said one day doesn't necessarily seem to pertain the next."

Allen shook his head wearily. "One of the problems, David, is that you want all this control, but you'll be gone in two years' time under the present terms of your contract."

"What I need most of all is the assurance of your support while I'm here," David replied.

"Support? What support?" Allen asked, suddenly finding his voice. "I *have* been supportive. And it really doesn't matter if we support you or not, just so long as you make good movies. That's all that counts, that's all you were brought here for. David, I'll be frank. I'm against a lot of what you've been doing because you're hurting this company and its assets. You have no right to leave us with bad relationships with all these important people. That's not fair, particularly when you're here such a short time. You're killing us with all these people who are against you. You're right on a lot of the issues, but these people are too powerful—you can't take them all on at the same time.

It's too many fronts, and you're not that strong. They're going to get you in the end, and you won't be able to pull that off."

Fay Vincent mentally ticked off the multitude of high-level complaints that had found their way to Atlanta. As he listened to his colleague's accusation, he knew there and then that Columbia was approaching its final curtain in its relationship with David. With every statement that David made, Fay became increasingly convinced that the man was unraveling. Even so, he was unprepared for David's next assertions.

"Hollywood is a despicable place," David said.

"If it's so despicable, why did you ask to work there?" Allen answered back.

David ignored the comment and continued, "The trouble with Hollywood is fear. Fear in Hollywood in general. Fear at Columbia in particular. It's a fearful company. People are fearful of their jobs." He looked directly at Goizueta. "Everyone at Columbia is afraid of *you*—and the Coca-Cola Company."

Goizueta's mask slipped. "That's nonsense," he snapped. "The truth is just the reverse. We are always being accused of being too kind and paternalistic. Nobody has any reason to be fearful."

"With respect, I think you're talking rubbish," Allen interjected, shaking his head furiously.

David turned to Don Keough, for whom he had developed a genuine affection. "Look, I don't want to spend the rest of my life worrying about what you, Don, think of me. We just had a conversation this morning about a misunderstanding, for I know that Fay thought I was going to resign. So I just want to say this: I hope you like what I'm doing and I hope the company is successful, but at the end of the day, I don't care whether you like *me* or not. It's not important—it's not an issue. I would become less of a man if I looked at myself in the mirror every morning and wondered whether Don Keough still likes me. That's no way to live any kind of life."

David saw the hurt in Keough's face, and he knew he had made a grave error. It was the startled expression of someone who had probably been worrying about exactly what David had just described on every single rung of the corporate ladder. If Coke had had any doubts before, they had none now.

"The meeting was a disaster," Fay summarizes. "His comment about Roberto was just bizarre. What we concluded was that *David* was afraid of him. One of the insights I took away from that meeting was that David simply has a problem with authority. He worried desperately about Roberto and Don and continually referred to them, not me; I guess he wasn't worried about me. By that point, everybody was quite negative about David. After that meeting, he really was finished."

David later maintained that he had been asked at the meeting to extend his stay to five years. ("Coke was simultaneously trying to induce him to sign a five-year contract," *Vanity Fair* reported after talking to him.) Fay refutes this. "*Nobody* asked him to stay for five years. It's not *true.* It was exactly the *reverse.* Coke's position was, he should go and how do we work that out? There may have been some *conversation* about being a producer, but certainly not about running the studio. There was no way he could stay in that job. It was *over.*" (In August 1988, David admitted, "They may not have said in so many words 'What about a five-year contract?' I'm sure they didn't.")

After the meeting, Herbert Allen apologized to David for his outburst. "Someone has to be the devil's advocate." He shrugged. The board meeting itself went without a hitch. Frank Biondi, Jr., was ribbed about rumors that he was leaving to join Viacom. After the lunch that followed, the participants went their separate ways.

At a Coke budgetary meeting in August, Biondi confirmed the Viacom rumors and resigned, amid word that the TV Operations of Coke's Entertainment Business Sector was going to be around $50 million short of its forecast—a major disappointment. Fay went off to a meeting with RCA, where an attempt was made to renegotiate Columbia's end of the joint RCA-Columbia video deal, continuing a running dialogue that had taken place for over a year.

In mid-August 1987, when Debbie Puttnam arrived with Patsy's mother to spend a couple of weeks at Coldwater Canyon, she was struck by the change in her father. At their reunions at Kingsmead Mill since he had joined Columbia, he had seemed distracted and distant. The warm, loving parent she adored had seemed gone. "What's up with Dad?" Sacha had asked the previous Christmas. "He's walking about, but he's not taking anything in." Now in Los Angeles he seemed quiet and thoughtful. While pretending to listen to Debbie's stories of home, he would switch off halfway through. He spent little time with her; during the first week, he came home once for lunch and they enjoyed an evening out together at the Bolshoi Ballet. But apart from that, it was business dinners every night. Debbie began to feel that she might as well not be there. The only saving grace was that he seemed to be not depressed—just preoccupied. The second week that changed.

David phoned Fay Vincent on August 24 and was told by his secretary that he was in Atlanta. This was a precedent—Fay had never gone to Coke's headquarters before without letting him know. On August 26, before David was due to fly to Montreal to attend a lunch in honor of Cineplex Odeon chief Garth Drabinsky, he tried to set up a meeting with Don Keough at the event. His call was not returned.

At the lunch, Keough was seated near David, and he greeted him jovially enough. "Are you free for breakfast next Thursday?" he asked. David replied that he was. "Good, Roberto and I will be in Los Angeles, and we'll see you then." Later, he departed without saying good-bye. Dick Gallop, who was seated in the middle of the room, avoided David altogether.

On the way to the airport, David had time to reflect. Goizueta and Keough normally came to town only for big occasions—a tour of the studio, the Oscar presentations. This time they were coming for *breakfast*? By the time he had arrived back to Los Angeles and was making his way to Coldwater Canyon, his mind was in a turmoil. Debbie had never seen her father look so cold, withdrawn, and utterly exhausted. As soon as he could get to a phone, he called Fay Vincent.

"What's going on, Fay? You never told me you were going to Atlanta."

"Didn't I? Well, something came up. You know, David"—Fay sounded totally demoralized—"this is a really tough business we're in, isn't it? Really tough. It's this RCA deal that kills us, really kills us—"

"Fay, what are you talking about? Something's wrong. What is it?"

"I'll tell you next week."

David phoned Fay again on the afternoon of Sunday, August 30. By that time the grapevine was buzzing with rumors.

"Fay, I've heard you're moving to Atlanta."

"It's not true."

"Then what is going on?"

"I can't say any more right now. I'm sorry, David."

Patsy watched anxiously as David put the phone down. "I've got to leave now to run Mum and Debbie to the airport," she said.

"Okay, darling. I'll come through with you to say good-bye."

Roberto Goizueta and Don Keough at Coca-Cola had placed a phone call to Victor Kaufman of Tri-Star on Saturday, August 29. Could he fly down to Atlanta for a secret weekend meeting? "Maybe they're going to fire me," he is reported to have thought. Coke's new plan was a sleight-of-hand dreamed up a year earlier. Coke would devolve its 100 percent ownership of their Entertainment Business Sector [including Columbia Pictures Industries and Coca-Cola Television] and its 37 percent ownership of Tri-Star. The first stage of this process would be to increase its 37 percent stake in Tri-Star to 80 percent and form a new entity, Columbia Pictures Entertainment. The second stage of the devolution process would be to distribute shares in the new company to shareholders as a one-time dividend and reduce Coke's holding to 49 percent. "Fizz" would thus be considerably devolved from "show-biz," Coke's balance sheet would no longer have to take the full hit on write-offs like the $25 million on *Ishtar*, and the shares in Columbia Pictures

Entertainment would be a more attractive proposition on their own, trading purely as a movie company glamor stock. Within forty-eight hours, all this—together with the results of the concurrent power-plays—would blow up in David's face.

Valerie was waiting when David got back at 3:45 P.M. to continue the day's dictation. "Are you remembering that Andrew Yule is due at four P.M.?" she asked.

"Christ, that's all I need." David sighed.

23

As a personality as well as a filmmaker, David Puttnam had always seemed an intriguing subject. Intriguing, yet daunting—and quite enigmatic.

I had conducted numerous interviews with his British associates, most of whom spoke of him with great deference. In England, he was director of a radio and TV station and knew the heads of both Channel 4 and BBC 2 television, the editors of various important daily and Sunday newspapers, and the heads of publishing houses. He was, in fact, a regular Ray Stark of his own patch.

In the months leading up to my initial meeting with David, a large number of "NFA" (not for attribution) quotes from various industry and media figures had cropped up. One had echoed Don Boyd's criticism of David's distancing himself from Goldcrest's difficulties: "Toward the end, David talked as if he was just a producer who'd been done over by James Lee. But he wasn't, he was on the board, and he can't wash his hands of that. David doesn't have that sense of corporate responsibility."

A reporter had told me, "When you meet him, you'll find that he's so incredibly open. If he feels depressed, he's going to tell you he's depressed. If you happen to be interviewing him that day, you'll get the whole story."

A director: "One of the worries that David has is, 'Why do I keep losing my directors?' Their first film with David has been their best film, then they feel they don't need this guy around. It's their mistake and David's tragedy."

A reporter: "He would like to be an intellectual, but knows he isn't one."

A colleague: "David's not emotionally sophisticated, he's not gone through an enormous amount of emotional experiences. He has a safe marriage, a very few friends, a lot of relationships. That's why his films are hollow at the center—they don't have the emotional resonance."

A scriptwriter: "Ultimately he's an advertising executive who got into the movies, one never gets away from that. If you are an advertising executive per se, you cannot be a profound film producer. Looking at David's films; it is possible to believe he's only ever read three books—*The Ovaltiney Annual of 1949*, with their games for boys and little fair isle–sweatered heroes, Vance Packard's *The Hidden Persuaders*, and Dale Carnegie's *How to Make Friends and Influence People*."

As forewarned, David did appear incredibly open, even warm—and certainly ready to talk. He looked relaxed in an open-necked short-sleeved shirt and casual cotton slacks and showed hardly any sign of the enormous strain he was under, other than an occasional tug at his pepper-and-salt beard. He also displayed a tendency to stare directly at his questioner.

There were basic points to be gotten out of the way concerning the book's construction, such as the understanding that David would have no control over the final manuscript. He demurred at length. "I believe at the end of the day [that] if anyone assesses who or what I am, it only has any value in terms of its effect on other people's lives. I'm not a director, I'm not a writer, the impact of my life is its impact on other people's lives. You know what I'm saying? I'm a conduit, and I'm very, very aware of that and perfectly proud of it, incidentally. I would like to be judged by what I've meant to others. Does Bill Forsyth regard me as someone who's important in his life? I mean that in the *best* sense. Does Alan Parker? Does Michael Apted? Does Roland Joffe? Am I someone who, by and large, has treated them fairly, behaved honorably, delivered what I said I would deliver? Not *always* possible, alas—one simply isn't always able to.

"All I would like (and I know this is going to sound horribly pretentious) is to try and set a standard of dealing and a standard of behavior rather like the standard my father tried to instill in me, in an industry which at times skates around that. That's really what it comes down to. So if the consensus from the Bills and the Alans and Ridleys is that I have, then maybe that will encourage other people to see they don't have to lie and cheat and steal and behave as if every deal is the last deal and that there is the potential for decency and consistency. It doesn't work all the time, but it does work. I'd like to think 90 percent of the time I've done what I said I'd do—and, amazing beyond belief—I've made some money, I've had a very nice life, and therefore you don't have to be a gonif to succeed."

He continued to talk, touching on many subjects. He talked at length of his parents, his childhood, and his first jobs, how he started the photographers' agency, met Sandy Lieberson, and broke into films. In only a couple of hours he had produced an intricate word-picture of his life.

He talked about Kingsmead Mill and what it meant to him, his "little piece of England," a shrine he had built in the garden for his father. "Patsy was surprised how much I took to the Mill," he said. " 'He's going to hate it, he's an urban person,' friends told her. Outside of Patsy, people who think they know me really well don't know me at all. Alan Parker was one of the most vocal, it was a wank and I was just kidding myself. I just think it's illustrative of the fact I think I'm a significantly different person from the person I maybe present myself as, or as most people think I am. Kingsmead saved my life. Columbia came at the completely wrong moment, when I was enjoying the Mill. I remember shortly before I left to come here, I was fishing and I thought 'I must be out of my mind—what on earth am I doing?' On the other hand, the three years at Columbia spelled independence and Patsy's security."

He talked about Peter Guber, his executive producer on *Midnight Express:* "We rubbed against each other all the time, didn't get on. We get on very well now. What it boils down to is, I don't like working for anybody. The differences with Peter were a matter of style—we have totally different styles."

He talked of Alan Parker at the time of *Bugsy Malone* and their differing views of U.S. success: "Alan had an obsession with *Bugsy* being successful in America. I had a huge argument with him. 'I don't give a fuck,' I said. 'If it happens to work there, that's great; if it doesn't, it doesn't.' It comes back again to ambitions. I didn't have the same obsession of cracking America as Alan had. I was far more interested in the Cannes festival and Europe, especially France, because I'd admired French movies. *Chariots of Fire* is a perfect example, not one single concession to America."

He talked of the process of making a movie, providing a glimpse of just how frustrating so much of the Columbia year must have been, removed from the actual moviemaking process he clearly thrives on, reduced to a "suit" pacing the corridors of power: "What I'm really looking for is someone who's better than me, because if I work with a director whose work I look at and think, *'I* could have done that,' then we're in all sorts of trouble. . . . I've never felt any form of frustration in that respect, that I don't direct, although I'm sometimes slightly frustrated in my writing. I'm a good editor, I think I write decent prose, but I can't write dialogue."

He talked of his discomfort with Hollywood: "I've never felt comfortable working here. It's sad, really, and I don't say that with any British chic. Mike Apted was quite right when he said that psychologically and in every other way, I'm the most inter-

FAST FADE

305

national, I'm the one who's traveled the most, I know more people than any of the others, and I'm certainly the one who's dealt with the most situations in my life—yet I'm the one who's found it hardest to assimilate. Most peculiar, I can't explain it."

Further on the subject of Hollywood: "It may come back to my concern with detail. I know there's an element in me that is unhealthily a control freak. I don't ever feel in control here, and it's not only that I don't feel it, it's that I'm *not*. No matter what you're called, chairman or producer, you're not in control here. The creative environment here denies control to anyone. There is a constant sense of turmoil, and I don't like turmoil. Some people do like it, some people are genuinely excited by the idea of change or turmoil. I'm not. I like order.

"If that was what I was working in and doing, that would be great, but the truth of the matter is that ninety percent of my time in the past year has been an attempt to restructure. I haven't spent fifteen percent of my time doing what I really have a skill for. Someone told me that what I've done here is, without knowing it, to transfer my sense of order to Columbia Pictures. He said I'd tried to make Columbia Pictures into a movie, that it *became* my movie. Right now, he said, you're still working on the rough cut. But you know, nothing—and I mean *nothing*—could give you any inkling of what I came to. It was not to be believed."

As David went on to talk with disarming frankness about the tussles with Ray Stark, Martin Ransohoff, Bill Cosby, and the *Ishtar* actors, it was impossible not to reflect on the unfolding phenomenon. I'd come to L.A. expecting to see a man one third of the way into his contract, reveling in the power that being the head of one of the five major studios brings. Instead, as David Puttnam related his story of the year at Columbia, it became apparent just how thoroughly demoralized he was, yet thankfully still prepared to talk his way through those difficult days. One of the great secrets of David's charm was being demonstrated. He was taking a total stranger fully into his confidence, as if he had divined from the first moment that here was a person he could trust. It was a heady awareness, very flattering. At the same time one had to wonder, "Why is he telling *me* all this?"

Why, in fact, had he been so open with the community from the outset, broadcasting his plans for all to hear? That was his way, he replied.

What he didn't tell the total stranger, because he hadn't fully realized it as yet, was that his reign at Columbia was effectively over. Victor Kaufman, at forty-four, was about to be installed as the new head of the entertainment colossus that Coke would create. As David flew back to New York from Atlanta, his head must have been spinning. Kaufman, the legal counsel who had hung in through the David Begelman difficulties in the 1970s, was being well rewarded by Ray Stark and Herbert Allen for his pains. He was about to step into the shoes of the man who had once declined to fire him, Francis T. "Fay" Vincent.

The next morning there was a session with Patsy, again at Coldwater Canyon. "It's the first time I've been interviewed," she told me, before proceeding to talk about her husband, his career, their life together. Listening to Patsy confirmed earlier reports that she is the fountainhead from which David draws succor, comfort, and refreshment. She had drawn the moral guidelines in their marriage and had steered her husband with infinite style and compassion through their rough patches. If David was the driver, Patsy was the navigator.

Then there was Patsy the cheerleader. Without a hint of makeup on her face, her cerulean eyes lit up and her cheeks glowed radiantly as she spoke of her husband and his achievements. Clad simply in a loose-fitting linen top and skirt, she sat opposite me in their comfortable den and reminisced of her years with David.

She spoke of their early struggles and pain: "My loss of identity was in danger of becoming permanent. We got together again just in time."

On what keeps David driven: "He wants to *show* anyone who underestimates him how wrong they are. He wants to please me and our parents more than anything else in the world. . . .

If he's going to go down in future, he vowed, it will be his doing, and not someone else's cock-up. At the same time, he realized that our failures teach us more than our successes."

On David's motivations: "It's anger—there's *always* the anger. The Cannon thing, watching as they were welcomed by people who should have known better. Warners' rejection of his little $6 million *Stars and Bars.* They should have done it anyway, even if they hated it. They owed it to him. Once again cap in hand, talking to people half his age. 'I am fucked if I'm going to do this anymore,' he told me."

On David's personal and private faces: "He's unbelievably warm, terribly affectionate. He hugs, touches, shows it. He's always been a warm, huggy person. I've always loved the warmth of David and his family. He puts on a mask for people outside, he's a *totally different* person when he's outside, when he shuts that door. He worries about how much he only basically loves a handful of people, he thinks there's something wrong with him."

On David's vindictive side: "Often what sets it off is other people getting the blame. In Ed Victor's case, he made it look as if David's secretary, Lynda, was lying. She was the one who was there, Lynda had to put up with it. From incidents like that David carries a list in his head that's ineradicable."

On the Harvard idea: "It was to do with how he felt coming off *The Killing Fields,* not the Enigma situation. He felt he had to take stock of his life."

On what attracts David to a project: "It's always the same. Some little idea that could be summed up on the back of a postage stamp. Whenever he deviates from that, there's trouble —as there was with *Agatha.* There was just no reason for that movie. We had a hell of a fight over that one."

On the Columbia deal: "I told him, 'Look, David, do you really want to look back in ten years time and with four or five more pictures under your belt and recall that you once turned down an offer to run a Hollywood studio?' That started it. Then, when he thought there was a possibility of Columbia working: 'I'm free if I do this, I really can do what I want

afterward. I could become a teacher, or whatever else I decide.'
First it's the anger, then he has to justify himself. Then there's
the trap! 'What if I really could beat the system?' "

On his first few months at Columbia: "There're so many people here prepared to lick ass and stir the pot. Every day he rang
me when he first arrived—it was terrible. 'It'll be all right,
David, you can do it,' I told him. 'It's just that you can't see the
wood for the trees.' I'd never heard him like that before. Then
that debacle with his office! Of all the things that could have
helped him, that was it. When he's got everything laid down
and organized, with every last drawing pin perfectly placed,
then he can work. He needs this perfect order before his brain
can function. If he doesn't have that, he's not at the starting
point to work. World War Three could be going on outside, but
his room has to be perfect."

On the moments of despair: "Twice we sat up and talked all
night. He wanted to go home—he wasn't just running a studio,
he was changing a studio, and it wasn't working. A sneak was
leaking stories, he never knew who. Agents were all trying to
trip him up. He was going to bed and dreaming of work. All
the cards were stacked against him. Each time we got over it,
and things ironed themselves out for another week or so before
the next upset."

On different versions of the same tale: "So many stories get
distorted here, like the *Jagged Edge* sequel. Yes, David turned
down Ransohoff's script—it was appalling! A wonderful idea,
he thought, to make a sequel, but the script was shit."

A further interview with David had been arranged for the afternoon at his Columbia office. At five o'clock, David took a call
from Fay Vincent in New York. Fay told him, "There's going
to be an announcement in *The Wall Street Journal* tomorrow
morning that'll clarify what's happening."

"No details, Fay?"

"No details, David."

That night there was a screening, followed by dinner and
more interviewing, all of it very casual, very relaxed, very in-

formal. Yet David seemed fairly preoccupied and restless throughout most of the meal. "David, what is it?" Patsy asked at one point, clearly exasperated.

"Nothing, Billy," he replied. "Well, there's a call I have to make later tonight, and generally all that's going on, I suppose."

A breakfast meeting was arranged with David for Wednesday, two days hence, followed by another interview with Patsy in the morning, then a further session with David at Columbia.

The next morning, on the front page of the business section of the *Los Angeles Times* the headline read, COKE TO COMBINE COLUMBIA, TRI-STAR, TV FILM HOLDINGS. According to the story, Coke would initially hold a majority of the combined new operation, then their stake would be reduced to 49 percent, with the balance distributed to Coke shareholders. Although no name had been selected for the combined companies, one executive gave the assurance that "the Columbia name will be in there." Fay Vincent was expected to move over to Coke's 49 percent-owned bottling operation.

That whole day at the studio, where interviews had been arranged with David's co-workers, little else was discussed. There had been not a single mention of David in the *Times* story. One could only wonder how he must be feeling, although when he appeared later that day, he looked refreshed, confident, and totally on top of his game. The man was a walking contradiction.

The Wednesday morning interview was held at a delicatessen near the studio. Other Columbia executives were seated around the restaurant, each one of them anxiously studying their copies of the daily trade papers. TRI-STAR AND COKE JOIN FORCES IN $3 BILLION COLUMBIA VENTURE, ran the headline in *The Hollywood Reporter*.

It'll be the "reel" thing for Coca-Cola's Entertainment Business Sector when Coke combines its Entertainment Business Sector (EBS) operations with Tri-Star Pictures to form the $3 billion Columbia Pictures Entertainment Inc. According to

Coke president/CEO Donald Keough, the new combined entity should be in place by January 1988, with Victor Kaufman, current chairman of Tri-Star, as its president and chief executive officer. . . .

"All production activity currently under way will continue during the transition," Keough said. "Any [future activity] will be under review. During the [expected 90-day] interim, all offices will operate via a committee composed of me, Kaufman and others."

Reaction from Hollywood and New York was swift. "It was a shock to me and a shock to people higher than me. . . . Nobody had an inkling," said one highly placed Columbia staffer when informed of the deal. Others at Tri-Star indicated they had "heard rumors" for months, but were surprised that the deal had fallen in place at this time. "I read it in the papers, like everyone else," said one.

Sources said that even the likes of Columbia Pictures chairman David Puttnam and David Picker, the company's president, had no idea that a Tri-Star deal was imminent. Puttnam could not be reached for comment at press time.

As David entered the busy restaurant, he waved toward me with his own copy of the paper. On his way over, he was stopped several times by concerned colleagues. "What's it mean?" one asked him. "No idea," David replied with a nonchalant shrug. He gave the impression of a man under pressure who was behaving superbly well. "I know as much as you do, just what I read in the papers. See you later."

He sat down opposite me and ordered an omelette, tea, and toast. He beamed at me. "Can't get a moment's peace. What's up, Andrew?"

"Nothing," I replied, "except this desperate news. They're even giving out assurances now that they'll definitely keep the Columbia name."

"We can't put anything past them," said David. "I expect I'll be hearing all about it at tomorrow's breakfast meeting at the Bel-Air with Goizueta and Keough. Look, why not spend the morning at Columbia with me now? I'll phone Patsy and tell her you'll be over this afternoon instead. You can meet quite a few people you haven't yet spoken to and get the general reaction to this. Now—when are you coming back to L.A.? If you let me know well in advance, I'll get interviews set up for you with anybody else you want to meet."

The morning at the studio was like a wake; the news had thoroughly sunk in. Everyone seemed weighted down by the dreadful uncertainty brought about by Coke's decision to remove Fay Vincent and have Victor Kaufman run the show. What about David? What about the Puttnams' future?

For all his candor, David had not let on that he and Patsy had been awakened at six-thirty the previous morning—Tuesday, September 1—by a call from Tom Lewyn in New York. Lewyn had studied the *Wall Street Journal* "leak" on Coke's plans. "This action of Coke breaches your contract," he told David. "You can walk away with your $3 million." David and Patsy had hugged each other with delight and danced around the bedroom. For them, the nightmare was over.

24

Breakfast at the Bel-Air with the Coke bosses and Fay Vincent on Thursday, September 3, was generally a low-key affair, although the visit had begun somewhat disconcertingly. David had arranged to meet Fay in his room at the Bel-Air before going down to join Goizueta and Keough for breakfast. But as soon as David parked his car—before he could cross the bridge over the Bel-Air's swan lake—one of Goizueta's assistants, whom David recognized, approached.

"You're to go straight through to breakfast, sir," David was told.

"But I've arranged to meet Mr. Vincent first."

The messenger was polite but firm. "Mr. Vincent will be making his own way, sir. It's no problem." Then he proceeded to usher David through to the breakfast meeting.

"We planned this a long time ago," David was told as the

meal proceeded. "We wanted to do it last year but missed the sixty-day regulatory period. There's no reason the move should particularly affect you, but we've given the running of the show to Victor, and you'll have to sort it out with him how you're going to work together." That Columbia and Tri-Star would be run as two separate companies was repeatedly stressed. There was no reason for any of David's staff to feel in danger, although there could be "a little rationalization in the service areas." David was told, "It's your job to make everyone feel comfortable,"

"You know what they're saying all over town?" David asked. "That Ray Stark's behind all this." Goizueta and Keough dismissed that suggestion with laughter.

Later that day, David found himself "doorstepped" by a reporter from the Los Angeles *Daily News*. The vast majority of David's staff lived in the Valley, where the *Daily News* had its widest circulation, so David proceeded to give a bullish version of their futures, along the lines of the assurances he had just received. As for himself, he claimed that Coke had given him "a massive vote of confidence," adding, "The only stress you come under is that in an environment in which people prefer to think the worst rather than the best, immediately there is a sense that the sharks start circling. In this particular instance, if the sharks are out there, they're going to be miserably disappointed over the fact there's no blood."

The reporter pointed out that David had first read of Coke's plan in the papers. David brushed it off. "I come from a noncorporate background. I am a film producer. If someone explained the Coke deal to me in detail, I wouldn't have understood it. I can now see—even *I* can see—that from Coca-Cola's point of view, it's an extremely good move. It makes absolute financial sense. It's very much my job to carry back to the staff the assurances I've been given by Goizueta and Keough. And I absolutely accept those assurances. I don't think I'm being naïve. I've known Roberto and Don for a little over a year, and they've been consistent."

The validity of Coke's assurances was questioned immediately by many in Los Angeles, especially by those who had been in the thick of it for more than a year. "It depends what David means by *consistent*, " said one reporter. "If they act consistent with their winery performance, they'd better look out at Columbia. They bought the wineries, then sold them off when they couldn't make them pay. The workers were all told, 'Go home, folks. Sleep in your beds, secure in the knowledge that your jobs are safe.' The next day when they reported for work, Coke had locked them out! Coke's paranoid about Los Angeles. It's an area where, ethnically, they should be number one, but they're not. They used to be, but Pepsi has them licked now. It used to be a big thing for graduates to get a job in Coke's big, beautiful boat-shaped L.A. plant. Not anymore."

Although David had been assured by Tom Lewyn that in principle Coke had breached his contract, no formal approach on this vital topic had yet been made to Coke. As for his staff, David was not unaware of the industry norm that large quantities of blood—not cola, not wine—invariably flow along movie executive corridors when a Hollywood chieftain exits.

David wrote a letter to Don Keough after the meeting at the Bel-Air that was a strange, confused mixture of the obsequious and the naïve: "I wanted to write and thank you, Roberto and Fay, for taking time out of what must have been a horrendously pressured week to meet with me. . . . I was delighted to be able to carry back to the studio your broadly encouraging words with respect to the future, and I doubt if I can adequately express the sense of relief they engendered among the staff." It was also unctuously humble: "Believe me, I have done my best to use yesterday's meeting, and the personal and corporate assurances you were able to give, to calm matters and alleviate fears, but frankly I have no experience in this area and I'm concerned that I'm seriously out of my depth." And it was also frankly pleading: "Please stay in touch. I specifically need your personal help in ensuring that by energetically carrying out your instructions I don't find myself endangering my personal or professional reputation."

Because of Coke's supreme arrogance in allowing David to

read of Victor Kaufman's ascendancy—and the small matter of the breaking of his contract, along with everyone else—in the newspapers, Keough may well have been a little surprised at David's piety. What had happened to the two-gun kid? David's letter went unanswered.

David quickly reached the conclusion that it would be untenable to sit out Coke's proposed ninety-day moratorium period. He indicated that by a deadline of October 12, he expected to know what his new budget allocation was to be. If it proved unsatisfactory, he would have the choice under the terms of his contract to reject the proposal. This, he said, he was reluctant to do because of his deep sense of obligation to those colleagues he had brought to Columbia and who were therefore tied to his personal fortunes.

"What obsessed me in the next two weeks," he later confided, "was how to get out elegantly, to take advantage of what had happened to get myself out as nicely as possible. I had to play a slight double game. I had to be one person at the office, while I talked to Tom Lewyn every day about the extrication process."

When Victor Kaufman noted David's new deadline, he decided to do a bit of preempting of his own. On Wednesday, September 9, 1987, in a move perfectly calculated to bring about the swiftest possible reaction, he announced the return of Patrick Williamson to run Columbia's International Marketing and Distribution setup. David rose immediately to the bait through his lawyer. "There's no point in taking six weeks for something that can be sorted out in a week," Lewyn told Kaufman, who hastened to agree. A meeting with David on Friday, September 11, was set, when David would be on his way to Toronto to address the Trade Forum at their Festival of Festivals.

According to David, the meeting opened with an almost ritual exchange of unpleasantries. First he himself harangued Kaufman about bringing Williamson back. Kaufman was all innocence, and he had a complaint of his own—that David should not have commented to the Los Angeles *Daily News* on the future of the Columbia staff. "You'd have been better saying nothing," he told him. "I was only repeating what Coke had said," David retorted, "I was only doing the job they should have done."

With these preliminaries out of the way, the nitty-gritty began. "I know you can't live with my existing contract," David claims he told Kaufman. "But I'll continue if you give me a smaller stockade with higher walls." (David says he had in mind a $23 million ceiling instead of the $30 million in his contract.)

Kaufman replied, according to David, that since the new company was about to prepare a public stock offering, it simply would not do for it to have a CEO with only eighteen months to go. The nature of David's autonomy, rather than a lower ceiling, was the other major problem. And Kaufman intended to go back to big star projects and packages. Was he trying to tell David something?

David says he then told Kaufman he would resign. He maintains he extracted a promise from him that there would be no staff changes "in the foreseeable future" and that all executives would get the opportunity "to prove their worth." David later stressed to Will Tusher at *Variety* that he believed these were not meaningless promises, since they had specifically been sought by him as a quid pro quo for what was in effect the nub of the meeting—in David's terminology, his "voluntary agreement to expeditiously remove himself from the scene." (Curiously, in David Picker's account of why David had fallen out with Ray Stark, he claimed that "Ray works on the basis of quid pro quo, but there are no quid pro quos in the world of David Puttnam.")

There was another sting in Kaufman's tail. "You won't be writing any more letters, will you?" Kaufman asked. "Don Keough was irritated that you wrote to him about his promises concerning the staff. He felt you overstated the case." This immediately deflated David. If Keough had a complaint, why was he making it through Kaufman instead of directly to him? As David got up to go, a gnawing sensation took hold in the pit of his stomach.

"Can I tell Roberto and Don you're leaving?" Kaufman asked.

"Of course."

"Fine. I really should tell Herbert Allen as well."

"I'd rather you didn't."

"Well, it would be very difficult not to—"

"If you tell him," David conceded, "you mustn't tell another soul. If you start talking to people, so will I."

In his speech at Toronto on Sunday, September 13, even with his "resignation" handed in to Kaufman, David kept up the double game. He had a "big" decision to make regarding his future at Columbia, he told his audience. "Is it fair," he agonized, "to put the studio through the same thing eighteen months from now it has just gone through?"

Wednesday, September 16, found David back in Los Angeles. A call from Tom Lewyn in New York at one-thirty confirmed that settlement negotiations were satisfactorily completed with the Coca-Cola Company—the $3 million golden parachute was fully open. Later in the afternoon, at five o'clock, word came that the story of David's departure had been leaked to *The Wall Street Journal* and would appear the following day. Infuriated by this breach of faith, David decided to announce his departure at "The Reel Truth" seminar, which was already due to take place at the studio that evening. A showing of Ridley Scott's *Someone to Watch Over Me* was lined up, together with a presentation to Frank Capra that would be accepted by his son. David had a call put through to Will Tusher at *Variety*. "If you're ever going to come, make it tonight," Tusher was told, "and hold the presses for a story."

After *Someone to Watch Over Me* was shown—about which David declared himself "unbelievably proud,"—Ridley Scott spoke for a while about the making of the film. A touching tribute to Frank Capra followed. Then David broke the news of his "resignation."

"When we originally organized tonight," he told the audience of two hundred, "I was going to give you a rather odd speech about what we'd achieved and how it wasn't nearly enough and what a lot more we had to achieve. I guess both are true. But the last few weeks have been trying, very difficult. Life's like that sometimes—it's been a bit like trying to gather yourself together after Pearl Harbor. Anyway, the upshot of all this is, there's a piece going to appear tomorrow, and I wanted to read this to you first if I may:

" 'The Entertainment Business Sector of the Coca-Cola Company announced today that David Puttnam, chairman and chief executive of Columbia Pictures, a division of the Entertainment Business Sector unit, and Victor Kaufman, chairman and chief executive of Tri-Star Pictures, Inc., have met concerning Mr. Puttnam's relationship with Columbia following the anticipated combination of the Entertainment Business Sector with Tri-Star. During that meeting, Messrs. Puttnam and Kaufman agreed that in view of the anticipated combination and Mr. Puttnam's original and irrevocable decision to vacate his post no later than the summer of 1989, it would be in the company's best interest to plan for an orderly transition now. Both men stated that in their view this approach would probably facilitate the organizations's long-term goals and allow a settled structure for the newly combined company. Accordingly, Mr. Puttnam will remain as chief executive officer until the consummation of the combination and will shortly afterward relinquish his position.' "

As David spoke and the words *relinquish his position* echoed through the small theater, the video cameras recording the event panned over the shocked, tearful faces of many in the audience.

"Well," David continued, "this is not—obviously, I hope it's not thrilling for you. I'm not delighted, but it's correct, what the statement says is absolutely accurate. I came to the conclusion at the weekend that it's not right in any way, shape, or form to put you all through three months of uncertainty while this particular situation gets sorted out, and put you through the entire thing again in sixteen or seventeen months when I go back to England. And I think it's sensible and correct—I mean obviously, I'm sick to my stomach, because one thing when I came over here I didn't reckon on was, thanks to Frank Capra and all of you, falling in love with the Columbia lady. That was never part of my plans. So it's a bad day. What is most important is this studio and that it continues into the future. For me this studio is—and it's not a joke, sadly—a bit like Poland. An awful lot of people over the years have felt they've owned it, and it continually gets knocked backward and forward and sideways by continuous invading forces. Victor has his own opportunity, a real opportunity, to stop that happening ever again. And in order to consolidate the studio and make it work and make it prosperous and make it all the things that you and I would want it to be, he needs time and a very clear run, and it's up to all of us to give him that.

"I've had the most wonderful year," David concluded. "Three months ago, I was wondering really if I'd even made the right decision, but in the last few months it's got fabulous, and Patsy and I will take home a bunchful of memories we'll never ever be able to forget or thank you enough for."

If he had not beaten Laura Landro at *The Wall Street Journal* to the punch, the world would have heard the news first from the pointed headline, COLUMBIA ASKS PUTTNAM TO LEAVE POST.

"While Hollywood is notorious for the revolving doors in its executive suites," Landro observed, "Mr. Puttnam's imminent departure marks the shortest tenure of a major studio chief in recent history. . . . Dozens of projects he put into development may never see the light of day. Moreover, numerous executives hired by Mr. Puttnam, mostly British and Australian colleagues, may lose their jobs under a new studio boss." David furiously described Landro's article as "false from top to bottom. At no point was I asked to resign—ever. It's categorically incorrect, and it's documentarily incorrect."

Victor Kaufman phoned David next day and angrily expressed his displeasure at the *Variety* leak. More important, he had a key question for David. "What's all this shit about *Poland*?" he yelled.

When David traveled to the Tokyo Film Festival in late September 1987, he was uncharacteristically quiet. ("I'm not going to say a word," was the only statement he made, "about *anything.*") One night in Tokyo, in another uncharacteristic departure, he indulged himself with Alan Parker (who was serving as a jury member at the festival) during a nighttime visit to Tokyo's red-light area, Roppongi. Both men reportedly downed fairly liberal helpings of sake. ("I've never seen him drink so much in all my life," says Alan. "He hasn't got that outlet, he's very disciplined in that area. It's always me that used to stuff the kirs down for an instant personality change.")

Before traveling back to Los Angeles, David spent a few days in London and invited his daughter Debbie and her husband Loyd Grossman along to dinner with Cineplex Odeon chief Garth Drabinsky. Debbie had dreaded the occasion, for she now thought of her father as the careworn, frazzled individual he had become during the year at Columbia. But to her surprise, he appeared totally relaxed and cheerful, pressing upon her a multitude of sweet and silly souvenirs that he had purchased on his Hong Kong stopover. No business was discussed at all at the dinner, which was a joyous, lighthearted affair. Afterward, Debbie exclaimed happily to Loyd, "Thank God, my dad's been given back to me."

When David arrived back in Los Angeles, a bug he had caught in the East manifested itself with flulike symptoms that proved impossible to shake off. The doctor diagnosed mononucleosis and recommended complete rest.

After several weeks of silence, the many admirers of Ray Stark could keep quiet no longer. Although Ray modestly denied newspaper claims that he was a "power guy," an anonymous "major studio executive" contended that David had made an enormous error in dismissing Stark as "a relic." "It was a matter of respect," he declared. "Ray wanted respect for his body of work, and David wasn't willing to give it."

"Ray was angry, not just for himself but for the community," an associate claimed. Another added that Stark had found

Puttnam "too callow" to appreciate the irony in his own pronouncements. "Ray would say, 'When I was David Puttnam's
age, I wasn't producing *The Mission* for $28 million and then
complaining that the studios let me spend the money.'"

"There had been a sense of depletion and disappointment,"
one of Stark's friends admitted, referring to the producer's
years of agonizing failures—*Sylvester, The Survivors, The Slugger's
Wife, Violets Are Blue, Amazing Grace and Chuck,* and *Brighton
Beach Memoirs.* "But to come back like this is really amazing."
Apart from the $65 million grosser *The Secret of My Success,* Stark
had enjoyed two small hits with Tri-Star during the year, *Peggy
Sue Got Married* and *Nothing in Common.* "I told Ray at one point,
'You have had the ultimate revenge. You've done three pictures
away from Columbia, and they've all been hits. Why don't you
relax?"

"I adore Ray," said fellow septuagenarian David Brown (of
the Zanuck-Brown *Jaws-Sting-Cocoon* team). "He's been through
all the onerous things that all of us endure. Presenting projects
to people of one third our age and one eighth our experience.
But he's never been defeated. He's never become cynical." (If
he hasn't, his associates have. When Don Safran, Stark's assistant, was told that a Puttnam biography was in the works, the
sarcasm of his response was thick. "Are you sure there's enough
in Puttnam for a whole book?" he sneered.)

Victor Kaufman—who was said to be already struggling to
keep up with Ray's constant phone calls—took time off to deliver his encomium. "Ray has always been a great adviser to
me," he asserted. "I've talked with him as a friend, and he's
taught me a lot about people."

Coca-Cola chose this point to reveal that Stark had been quietly under contract as a consultant to Columbia for the last five
years, but it fervently denied that Stark had carried out any
maneuvering behind the scenes to effect anyone's removal. "It
is really off the wall," said a spokesman, "for anyone to tell you
that Ray Stark or anyone else in Hollywood had anything to do
with Fay Vincent's change of assignment." How about David
Puttnam's removal? There was no comment on this from Coke.

Despite his illness, David agreed to be further interviewed in October, again at the Coldwater Canyon house. He made a temporary recovery, then the illness struck again. His doctor warned him that this could be the pattern until the virus burned itself out and that undue strain would only serve to shorten the time between the attacks and make them more acute. He looked wasted with fatigue.

One night, David talked at length about his plans for the immediate future. He was to spend the months ahead, until April 1988, in Los Angeles, overseeing the release of the movies made so far. Then, most likely, he would return to independent production, and he looked forward to "knocking the spots off my competitors." He ruminated about the role of a producer: "Someone in France decided film was a director's medium." A shrug. "And with the gleeful participation of directors, the press swallowed it. This puts me in a difficult position vis-à-vis me and Roland and Alan. It'll be a real problem for Roland if his next film doesn't work on his own, which is what happened with Alan. Alan's obsession with working with me would be to do a film that would be the biggest hit since he's had with *Midnight Express.* He'd really be fucked, because people would say he's fine when he's working with Puttnam. And that would really kill him."

When the subject got around to the delicate matter of his demise at Columbia, the mood grew darker. He mused, "Maybe what divides me from the likes of Ray Stark is my being prepared to be judged by history and his not being prepared for this. . . . Maybe that's an area that divides people, one of the great dividing lines. Because I've always been, rightly or wrongly—maybe wrongly—totally comfortable with the idea that in the long run, when my contributions are added up and assessed, I'll come out looking good, or certainly on the right side. I've been absolutely confident about that always, whereas someone like Stark—he needs to have these little day-to-day victories."

The next day it was Alan Parker's turn to talk about David,

which he was more than willing to do. "What do you like best about me?" he had once asked his friend. "Your devastating honesty," David had replied.

"He's my best buddy," Alan said now. "We phone each other pretty well every day. I'm like a nagging mother—if he doesn't phone, I get irritable. In the end, what I like doing with him most is laughing and slagging each other off, not taking ourselves seriously. In the latter years he's done that far too much. All I ever did was try to redress the balance, because I do think we're a couple of lucky yobbos, him from Southgate and me from Islington. We've had this fantastic privilege, this wonderful opportunity to make movies. What we say we should say with our films, up there on the screen.

"*That's* what David should have done, but in order to justify why he was doing the Columbia job, he had to turn it into a crusade—it was the only way he could get that little extra dignity out of doing it. Then he made the mistake of conducting the debate in the press. And when he's doing an interview, he's so zealous about what he believes in, he's no longer talking to a journalist but someone who has to be convinced. The problem is that you're not talking to one person, you're talking to the thousands of people who are going to read it. He could never make that differentiation.

"I can't imagine why David would want to take Ray Stark on at the beginning. In the early days, Ray always admired David —he said he was one of the only producers he ever had any time for. And in a way I think David quite admired Ray and what he stood for, as a very powerful producer of the old school, a very powerful man. The housekeeping clear-out was to get rid of a whole lot of people who shouldn't have been there but not Ray. He might have had the most expensive deal, but it turned out to be a very costly error. It'll take a while before David acknowledges that in the tactical way he went about achieving his aims, what happened to him was his own fault."

The next day, Hugh Hudson was equally forthcoming as he gave his side of the *Chariots of Fire* and *Greystoke* controversies. His affection for David was obvious despite his criticisms. He saw a parallel between recent developments and his being left holding the *Greystoke* baby.

"He's done it again," Hugh said, "walking out of Columbia. You could argue that he's left a lot of people in the lurch. A lot of people who brought their films to him—you could argue, now they'll never get made. Because *he* feels uncomfortable, because *he's* not prepared to go on, that's fine for *him*. But what about all the other people he's left in a very uncomfortable position? And David's making a tremendous amount of money. He hasn't sacrificed the money by leaving, but all those people who had their hopes pinned on him have been sacrificed. He hung himself by not being the diplomat he was as a producer, by being arrogant and self-righteous. In a way, he came here hating it, he came for all the wrong reasons. He came to take revenge and make a pile of money. Money had never been his motivation in the past, only power. He wishes he could direct films. The memory of his father drives him forward. He considers his father was an artist and wishes he could be one. But he likes power and control and now he needs money. So that's become part of the equation, and it sits badly with him.

" 'The gardener gets more pleasure from the Mill than I do,' he's said. You could say that subconsciously he engineered his demise without sacrificing the bread—because he's a real fastfooter. The things I say may sound harsh, but I'm trying to be the devil's advocate. There will be many others who won't have this voice through you and will be feeling hard done by, who would cast a very harsh judgment on him for leaving after a year.

"Why immediately upset Ray Stark, a man who's been making movies here for thirty years? It was completely self-destructive to do that, immediately inflammatory. So who gives diddly-shit? But he understands that the people he's brought to Columbia have value, and he brought their dreams to fruition, then allowed them to evaporate for his own amour propre. He talked too much. If you want to eat at the table again, you mustn't criticize the food unless you're the chef. You've got to own the restaurant to criticize the food, and nowadays nobody owns the store, only corporations. He was only another puppet, but he thought he wasn't. Vanity, vanity—all is vanity. It brings everybody down in the end.

"Nevertheless, I'm fond of him, and we're speaking again. I rang him up two days before he left Columbia and said, 'This is ridiculous, we must get together.' We met for lunch. There's an umbilical cord between the two of us. We're discussing the possibility of getting together on a film that's got a lot of special effects in it, like the ones he claimed put him off doing *Greystoke.* Of course you *have* to change, otherwise you're fucked."

25

The air of enthusiasm and camaraderie was gone from Columbia's staff. Most expressed anger and hurt at David's departure. Several offered what they called the "inside story" of the events, but these were wildly conflicting. Did Ray Stark and Herbert Allen have anything to do with it? "Absolutely not, that's a ridiculous suggestion." "Of course they did. These guys are so incredibly powerful." Equally conflicting were the staff's views on their boss's conduct, together with a hefty sideswipe at their new boss.

- "You won't find one person in this building with a word to say against him."
- "David was a minnow who thought he was a piranha."
- "David should have taken the cotton wool out of our ears and stuffed it in his mouth. He should have listened first instead of sounding off."

• "It's a damned shame. He had just gotten started. We were all rooting for him. Victor has perpetuated the myth of Tri-Star being successful. They've never had a real hit since they were founded except for *Rambo,* and they only acted as distributors for Carolco. If you count that as a credit, the fact that Victor picked it up—and it *was* enormously successful—you should also bear in mind the many, many disastrous pickups, like *Lifeforce* from Cannon, *Supergirl* and *Santa Claus* from the Salkinds. These films represented millions down the tubes. And *this* is the guy who's come out on top?"

Jim Clark, who had joined David from London as a kind of "project fixer," was looking forward to going home. "It started off more interesting than it ended up," he said. "The Cosby movie? I've spent a great deal of time on it, to very little avail. That aspect of the job, which I was aware of when I took it, I didn't particularly enjoy. I kept saying I'd rather make my own mess than clear up someone else's."

Despite the somewhat disappointing year he had gone through at Columbia, Jim saw the effect that David had had on the personnel there. "They respected him enormously," he says. "He really inspired people. It was the side of David that is a crusader that got him into trouble with the establishment. He wanted to change the nature of things, and there are so many people here who, in a sense quite rightly, were offended by a foreigner, an Englishman, coming over and telling them how to run their business. That side of David—his zealous, crusading side—does occasionally get the better of him and makes him say or do things that are probably better left unsaid. However, among the people who worked here, when he resigned, I've never seen a greater display of public emotion."

Fred Bernstein, David's worldwide head of production, was likewise quite reflective regarding his boss. "I would have to guess this has been the worst year of his life. He is the most opinionated man I've ever met; he is also the most self-assured man in his right to be wrong in his opinion. I really think he doesn't care. Most of us are very cautious about rendering our opinions, because invariably our opinions are a reflection of ourselves. David doesn't care, right or wrong. He puts himself on the line every day, and it staggers people."

How did he feel about David's public pronouncements? "There were a couple of times I winced," he admitted. "I would have done it differently, but you've got to look at the whole record. David Puttnam never got anywhere biting his tongue. He truly believed there is a malaise in this industry, and he wasn't going to play the game. Could he have played the game and lasted longer? Maybe. That might not have been true to his own spirit. I think David made a fatal mistake, and it wasn't that he talked too much—that's David. The mistake was to take the management of the Coca-Cola Company at total face value. 'You do it, we'll back you up.' He didn't expect them to kowtow to the Hollywood pressures, and obviously they did. I don't believe the Coke transaction is anything to do with David Puttnam—it had to do with a big ball of wax. David was a detail. They wanted to do this transaction and David became a problem and they simply decided they couldn't have the two guys. Victor wants it, and David was leaving anyway."

Everyone also had a frank opinion about the films produced so far during David's tenure. *Little Nikita* and *Leonard Part VI,* even at this stage, were acknowledged disasters. *Pulse* was David Picker's utter folly—an idiotic, laughable horror film. Spike Lee should never have been handed $6 million for *School Daze. Zelly and Me* drew either blank stares or the comment, "a home movie." *Punchline?* Good movie, great performances by Sally Field and Tom Hanks, but could be a difficult sell. Oscar nominations for *Punchline?* Maybe next year, not this year. *The Beast?* Good B war film in the Sam Fuller mold. *Someone to Watch Over Me?* Should have been better. *Housekeeping?* Brilliant, but totally uncommercial. *Vibes?* Still a faint chance of being a good summer picture. *Stars and Bars?* Misfire, not funny. *Hope and Glory?* Quality film, tough sell, might just make it in the end. *The Last Emperor?* Dazzling, an unknown quantity commercially. Was there pride in the product? Yes, still, for the most part, but an element of realism was creeping in that had been absent before.

Since David announced his departure, several names had been mooted as his likely successor, notably Frank Price. Price was now an independent since his release from Universal following the summer 1986 disaster of *Howard the Duck*. (Why is it that movie bosses are remembered only for their failures and the hits that get away? Price had a major hit with *Out of Africa* in the same Universal season. At Columbia he was responsible for the brilliant *Tootsie* and the hugely successful *Ghostbusters*. But he'll always be chiefly regarded as the guy who wouldn't take *E.T.*'s calls at Columbia.)

On Wednesday, October 28, 1987, the uncertainty over David's successor ended with *Hollywood Reporter*'s headline, NEW DAY DAWNS AT COLUMBIA. David's post of chairman of the studio was being eliminated. Taking his place, but on a somewhat lower rung, as president, was Dawn Steel, the current production president at Paramount Pictures. "This is a job of a lifetime," said Steel. "This is the head of a studio. How could I turn it down? The fact of the matter is, they made me an offer I couldn't refuse." (The other fact of the matter was that Paramount executives could now get relief from exposure to Steel's well-known temper.) Also announced was David Picker's return to independent production in New York, producing for Columbia, and serving as a "consultant" to Victor Kaufman.

Before my departure from L.A., David had me given a copy of the "Truth" video at which he had told the Columbia staff of his leaving. Even at that first viewing, I had been struck by a false note that seemed to permeate the proceedings. At the time, I couldn't put my finger on what it was.

The roll-out of David's movie slate reminded the industry that this was the first time ever a studio head had left before a single film of his had been released. True, Marty Ransohoff's *The Big Town*, to which David had contributed the director, had brought in less than $2 million at the box office against a $17 million cost, but no one seriously claimed it was part of David's output. He says he was chary about releasing *Someone to Watch Over Me* only a few short weeks after Paramount's *Fatal Attraction* had hit the market, but he allowed his judgment to be overruled by his marketing people. Many felt the film was a nonstarter in any case, described by one critic as "gorgeous-looking, but dull and empty." Ridley Scott's "Give me a disco and I'll give you *Dante's Inferno*" style of directing had once again prevailed over pacing, character, motivation, and plot. At a cost of almost $17 million to Columbia, the movie faltered at $10 million box-office gross, a net return to the studio from the U.S. theatrical release of around $4 million.

Regrettably, Bill Forsyth's beautiful *Housekeeping* was next to take a box-office tumble, grossing a meager $1 million plus on a budget of $6.5 million. Despite its dazzling reviews (one critic described it as "as close to perfection as it is possible to get"), exquisite delicacy of touch seemed not enough to fan the film out to a wide audience.

All eyes were on Tri-Star as it released its father-son role-reversal saga, *Like Father, Like Son*, while Brian Gilbert was still knee deep in postproduction on *Vice Versa* at Columbia. The critical reaction to the effort Kaufman rushed through was terrible. *Variety* described *Like Father, Like Son* as a "messy, repetitive role reversal comedy . . . strictly sit com stuff . . . sloppy directing and choppy editing." One week later, the film took in over $7 million at the box office in its first weekend and went on to gross a very respectable $35 million total. The old Hollywood adage, "Do you want it quick, or do you want it good?" had once more been stood on its head.

The first bright ray of hope on both the critical and the commercial horizons for Columbia was John Boorman's *Hope and Glory*. The film had a tremendous amount going for it, and the slow roll-out Columbia gave the film was generally seen as appropriate, allowing as it did for good word of mouth to get around.

The second ray of hope was provided by David's other pickup. *Variety* previewed Jeremy Thomas's production of Bernardo Bertolucci's *The Last Emperor* as "a film of unique, quite unsurpassed visual splendor." It paid special tribute to producer Jeremy Thomas for the "enormous, impressive job he pulled off . . . in organizing such an ambitious production . . . without up-front involvement of any major studio." The film went on to open to hugely enthusiastic reviews and brisk business. By Christmas 1987, it was playing at ninety-two theaters and taking in $1 million a week. As for *Hope and Glory*, the plan was to go wider when the Oscar nominations were announced.

All the postproduction resources at Columbia's command were poured into making *Leonard VI* work. Choruses of frogs croaked on cue, lobsters leaped, turkeys trotted, and fish flew as Paul Weiland anxiously assembled the first cut of the film back in London. When Bill Cosby heard that David Picker was flying over for a viewing, he banned him from seeing the film; under Cosby's contract, no Columbia executive was allowed to preempt his first viewing. He was so pleased after seeing it that he insisted on a third credit. As well as "producer" and "star," he now claimed "original story." "It will take in a hundred million dollars," he told a punch-drunk Paul Weiland. Cosby relayed the same message to Fay Vincent in New York and to Don Keough in Atlanta. But as far as Paul was concerned, the film had no heart, no soul, and an unsympathetic star.

Two audience previews of *Leonard Part VI* were held, neither of which Cosby attended. After the first one went badly, doubts and not a little panic began to spread. Why wasn't Cosby funny? Editor Gerry Hambling was blamed: He'd cut away too fast from Cosby. ("We did that to get off him because he wasn't funny," says Paul.) "You should let the camera linger on him, let him wait for the laugh like he does on TV, let him burn," Hamblin was told. Hamblin dutifully reassembled every scene, then a new preview was set for San Bernardino. "David hugged me, put his arm around me after this," says Paul, "in commiseration. I was broken. The audience *hated* it, you could feel the hatred. Jesus Christ, a rainbow trout got a bigger laugh than the great God Cosby!"

There may have been despondency among Columbia production executives about the film, but the marketing people set about promoting it as if they were in another dimension—one in which only hit movies exist. Integrally built into *Leonard* were crateloads of onscreen Coke, together with other "product placements" like Porsche cars. "This is a whole new ball of wax," a marketing head enthused. "We devised a couple of premium items and placed them in the film, products you can get only with the purchase of Coca-Cola. Seven or eight characters from the film will appear on collectible badges, T-shirts, and mugs. A Porsche was featured, so apart from in-store displays, we plan to give away some Porsches as well." Hollywood's ever-tenuous hold on reality seemed to have snapped completely. In the jargon of adspeak, "some Porsches" will forever be immortalized—as will the "synergistic" *Leonard*-Coke advertising campaign on which the company was estimated to be blowing upward of $15 to $20 million. Marcio Moreira of Mc-Cann-Ericson Worldwide, the agency responsible for handling the blitz, declared the strategy had "created new energy and excitement in the studio." Sure—and record billings too! If the final figures were to be believed, Columbia and Coke between them had more than $40 million wrapped up in *Leonard Part VI.*

The film was due to open in December. But after studying the results of the two previews and listening to his wife's advice, Cosby had a change of mind regarding the film's prospects. His wife hated it. Even after a final panic-induced recut by Jim Clark, the film was clearly going nowhere. On the eve of the movie's opening, Cosby decided to disown the project and flush Coke's advertising campaign down the drain—Porsches, placements, and all. One night, viewers of Larry King's TV talk show were startled to hear Cosby say, "It took an awful lot, Larry, to come on this show and say to people, 'Look, I don't know if this product is good enough.'" Humble pie? Not a bit of it. "It's not my picture," he hastily added—despite the fact that his name was in the credits three times over.

"Puttnam asked for the director," he enlarged later. "Puttnam asked for the line producer, who then went on and hired people. Puttnam calls me and says, 'Listen, you're a partner on this,' and I find I'm not really a partner, man. I think part of the problem was that these people came from England and in a way were saying, 'We understand he's very big in America, but we have to have our control.' "

Variety wrote, "Perhaps no studio deserves two *Ishtars* in a single year, but Columbia has turned the trick, with *Leonard Part VI* opening as its Christmas release. Bill Cosby is right to be embarrassed by this dud, but the result can't have come as a total surprise to him, since he wrote the story and produced it."

Public reaction supported this view. Seven days later, 1,142 theaters reported a rock-bottom $1,153 average for the opening weekend. (For the record, *Ishtar* opened at the same number of theaters and took in a $3,803 average—and *that* was considered a disaster.) The total U.S. take came to less than $5 million.

Yet Paul Weiland's recollection of Cosby is far from totally negative, for the relationship between the two had survived all the vicissitudes on the film. "Bill's a big baby," Paul maintains, "who needs to be cuddled and mothered. And he's got all the normal hang-ups, although in his case they're *billionized* because of the enormous power he wields. He's got a huge ego and is paranoid about two main items: Eddie Murphy—and critics. The reviews must have crucified him."

Paul felt seduced and abandoned by David and Alan Marshall, in a sense the sacrificial goat. "I'd been drawn into making a *product,*" he said, groaning, "not a movie. Christ, I make product commercials all the time. The last thing I needed was a megabudget product. What I could have used for a first Hollywood film was something smaller, controllable, and if it had bombed, it would have been my fault. Instead, I was made caretaker over a fucking disaster. The ship was going down, and there was little me, trying to plug up this hole. It must be the biggest first film any director's ever been given. 'Are you sure this is right, David?' I kept asking him. Even Alan Parker told me, 'Take it, Paul—you can't fail.' In the end I believed them. I should have followed my own judgment instead. Puttnam and Marshall certainly should have known better. It would have helped if just one of them had said it was dreadful.

"Am I angry with David Puttnam? To a degree. He gets people wrong. His character assessments are sometimes way off. Nathanson's friendship suddenly cooled when the shit hit the fan. 'You've done a brilliant job no matter what happens with the movie,' David told me after the first preview. 'You're making me look smart,' he wrote to me later. But then his associates withdrew all their support and left me on my own.

"I'd like to work with him again on a one-to-one basis—that would be brilliant. To sit down with him and go through ideas, to be his friend, like Roland and all the others must have done— that would be great. But to have him as an executive, was a total —I mean, it wasn't working with David Puttnam. He's a very honorable man, and on the other hand, he's not so honorable. He's a bit of an enigma."

When Cosby announced in a huff that his next film would be made at Warners, one Columbia executive dryly commented, "Don't dress for it."

One night in November 1987, a bizarre encounter took place in Giardino's Restaurant on Third Street, west of Doheny in Beverly Hills. David and Patsy had arranged to meet Columbia's business affairs executive, Lyndsey Posner, there for dinner. Lyndsey arrived first and found that their table was close to another occupied by Ray Stark and Barry Diller. She had arranged for a diplomatic change by the time David and Patsy arrived.

When the threesome were halfway through their meal, Stark and Diller got up, passed their table in silence, and left the restaurant. A moment later David, Patsy, and Lyndsey were treated to the spectacle of Ray Stark squinting through the glass doors at them. When he saw he had been spotted, the indomitable Ray was not to be defeated. He promptly reentered the dining room and strode up to address two men seated at a table next to the group. The two looked totally perplexed; they obviously knew who Stark was but appeared to have no idea just why they were being so honored. After a few minutes of this charade, Stark turned from their table.

"Oh, David," he said, laughing, "I nearly walked straight past you."

"Yes, Ray," David replied quietly, without looking up. "And that's how I want it to be. Let's leave it that way, shall we?"

Stark scowled, thoroughly discomfited. This wasn't the line he'd expected. "Yes, but"—he stammered—"I wanted to let you know I'd walked past you and didn't acknowledge you. I did it deliberately!"

It was Lyndsey's turn. "We know, Ray," she cooed, "but you had to come back and tell us, didn't you?"

He glared at her for a moment, then at David and Patsy, the veins on his forehead pulsing. Where, oh where, was Neil Simon with that perfect exit line? Stark was left to stumble toward the door, having shot himself neatly in both feet.

"We can't believe it," said the two men he'd been addressing. "We've never actually spoken to Mr. Stark before."

"You're lucky," said David, smiling at his companions.

After that first reassuring phone call from Tom Lewyn in September, when David and Patsy had gone into their little dance of joy, fears regarding the fate of the executive team at Columbia were banished, if only for a few carefree seconds. In early December, Coke's assurances and later promises that David thought he had extracted from Victor Kaufman were still ringing in his ears, despite the departures of David Picker and later Greg Coote. David and Patsy had consulted a psychic specializing in "astral plane" projection just a week earlier. When the seer predicted a dreadful time ahead, David and Patsy thought the seer must be a little late with the news. Surely they had already been through the worst?

Then the wholesale slaughter began. AXE FALLS AT COLUMBIA PICTURES, ran *Variety*'s headline for December 9, 1987, and it went on to list a "massive first wave of anticipated firings. . . . Columbia reverberated with shock and apprehension over the wholesale payroll lopping. . . . Executive suites from one corridor to another were swept out. . . . Despite the claim that Columbia is divesting itself of 'superfluous employees' there was no doubt that almost all personnel fingerprints left by Puttnam are being—or appear to be being—systematically erased."

Two days later, *The Hollywood Reporter* noted, "Another round of firings at Columbia Pictures resulted in a clean sweep of the studio's creative production staff both in New York and London. The terminations, which come on the heels of ongoing firings at both headquarters in Burbank, signal the virtual disbandment of production operations."

A week later, *Variety* provided an update, revealing that as many as five hundred of the new Columbia Pictures Entertainment's thirty-five hundred employees were being dismissed in a restructuring aimed to reduce overhead costs by $40 million annually. The key expression used for the cutback was *to the bone*—in total and painful contrast to Goizueta and Keough's "little rationalization" in the service areas.

The bloodbath at least ended the uncertainty for the many of the Columbia personnel who had either been recruited by David or judged favorably by Victor Kaufman. Kaufman had proved himself a master of timing. Merry Christmas, folks!

In the same week as this slaughter of the innocents, Ray Stark had a cheerier Christmas message: a $236 million slate of eighteen features was ready to roll, of which ten so far were either at Columbia or at Tri-Star. *Annie II* was going ahead. *Revenge* was with New World at a budget of $12 million (this was later boosted to $20 million and turned into a co-production with Columbia). *Sweet Libby* was being made for Home Box Office. Stark's president of production, Doreen Bergeson, was in an ebullient mood on the rapport the company had regained with Columbia. "I think we'll put about eight projects into development with them," she trumpeted, "starting right away. We're going to be doing a lot of business with Columbia." Right *on*, Ray!

In the movie *Broadcast News*, William Hurt plays a newscaster who at one point interviews a rape victim on film. Toward the end of the filmed interview appears a close-up of Hurt brushing a stray tear from his cheek. Later, it is discovered that the news-caster had the tear-stained reaction filmed separately after the interview, then spliced in for maximum emotional voltage. If life imitates art, this parallels what David perpetrated on his "Reel Truth" audience with his "resignation" speech. The parallel exists in more ways than one, for instead of planting the tear on his own cheek—he was totally in control—he planted it on the cheeks of his audience and captured their emotional reaction for posterity with a bank of zooming, panning cameras.

Although David modestly claims that as a producer he can neither write a good enough script nor direct a movie, here he was doing both with a supporting cast of two hundred. He pressed every single patently loaded emotional button (he "fell in love with the Columbia lady" . . . "the most wonderful year" . . . "it's got fabulous" . . . "bunch of memories"). Indeed, why couldn't he just have told them the truth—that he was going back to England with $3 million in cash and Coke shares and leaving them to Victor Kaufman's tender mercies—and that, yes, if it hadn't been for his posturing they would still be reporting to him. But maybe then his audience would have loved him less.

Of course David was going through a dreadful time—of this there was no dispute, whether or not he had brought it upon himself. He needed the approbation of his Columbia colleagues and the wave of emotion and love that washed over and soothed him. And if the price was a manipulative tug on the heart-strings, what of it? David wanted the best of all possible worlds, the cash *and* the kudos. Cry for me, Columbia—on cue and on video.

When *The Sunday Times* of London published its 1987 year-end list of "Risers and Fallers," David had close connections with everyone in the Hollywood section. One Riser was Ridley Scott's brother Tony, who had directed two of the biggest hits of the year, *Top Gun* and *Beverly Hills Cop II*. David had begged Tony not to undertake the *Cop* sequel, arguing that one sellout was enough. The second Riser was Adrian Lyne, with whom

David had fallen out after *Foxes* back in the 1970s. The *Times* described Lyne as "Hollywood's hottest director" after the phenomenon of *Fatal Attraction*.

In the "Fallers" section were the "Go-Go boys," Menahem Golan and Yoram Globus of The Cannon Group, rescued, according to the *Times*, "by a Madrid property company to avoid bankruptcy." And to prove that fate makes strange bedfellows, the other occupant of the "Fallers" list was David Terence Puttnam himself.

26

Which had come first—the Coke plan, or the decision that David was leaving? "The thought process was that David was going to go," Fay Vincent recalls. "The first issue was, what does Coke do with its entertainment operations? You either have to put more money in, or you have to stay where you are, or get out. My argument was that to get into the 1990s you're going to have to make a much bigger investment. That didn't seem to be very attractive to the people in Atlanta, because they have a huge soft-drink business and to build entertainment to where it's competitive with soft drink wasn't in the cards. So the first judgment had nothing to do with David. It was time to get Coke's entertainment division in a different position.

"Point two was what we did about it, and I came up with the scheme to spin off half the business to Coke's shareholders and get Columbia into a position where it was not a wholly owned division of Coke and they'd get back all the money they'd invested in it. Financially, it turned out to be a very good deal, but David *could* have stayed on to run Columbia through all that.

"The coincidence was that while Coke was making these strategic moves, David's problems were also coming to a head. So having decided we were going to put all of entertainment together and have Victor be the chief executive, then the question of David became very clear. . . .

"Ray, I'm sure, was out trying to do Puttnam in very early on, but he couldn't have done it if Puttnam hadn't cooperated so well, because Ray went after a lot of things around here over the years without success. Puttnam just made it easy for him by giving him so much ammunition."

Patsy and David went to Thailand on vacation, and then a spell on safari in South Africa. Back in Hollywood, Patsy appeared to be enjoying life, despite the outcome of the fight. Now she could see where their trust had been misplaced. Surprisingly, it was not the big stars or agents that drew her fire but the creative community.

"They used everything to trip David up," she says. "Take the Edith Wharton stories. I'd been at him for years, saying they'd make wonderful films. I kept banging on about them. At the right price, I felt, they could be extraordinary for the *Room with a View* market. So here's an example of how David wanted to try and build the studio up. He went to Tina Rathborne, after supporting *Zelly and Me*; how would she feel about tackling an Edith Wharton story? She knew and loved *Age of Innocence*, as it turned out. Meantime, Lyndsey Posner had been working for three months to get the rights to the books through an agent that David knows. When David was out of town in Atlanta— for *one* day—the agent phoned Columbia. He had to have David's offer *that day* or the rights were going elsewhere. David Picker didn't know what it was all about—he hadn't been told —and Lyndsey was away, so we missed the deadline. Who got the rights? Martin Scorsese. . . . Nobody had even *heard* of Edith Wharton until then. David said he'd never speak to that agent again. And do you want to know what's funny? Scorsese in the end let the rights go! It was about the same as the *Toys* saga, which I've just heard is no longer going ahead at Fox— another perfect example. As soon as David showed interest, they wanted it. Creative community? There's no creative community.

"Greg Nava, who'd made only *El Norte* before, made *Destiny* for us. God, you should have heard him—'David did this for me, David did that for me.' $800,000 he got for *Destiny*. When David asked him what he wanted to do next, oh, he was off elsewhere—for $1.1 million. For $300,000 he went with someone else! And he's already gotten screwed! There's just so much greed, you can't build anything. Someone who owes everything to you—they'll sell out for $300,000. Fuck them—they're not worth it. It's *impossible* to deal with that. David wanted to nurture people, do it from within, but you can't do it with that society. They say nobody supports them, but nobody supports them because they don't give any loyalty. . . .

"Looking back, it's wonderful," she continues. "Now that all the rage, the cynicism, the betrayal is over, it's wonderful. I can now look and say, he did it for a year, a year and a half. He's come away with all his money in a year and a bit instead of three years. 'We're a year and a half ahead,' he told me. 'Now we can get on with whatever we want to do.' It's the first time he's shown that cynicism; he's never had it before. And the enjoyment of Thailand, on holiday, *free* from Columbia! We've been on holiday before, but it wasn't as sweet as a *paid* holiday. It was another way of saying, 'You didn't *really* get me! I came out ahead!' Because he needs to feel that, however disappointed he was. Jim Clark told him he'd never have survived through three years at the rate he was going, burning himself out. He would have had a heart attack, never mind mononucleosis. So he has to weigh one year's satisfaction against three. And Goizueta and Keough are already working hard to mend the bridges. David's not someone they don't want to get on with.

"Yes, he's got decisions to make. The role of executive producer—that's not open to him. It doesn't work for him. If he's
going to stay in the film industry, he'll either have to line-pro-
duce or set up his own mini-Columbia. I used to fantasize that
when David was finished at Columbia, his relationship with
them would be so good, they'd say, 'Whatever he wants to do,
we'll follow him'—like going back to Europe and opening a
European filmmaking studio with their money."

The irony of Patsy's last remark struck a bleak chord, for
wasn't that one of the things Fay Vincent had had in mind from
the beginning?

Many people, of course, had opinions on why David Puttnam
failed; some were less generous than others. Agent Marion Rosenberg had kind words for the manner in which David had
handled a problem with one of her clients, Daryl Hannah.
"One of the things David did wrong, though, was serious," she
added. "He knocked this town, and he shouldn't have. He
seemed to have just no sense of tactics—everyone was astonished. A lot of support he had at the beginning quickly cooled.
The consensus is that if David had just done his job, he could
have *owned* the place."

Another friend had reservations about David's choice of executives at Columbia. "None of them came from the mainstream
pool that moves sideways and occasionally marginally up and
down—'Get me so-and-so on the phone, where is he now?
Wasn't he at Paramount?'—that group. The bottom line is, it
doesn't really matter where they are. They're all pretty efficient
at what they do, and if they didn't have power at one place,
they're not going to have it at the other place. But they do
perform a function, and David, I believe by design, never
hooked into any of those people. He chose people who had not
done these jobs before, with the exception of David Picker,
which was also an odd choice—he was Old Hollywood.

"It's hard to go for what's positive about David Puttnam
without emphasizing what's wrong with the rest of the business. You can't look at this business as a pimple on some corpo-

rate map and say, 'That's our movie division.' It's the only business you can't look at as a division. If it's not functioning on its own or generating its own power or feeding off itself, it can't exist. Ever since big business got in, the whole concept of the movie industry has changed. Coke, Kinney, Transamerica, Gulf + Western—there's always somebody above the studio who has to be answered to. The studio bosses are forever looking over their shoulders."

Another agent was less flattering and very specific in his criticism. "David was never *there,*" he maintained. "He was always at a film festival or a sales conference or abroad somewhere. It was always, 'I'm going away, but I'll be back, we'll talk then.' You can't do that in this town, not when you're the head of a studio. You've got to be there every single day. You can't go to film festivals. It was okay for Sherry Lansing to do that as the head of Fox—she was *hired* to do that and never given any power. She was the mouthpiece, she was pretty, everybody liked her, and it enabled Fox to say, 'Look, everybody, we've got a woman president.' But David should have been there every day doing it. After a while you pitch a project to Columbia, and they say, 'David's away for two weeks,' so you say, 'Okay, I'll take it to Ned Tanen at Paramount or Jeff Katzenberg at Disney or Mike Medavoy at Orion.' It has a lot to do with staying on top of relationships, having access to the right information. You don't do that by being at a film festival in Sri Lanka. He turned himself into the Sherry Lansing of Columbia."

A producer agreed with this observation. "He didn't have time to return phone calls, but he had time to give every interview and speech. He attended every film festival that invited him."

"Part of my agreement with Coke was to internationalize the company," David protested. "The first time I told Don Keough I was going to get on the road, he said, 'Thank God. Frank Price's idea of a trip was to the beach!'"

David was infuriated when Victor Kaufman announced that the newly formed Columbia Pictures Entertainment was writing off a staggering $105 million post-taxes on a slate of twelve of his movies. "They're doing nothing with the films!" he raged, "They intend to do nothing with them, and then they turn around and say the films have no value. It's transparent, it's ridiculous, and unfortunately it's the filmmakers who will suffer most from it." Financial analysts recognized Columbia's write-downs as all-too-familiar normal procedure in any studio shake-up: all losses are conveniently shunted into the old regime. That way, any business the movies subsequently generated would be money from home.

Kaufman publicly claimed that Columbia would take a "considerable loss" on *Hope and Glory.* For this, he later profusely apologized to John Boorman, who was never a director to take statements of this nature lying down. Another Columbia executive described *The Last Emperor*'s acquisition as "a dumb deal" and the movie itself as "a huge-budget art-house film. You're condemned to a loss. You have to support it, or you're seen as an enemy of the arts."

At first Columbia had supported *The Last Emperor* in fairly regal style, beginning with its carefully structured release in November, when it opened in five theaters. It took in an encouraging $30,000 per theater. The strategy was to roll the movie out slowly, conserving its strength for the February Oscar nominations—a plan that was only too familiar to David, who had benefited from the same decision at Warners as far back as *Chariots of Fire.* By Christmas, *The Last Emperor* had been spread out to a still-modest ninety-four theaters, but the per-screen average was brought down to a less glowing $8,000. This tended to confirm Columbia's suspicion that without Oscar nominations or awards, the movie would die in the sticks. To its credit, when nine Oscar nominations were announced, *The Last Emperor* was showing in 377 theaters, although by this time the average was down to a none-too-bright $4,000 per theater.

One week before the award ceremony, *The Last Emperor* was on its last pre-Oscar legs in every sense. Screens were up to 460, and the average take was down to under $2,000. On Oscars night, April 11, 1988, it made an astonishing sweep of the board and won in every single category for which it had been nominated. Following this triumph, Columbia—arguably one week late—raised the number of screens to 882 and spent millions of dollars on an advertising blitz. But the results were disappointing. "The film plays well in major markets," said distribution executive James Spitz, "but in the smaller markets, the urgency to see the picture is just not there, even with the panache and cachet of nine Academy Awards." In other words, "nix from the stix"—which had been the studio's feeling all along.

"There was every opportunity for a good distributor to make a lot of money out of the film," David had asserted as Kaufman made his write-down. Although producer Jeremy Thomas was initially critical of Columbia's handling of the film, he conceded his satisfaction with its efforts in the end. It's an age-old quandary. Throw the film on the mass market, and if it doesn't click quickly, it's yanked forever; roll it out slow, and you're not giving the movie enough exposure. You're damned if you do and you're damned if you don't. The final take in the United States for *The Last Emperor* appears to be in the area of $44 million, a fairly commendable haul by any standard. Columbia would do well to have more such "dumb deals."

Its 1988 Oscar tally had been surpassed only in 1960 (by *Ben-Hur*, with eleven wins) and in 1962 (by *West Side Story*'s ten) The 1988 awards night should really have been dubbed 'The Last Emperor's Picture Show.' When one reporter asked the film's producer, Jeremy Thomas, why none of the award winners had mentioned David Puttnam in their acceptance speeches, he replied, "I don't understand the question." Then he was asked directly why he had not thanked Puttnam. "There was no reason to," he said. "This is not an award for David Puttnam. He didn't produce the film. I did." After Jeremy's years of patient struggle to bring director Bertolucci's vision to the screen, his reaction was understandable and in keeping with David's own philosophy. After all, David's 1982 triumph had never been regarded as "Alan Ladd's *Chariots of Fire*," although Laddie had performed exactly the same function in that film's U.S. release as David had with *The Last Emperor* at Columbia.

Understandable and somewhat predictable were David's reactions to the awards. His joy was apparently undiluted by murmurings that he had bought the awards rather than produced them, or by *Hope and Glory*'s being overlooked despite four nominations. He managed to make every barbed line count. There was one for the Coca-Cola Company: "I was asked to join Columbia to give the studio some prestige, and I have to believe the Coke people are proud tonight." There was one for Hollywood: "We tried to make the studio international, and tonight twelve of the awards went overseas." There was one for Columbia: "At every studio there's an obligation to distribute their films with as much effort as went into making them." Then there was a somewhat self-serving nod to Fay Vincent, "who has suffered more than anyone in this whole mishmash": "I'd like to think this begins to vindicate the decision he made to bring me to the studio." (Missing was any word of congratulation for Norman Jewison, whose *Moonstruck* had garnered three Oscars for MGM.)

Fay Vincent was somewhat more sanguine about the outcome when I asked for his feelings on the awards and David's reaction to them. "I think David should feel very proud," he murmured, "and I'm happy for myself because it's another Columbia award to add to the others in my ten years. The fact is, though, it doesn't matter. The chapter's over, he's out, it's all history, and all that matters is the future."

So the roll-out of David's production slate continued, Kaufman's decision to write off the films' costs seemed fully justified, despite David's claim that the action represented a "self-fulfilling prophecy." *Variety*'s reviews and the films' grosses told their own story.

- *Zelly and Me:* "This precious story . . . will be as off-putting to some people as it will be moving to others." The film cost $2.3 million to make and took in precisely $55,000 gross.

- *School Daze:* "A loosely-connected series of musical set pieces . . . the film is a hybrid of forms and styles that never comes together in a coherent whole." I was with David in Los Angeles the Monday after the movie's opening weekend and when we checked the figures David declared that the $7,000 per cinema average take was better than he had expected. At a cost of $5.5 million, the film grossed a good-for-its-budget $14 million. Still, director Spike Lee claimed the film had been mishandled by the new Columbia regime. Although Victor Kaufman had approached him for his new film, he announced that under no circumstances would he work with Columbia or Tri-Star again. "All of Puttnam's films," he declared, "have been treated like illegitimate stepchildren."

- *Little Nikita:* "never really materializes as a taut espionage thriller and winds up as an unsatisfying execution of a clever premise . . . narrative unravels in the latter third of the film as chaotic and jumbled action takes over completely." Sidney Poitier's comeback film cost $15 million to produce and grossed a meager $1.7 million.

- *Stars and Bars:* "In David Puttnam's film legacy *Stars and Bars* represents a major faux pas. Unfunny mix of farce and misdirected satire has no conceivable audience apart from undiscriminating pay cable viewers . . . pic self-destructs rapidly. Helmer Pat O'Connor evidences no feel for comedy, having the cast overact unmercifully. Daniel Day Lewis is downright embarrassing." *The Village Voice* chipped in with, "The luckless *Stars and Bars* just lays there, gross and depressing. . . . David Puttnam . . . who commissioned the movie, must have thought the subject foolproof—a fish out of water comedy with something real to say about America. In the 18th century, people were tarred and feathered for less—now they get the golden parachute. Who says the Yanks haven't been civilized?" Cost: $8 million; gross: $100,000.

- *A Time of Destiny:* "A heavy-handed melodrama . . . stumbles awkwardly over a stiff, conventional screenplay laden with tedious and lachrymose plot." Cost: $9.5 million; gross: $1.2 million.

Normally a distributor stops reporting films' grosses when they fail to rise above a certain low level, but Columbia was not prepared to do this, apparently determined that maximum mortification be generated. *Variety* was constrained to note in late June that, "for some reason, distrib continued to report embarrassing figures for some of its major releases: *Stars and Bars* made $3,599 in six theaters; *A Time of Destiny* had a date with $1,758 in seven foxholes and *Zelly and Me* did all of $241 in four situations." By the following week, Columbia seemed to realize it was making an ass of itself and did the decent, sensible thing, reporting no further figures on the three films.

Hopes for Brian Gilbert's switched father-son saga were also cruelly dashed. "*Vice Versa* doesn't even have the pep of *Like Father, Like Son,*" wrote David Edelstein in *The Village Voice.* "It's drably tasteful . . . a lame affair." One former Columbia executive now felt able to talk freely about the first time he saw the movie: "David was talking as if Brian had worked a miracle, the new Capra, all that. It scared the living daylights out of me when I saw the film, because I thought, well, either I'm losing my marbles or—it just *wasn't funny.* I said to myself, 'What the fuck is going on?' It was like in advertising agencies, when they *have* to believe in their product—the power of positive thinking, mass hysteria. There was an element of that in David's reign." At a cost of $13 million, the box-office gross came to the same, bringing a net return to Columbia of $5 million—not even enough to cover the marketing costs.

Despite these reviews and box-office figures, David kept up his attack on the new Columbia regime. "They are strangling my pictures at birth," he claimed. "They're making absolutely sure the slate doesn't make money. They can deny it, but I'm saying it." Dawn Steel felt constrained to issue a cool rebuff. "Columbia Pictures and David Puttnam have one thing in common," she averred, "a need, desire and obligation for the pictures made during his administration, to succeed."

Several films that David left in the can have interesting potential, perhaps none more than Terry Gilliam's *The Adventures of Baron Munchausen.* Will this teller of tall tales ride to the rescue of David's beleaguered slate? Only time will tell.

As for the movie David had turned away—Marty Ransohoff's *Switching Channels:* In the same week that critic Edelstein flattened *Vice Versa,* like many critics he also pounded Marty's movie. "There is nothing particularly wrong with *Switching Channels,* except it has no taste and no bite," he wrote. "A flop on style alone, it moves with the bleary desperation of bad dinner theater." Tri-Star's release of the movie had Victor Kaufman licking his wounds with a puny $8.5 million gross, $3 million net—possibly enough to defray half the movie's marketing costs.

The $80 million gross of Norman Jewison's *Moonstruck* reopened the question: Could this have been a Columbia movie? It would certainly have sweetened the pot considerably, although no one would suggest that rejecting a Norman Jewison project is tantamount to turning down a fortune. Good filmmaker that he is, Jewison's last real hit is lost in the mists of time. At several times since the film opened to its dazzling reviews, David asserted that neither he nor Columbia had been offered the picture. But *Variety* provided "an update" on the subject in May 1988. "I'm now told the studio read *Moonstruck,*" David admitted. "I don't know if the studio did, I certainly didn't. I mean, it certainly wasn't submitted to David Puttnam."

Norman Jewison was equally adamant that it was. "I submitted it to Columbia to David Puttnam's attention," he insisted. Then he dropped his bombshell: he had proof—in the form of an actual rejection letter from David himself. *Variety* contacted David for a third time.

"I've got one thing to clear up," he now said, "because I did some checking up on my own. While I was at Columbia, we did turn down a film called *Moonglow,* which did eventually become

Moonstruck. ["It was called a lot of things," Jewison acknowledged, "and at one time it was called *Moonglow.*"] The letter I
sent out to Larry Auerbach, Jewison's agent, was the 6th of
September, which means it was at the end of the first week I
was there. As we got 4,000 scripts in, and as I'd done nothing
but read in the previous few months—I only read scripts—it
could have been one of the ones I read, I have no idea. In the
letter I sent, it sounds as though I did. I said, 'I'm pretty sure in
my own mind that this is the one decision I'm going to regret
and at least half of me hopes I will regret it.' It's an unusual
letter, the only one like that I wrote. It sounds to me as though I
must have been right on the edge." It sounded to a lot of others
as if David—to borrow one of his own cricket expressions—had
been fairly and squarely caught out.

David's own account of what was perhaps the origin of his
downfall—his three-year declaration—provided, as ever, only a
tantalizing, half-revealing glimpse into his motivation. "I had to
deal with this sense of selling out," he claimed in the May 1988
interview with *Variety.* "I'd said a lot of stuff in my life about
not wanting to go back to Hollywood. For the sake of my own
dignity, I had to time-cap it. It was very, very important to my
dignity that I hung on to this three-year notion. There was a
50-50 chance I'd never even complete the three years. In effect, I
was saying, 'You can't fire me, I'm already leaving.'"
  But the astonishing reason that David had given Fay Vincent
eighteen months earlier tells the *whole* story. "David's real problem from day one was that he was very frightened of failure,"
Fay reveals. "He said it was psychological. He was very, very
worried about failing, and he wanted to make it clear to everyone that he was leaving. It was all caught up in his own psyche.
He felt that by telling everybody that he was leaving in 1990,
that no matter what might happen, that was it. If he'd put over
my view that he was going to continue at Columbia *after* the
three years—and that hadn't happened—then it would be perceived that he had been fired. So he was anxious about that and
defensive from the outset. The point here is that David was

saying he can't have a superior officer. It was just too terrifying for him to think about failure. The fact is, he got into a mess very quickly. The moment he made that declaration about having his date circled made it appear that that was the day he was leaving the company completely."

David continued in his *Variety* statement, "When I shook hands with Fay Vincent and Dick Gallop in New York, something in my heart of hearts told me I should not be shaking hands with them. Really, what I would like to have done is got out of that room without having made a final commitment. But every little thing I had asked for had been agreed to. And I had no cause to procrastinate, and they said, 'We've got a deal.' I guess what I'm saying to you is, all things being equal, if I hadn't shaken hands at that moment, I would have picked up the phone and called Fay Vincent and said, 'Look, I'm making a mistake and I suspect you're making a mistake.' But we had shaken hands. And I felt obligated to Fay."

Fay smiles ruefully as he talked about David's account. "All he had to do was tell us," he said. "I'd have been disappointed, but it would not have been unsurmountable. It ties in with his terrific insecurity and his belief [that] he was going to fail, and says to you [that] from the outset David probably understood he was in over his head. He wanted the money, but he recognized he was taking a terrific risk with his own standing in his own career, and that really says, 'I shouldn't have taken the job, because I don't think I can do it properly.' If he'd said that to me, I'd have said, 'Then don't take the job, we'll give it to someone else.' But he told me he could do it. In fact, he told me he was very excited about it."

Since Dick Gallop had been involved with Fay Vincent in the negotiations that brought David to Columbia, David cited him to confirm that the subject of making money had never come up at this stage! Gallop, however, does not agree. "It *was* made clear to him from day one, and he accepted the fact that Columbia is a profit-making venture. There was no question—through direct conversations at our meeting—that making popular pictures and making the studio money was the essence of the assignment."

David demurred on this, allowing that the idea of making money had been only "implicit" in their discussions. Gallop came thundering back: "It was explicit," he insisted, "absolutely explicit."

Fay Vincent agrees with Gallop's recollection. "Of course it was explicit. After he started, there was one great moment when David said, 'We'll have the number-one record in box-office results in 1988.' I said, '*That's* the kind of thing I want to hear!' He and Coote suggested that we have our next distributors' meeting in Paris and take the whole group over as a treat if we reached number one. I gladly agreed. But that illustrates the schizophrenia in David's mind. On the one hand, I think he felt he had the ability and knew how to make pictures. On the other, there was this terrific insecurity and concern that he was going to fail.

"David didn't want to be put in the position where someday he could be fired. He had a tremendous anxiety about working for somebody who could fire him. He'd never done that before. I think the fear of being fired was really the thing that I missed completely. It explains the three-year thing, going public, circling the date in his diary—all of that. When he said that everybody was frightened of Roberto, he meant that *he* was frightened of Roberto. He was afraid that one day they were going to call him up and say, 'You're out,' and sure enough . . ."

When Fay bracketed his departure with the firings of McElwaine and Price, David violently objected. Fay conceded that of course, he had not been present at the fateful meeting with Kaufman. "I knew about McElwaine and Price, since I was directly involved," Fay said. "When Coke told me of the reconstruction, I knew it was their intention to fire David, I knew that he was not going to survive under Victor. David would go, he and Victor were not compatible, Victor was going the Ray Stark route, they wouldn't mesh. The problem is the word *fired*—people never use the word. I never used it to McElwaine or Price, I just said, 'I think it would be better if you left,' and I'm sure that's what Victor and David talked about. I think Victor would say, 'I fired David Puttnam.' It's a semantics problem, not a substance problem. The substance is that when the decision was made to put Victor in charge, everybody knew David was going to leave. However you characterize it, he was no longer going to run the studio, and that's what happened.

"The ultimate problem had to do more with the cumulative effect of all those things stacked against him. The effect of Ovitz, Stark, Murray, Aykroyd, Beatty, Cosby—it got to be a long list. I've thought about it, and I think there's a big difference between being a producer and being head of a studio. As a producer you can fight with people—that's how you live. It's your product, and there is no long term—it's just you. If you don't want to deal with Beatty ever again or with Murray or with Ovitz, fine. Running a studio is different, because it's all about relationships. It's an entirely different setup.

"And Columbia wasn't just any studio, but one owned by Coca-Cola, with a worldwide image to keep up. I think that probably David and I completely misjudged the circumstances when he came in. Looking back, I don't think I spent enough time coaching him. I assumed he knew a lot more than he did. I bear some of the responsibility, and he bears some too.

"I think David's reached a very serious level," Fay added. "He's hurt pretty badly. One of the things he's lost in this process is in terms of character and standing. He came over as a class act and a lot of things have hurt that. He's come face to face with himself."

Face to face or not, David continued to rail against the slings and arrows that were part and parcel of his Hollywood experience; they pierced him even after he had returned home. "I'm forty-seven years old and nobody ever asked me to leave anything," he insisted to *Variety*. "If anyone says I was asked to leave, there will be a lawsuit the next morning." Although earlier in the year he quipped that Coke had "bottled Fay Vincent," David clearly did not accept that he himself had been ever-so-neatly canned.

27

After less than a year at Coca-Cola bottling, Fay Vincent left to join his original law firm of Caplin and Drysdale. Many saw him as the main casualty of the Coke business plan; Fay, however, doesn't see it that way at all. "I'd been doing the job for ten years," he says, reflecting as he sat comfortably in his new office thirty floors above East Fifty-third Street in midtown Manhattan. "And I'm not really an entertainment person. Victor [Kaufman] views himself as a creative person, he likes to get involved with casting, reading the scripts, as a producer. I went the other way. What I did was build the company up, the earnings were very good, the stock went up, and people made a lot of money. I hired people—some did well, some didn't. I didn't interfere. Frank Price would argue that I did, but Puttnam and others will tell you that I didn't. I knew a lot about finance and acquisitions, and we built the biggest company, the most profitable entertainment company in the business in 1986. But the fact is that from my point of view, it was a job I was becoming tired of. So my move out of entertainment wasn't totally unexpected, since I'd been saying I'd like to do something else.

"I still think David was the right choice. The cynics say the only way to tell is to look at the movies. In fact, they haven't been terrific, and I think the opposition would say he was the wrong choice on every count. He didn't make good movies, he caused a lot of trouble in the community, he hurt the company, he hurt me. On what score was he the right choice? I'd say he was a terrific experiment in that he had a lot of talent, and you can't judge somebody by the first year in the job. Most of the people I've watched had beginnings that were not spectacular.

"Victor is very able, smart, and talented and has a very big job to do in a difficult situation. He's very different from me, too, in that he's closer to Ray, and Ray is much more involved in the company again. He's back to being a very influential and significant factor in Columbia." Fay was reminded of an incident in his relationship with Stark: "He talks to people in my position four, five times a day when relationships are good. He's on the phone constantly. Years ago he called and wanted to speak to me, but I was on the phone, and my secretary said I would call him back. On this occasion I was busy and didn't call him right back. He called again, and again I was on the phone. He got upset and said I was to call him right back. The third time he called, he said he was at the airport on a pay phone and he was running out of change and it was urgent. I excused myself from the meeting I was in and took the call. He was mad at me for something and went on and on and on, then after about two minutes he said, 'Wait a minute, there's a call coming in on the other line, hold on!' I think that explains Ray."

Regarding Stark's current rejuvenation and box-office success with *Biloxi Blues,* Fay smiles. "Lots of people thought he was finished. He fooled us all!"

Back in 1984, David Puttnam composed a witty and trenchant introduction to a collection of Alan Parker's devilishly satiric cartoons:

> Attempting to come up with a rational explanation of why I had tolerated (and even enjoyed) the past dozen years of humiliation, I turned to the dictionary to find:
>
> MASOCHISM: form of perversion in which person derives pleasure from his own pain or humiliation (opp: sadism; [colloq.] enjoyment in what appears to be painful or tiresome).
>
> However, even this doesn't adequately explain why I continue to open the familiar cream Pinewood-stamped envelopes with anticipation rather than dread. Worse still, finding that the current Screen cartoon spotlights someone else's torment, merely sets me wondering if I'm working hard enough, or if I've offended Alan in some way. In fact, all the symptoms of:
>
> PARANOIA: mental derangement with delusions of grandeur, persecution, etc.
>
> For the sake of my continuing sanity, long may I drink from my friend's poisoned chalice!

Sadly, the friendship is now over. Late in 1987, Alan did the unthinkable, the utterly unacceptable—he switched agencies and signed with Mike Ovitz's CAA, an action that David sees as the ultimate betrayal and the unkindest cut of all. If there is no going back, it will be a pity for both men. For David, the loss of his best friend will be yet another price he had paid for his sojourn in Babylon. Alan shrugged off the situation with the casual air of one resigned to losing something irretrievably precious. "He's warm, charming, concerned, helpful, and unbelievably generous," he railed, "and he's cold, callous, spiteful, selfish, and mean. I know more about him than anybody, and I know *nothing* about him!"

In April 1988, on the eve of his departure, David made an expression of farewell to Hollywood. Although there is no doubt his views were sincerely held, David was in the invidious position of one for whom the only good news is bad news. "I believe Hollywood is facing ruin eventually," he said. "But unfortunately it keeps having these series of comebacks when business is up, and the underlying cancer, which I sincerely believe is there, isn't being addressed. The patient keeps on showing signs of recovery. This, plus the tremendous comforts created by the people who are for the most part in power. No one is addressing the cancer, which is costs. From 1982 to 1986, costs rose 63 percent against a Consumer Price Index of 13 percent—five times as fast. The average cost of a movie now is $19.7 million. You know what I think sums up the present situation? At the end of all the bloodletting in the 1914–18 war, T. E. Lawrence observed the political maneuvering and manipulation that we now refer to as the Versailles Treaty. As he put it at the time, 'When the new world dawned, the old men came out again and took from us our victory. Then they remade it in the likeness of the former world we knew.' What ever gets changed without shouting taking place? I was misled—I was led to believe that the situation at Columbia was desperate. Clearly, Coke didn't feel it was as desperate as all that, or as they said it was."

A few days later, not content with being merely the California Cassandra, he delivered another farewell, this time to the United States itself, at a USC law symposium. "As I see it," he declared, "the U.S. is in genuine danger of becoming the lost land. . . . There is a disillusionment wafting through the heady winds of the American dream, as more and more people come to feel that they've had the experience, but somehow, somewhere, missed out in the meaning of it. It's as if there was a vision gap. Prosperity had bred contentment, but not enough to overcome this sense of drift. Something far less tangible than deficit assails the national spirit. Many Americans are concerned at the growth of influence peddling. . . . These same citizens watched in dismay as inside traders took over Wall

Street. They rightly question a system that allows the transformation, by greed and technology, of their stock exchange into a marketplace that functions much more like a casino than a financial institution.

"Reeling under the implication of problems of government and finance, some Americans turned to institutionalized faith for help—that's until they discovered that a new generation of religious leaders had merely set up profitable Disneylands, built in the name of Jesus.

"While all this was happening, Americans saw their place in the traditional world markets decline, as their interest was distracted from opportunities overseas; thus confirming the belief that in time of crisis there invariably looms in this country a very real form of parochialism."

David had learned the hard way the Great American Truth: Payback's a *bitch*. Ray Stark responded to his prognosis in his usual irrepressible manner. "How could he say the American dream is dead?" he asked. "He spent one year here and left with millions of dollars. Only in America!"

In Britain, the reaction to David's homecoming was muted. With another ten years under his belt, photographer Brian Duffy felt he could see where his friend had gone wrong: "David had worked the reviewers and press in this country brilliantly and got them on his side. In the end, they started writing eulogies to him, and he started believing their crap. He thought all he had to do was repeat the performance in America, but nobody there wanted to know that some smart-arsed Englishman was going to show them how to play jazz or save money. What they wanted from David was his brilliance of promoting. If he'd kept to that, he'd have promoted people's salaries and promoted the industry, but he had read the drivel these half-wits in this country had poured on him and swallowed it. He set up his own downfall in believing he could walk on water."

Alan Yentob at the BBC, another supporter, had watched in dismay. "The surprise was that David wasn't tactical. There was a sense of holier-than-thou. He was self-righteous, a bit pompous. He would make these long speeches and give the impression he was the only person who'd ever made a movie. You *have* to be tactical. Maybe he should have tried to let some of these popular films happen and then made the films he wanted to make as well. Then what he didn't reckon on was the revenge of Columbia. The wrath of Hollywood has just been merciless on him. It was *unprecedented* the way they went for him. What they did—it was almost *crucifying* him. Hopefully, when he's rehabilitated, he'll be able to look back on it as a pretty extraordinary experience. In the end, I don't think it's been that damaging to him. It may teach him some lessons. It's just hurt him, but he's got to come back and get on with it."

Photographer Terence Donovan saw David's Hollywood episode as just the latest installment in his career. "It's an industry where the square root of punishment is very high. The more successful you get, the more they loathe you. David hasn't got what he's got the easy route, lesser men would have given up. What's happened describes the nature of the weasels in Hollywood and Atlanta more than it describes David. In his career there's certainly been lots of gruesome. I hope later things will get less gruesome, but I suspect it won't, because filmmaking as a craft has got so much gruesome built into it. But to me it doesn't matter terribly in life what happens—it's how you react to it. You've got to keep going. And David will keep going."

If David is deep in many ways, he can be incredibly shallow in others. In one conversation, I asked if he thought he had a big ego. "It's a very unusual ego," he hedged. "Therefore it's hard to say whether it's big or small."

"Is there a difference between having a big ego and being egotistical?" I persisted. "Yes," he replied, feeling himself now on surer ground, "and I'd certainly go along with the idea that I've got a big ego. You couldn't do my job without it."

How does this manifest itself in his dealings with other people? "I'm obsessed with being understood for what I am and not for what other people judge me as. A useful quality, but very un-American, is my acceptance of the irresolution of life, that there are no answers, only questions. I understand the complexities of paradox."

Did he accept, therefore, the ambivalence of success? And how would he define it? "I absolutely accept it. I can't, for example, fully rationalize why being successful should make my life in the countryside more difficult.

"Something I find hard to deal with, because I don't have any, is envy. I find it an extraordinarily difficult emotion to comprehend. I come up against it a lot. What happens, tragically, is that it distances you from people. I genuinely believe that my career has been built on what I've done. I don't think it's a career of shadows. I'm a product of a lot of products, and so I've defined myself. It always annoys me, the fact that I've made some good films, which had been successful films, and I had to pay a price for that. That seems wrong to me.

"When people are envious of me and react negatively, what are they envious of? The fact that I've made successful movies? Enough successful movies to have been able to afford the things I've been able to afford and to have had the life I've had? Several friends of mine have a problem with how happy my marriage is. They think it's unjust, they think it's wrong, that I don't deserve this charmed life. They could deal with me being successful if my marriage was on the rocks or, God forbid, if I'd had personal tragedies in my life. I think what irritates people is the idea of someone who's successful, well known, and extraordinarily happy. I reckon that says something about the people it rankles, not me."

On a less philosophical tack, I queried, "If you could choose a director, anyone, living or dead, to film the story of your life, who would it be?" Would he pick Kazan? I wondered. Wilder? Bob Rafelson? *David Lynch?! Jonathan Demme?!*

"Brian Gilbert," came the astonishing reply. "I'd feel comfortable with Brian. He's absolutely a humanist. He would get on film those things that are important to me. Yes, Brian's middle-class humanism would tie in very well with what I think are my best qualities. I'd know I was in good hands, and I know I'd like the film. Alan would end up making Alan's film; so would Rolie. With Brian it would be a film about me, and I'd know it would be affectionate." (I'd met Brian and he's an enormously likeable, bluff character who I'm sure will go on to become a first class director, once he cuts loose from his moorings. However, based on *The Frog Prince* and the "drably tasteful" *Vice Versa*, the choice of Brian Gilbert seemed incredibly revealing. David clearly defined "good hands" as "safe hands.")

"You wouldn't go with someone who would bring out more of your undercurrents, for example?" I asked. "Or haven't you got any?"

"No," David replied very positively. "Because I'm sure that whatever undercurrents I have, Brian probably shares. I'm sure he does. He's a complex man, conflicted to a degree. He loved this last year in America but hated being away from his family. Yes, it's absolutely the right choice."

I was left to reflect that David's simplistic notion of human conflict was having to live in the country and work in the town, or enjoying a year in America while still missing your family. A bit superficial, a little on the thin side—or was he being disingenuous?

David is a prolific speechmaker. The speeches of Ray Stark, Mike Ovitz, and all the studio heads combined would make for only a slim volume; but David would be already deep into his second or third. Why? Has David got so much more to say, or is he simply ambitious in a different direction? His recent statesmanlike utterances, whether borrowed or otherwise, seem to indicate a move into politics, the conservation arena, or a combination of the two. Whatever he chooses, he would do well to heed the admonition that speeches measured by the hour also tend to die with the hour.

"My biggest single problem," David admits, "is that I'm not in show business, and deep down there's a bit of me that despises show business. I'm interested in what's behind the clown in the circus, what the clown's thinking, but I'm not interested in the clown himself and all that razzmattaz. I think a lot of people find me a rather mean-spirited person in that respect. I've never joined the Variety Club, I hate all that 'here we are again' stuff. I find it awful, sincerely embarrassing. That's why the role I've cast myself in is quite deliberately a role that—I've never said this before, never even thought of it before—while I went along with my dad's wishes that I didn't go into Fleet Street, maybe in the end I'm a journalist, and there's a part of me that still thinks like a journalist or biographer."

As Ralph Waldo Emerson stated in his journals: "until at last we find in some word or act the boy and the man . . . Straightway all past words and actions lie in light before us!" The basic conflict in David lay exposed—and the reason the Hollywood trip had been doomed from the beginning. For millions of dollars, he had blithely sacrificed himself and his ideals. The producer of films that deal with men in moral crises had turned himself into *a man in moral crisis himself.* A man who loathed razzmattaz had surrendered—indeed, offered himself—to the tinsel capital of the world.

To make his joining them palatable, David had portrayed the benighted Coca-Cola Company and its officers as an uneasy amalgam of the Friends of the Earth and Brothers of the Cross, with a touch of Amnesty International thrown in for good measure. Never could they simply be—even with all the cant stripped away—an enormous multinational soft-drink firm run by salaried executives responsible to their shareholders and watch committees, attempting day by day to turn a buck. If this was all they were, why on earth would David ally himself with such an enterprise? Three million reasons suggest themselves but provide no acceptable scenario for David to present to the world in order to justify his descent into the lower depths. No, it had to be a crusade, just as his leaving had to be portrayed as martyrdom. (He put to me the comparison of the "man alone," deserted by the townspeople and even by his bride-to-be, as portrayed by Gary Cooper in *High Noon.*)

Along with his "fuck-you" money, David wanted to be seen and heard and respected. The pity of it is that he had not yet learned to differentiate between attention and respect. The community itself had been bothering him for years. He had been constantly told, "This is the price—take it or leave it." The "other guy" had got the better of him all the time. David had paid all these dues, now he wanted them back—both emotionally and financially. He wanted to get even.

Then there was the second conflict—the guilt of uninvolvement. Few filmmakers in the world today have the inclination to make the sort of movies David does, and we should be grateful that there are some left. On the other hand, life would be tedious if we were fed nothing but a steady diet of Puttnam films. Fay Vincent, being the decent and honorable man that he is, may still think David was the right person for the Columbia job, or at least the "terrific experiment" he envisioned. This can be disputed. Just as in the so-called "Golden Age," studios were obliged to turn out a cross-section of movies that would appeal to the broad public—comedy, adventure, romance, drama, thriller—since most people go to the cinema to be entertained. The studios are in show *business* and have an obligation to their shareholders to make money. Some will choose to make endless *Rambos* and *Friday the 13th*s, others will not. Now and again a thoughtful, serious movie provides a welcome change of pace, and as an independent producer David will hone and polish his contribution to this oeuvre as close to perfection as he can through his tremendous personal enthusiasm. Others can pursue this course and still manage to find enthusiasm left over for the lightweight material. Not David. Faced with a *Leonard Part VI*, David has no idea how to approach the project, doesn't want to know anything about it, and is able to do next to nothing in order to make it better. For sure, he'll go through the motions, but basically he has no real enthusiasm for the kind of lightweight material that that comedy embodies to him. Bill Forsyth could bring off a *Local Hero* for his producer, but nothing could save the mismatched talent David cast on *Stars and Bars*. So what do "Puttnam's illegitimate stepchildren," as Spike Lee would have them, really constitute? Aren't they just as much the neglected *Leonards* and aborted *Stars and Bars* on the slate— films where he could have said, "It's no good as it is, but here's how we could make it better"—as the movies to which Lee refers?

Instead of punishing *himself* for his own guilt, he had picked on what he saw as the worst elements in the community—costs, deals, and individuals—and excoriated them instead. Mercilessly. Although every stroke of the verbal whip had made him feel that much less compromised, there was still no escaping his own responsibility, the damned spot that refused to budge. Knowing he was basically there under false pretenses, for all the worst reasons, his self-righteousness was an almighty din to cover the voice of his guilt.

In Europe, people listen to criticisms, or to what David would call his "debate." And some will say, "Well, we don't like it, but maybe we should listen. He's not saying things we want to hear, but we could learn from it." In the United States, where latent xenophobia is endemic—especially against Britons with a tendency to shoot their mouths off—the response was short and sharp: "Fuck you, David!"

The final element that blew this explosive confusion of emotions sky high was the dread David had been carrying about for years hidden deep within his subconscious—a neurotic, haunting fear of failure. Only he knew at what frightening a cost he had succeeded; to fail would be something too awful to contemplate. This was the secret that David had to deal with in Hollywood, the secret that illuminates his every action there.

"With every triumph," says one of David's detractors, "there are a thousand small betrayals in his wake." David's failure to behave in a predictable manner might account for this impression, for he creates an agenda for himself that is doomed to fail. When too many people are owed or promised favors, each shortfall or nondelivery constitutes a betrayal.

If David has finally been brought face-to-face with himself, he has not yet reached a stage where he can admit it. For the moment, the possibility that the Hollywood debacle was of his own making is utterly precluded from his consciousness. What Fay Vincent sees as David's "problem with the truth" reflects nothing more than the falsehoods we all create in our lives as a kind of binding agent to hold together the flimsy structure of our existence. In David's case, the process lies buried in a deep mistrust of himself. Can he ever live up to his father's ideals? For that matter, can he ever live up to Patsy's ideals? Or to use a movie cliché, will it forever be "one last bank heist" before he can "go straight"? The Columbia heist had certainly produced the money, but at a shattering emotional cost.

Another "welcome home" to Britain was the now-obligatory brush with the gutter press that many celebrities have to endure. Of more concern are David's plans for the future and the rebuilding of his shattered image in the wake of the Hollywood misadventure. A $50 million slate of features is soon to be launched, with backing from an international consortium including Warners in the United States and Japan's Fuji-Sankei. Possible projects include some shelf-clearing in explorer Ernest Shackleton's story and *October Circle*. A new addition is *Thumbs Up*, Jim Brady's account of life following the assailant's bullet that hit him in the head in the attempt on Ronald Reagan's life. David describes *Memphis Belle*, the story of a World War II B-52 squadron's twenty-fifth bombing mission, as a sort of thinking man's *Top Gun* with many of the same elements that first excited him about *Chariots of Fire*. Then there's *Gabriela*, in which the central character is a woman. Since women have been very much the dark continent until now in the Puttnam Universe, the question was put to David if this was not an unusual project for him. "Not really," he claims.

"But we don't have women in Puttnam films. What's going on here?"

"We're going to change all that," he laughingly replies. "I'm really embarrassed. The only excuse is that I've got a problem with characters whose motivations I don't understand. So because I can never understand women . . ."

He talks enthusiastically of his chairmanship of the National Film and Television School, an organization he has supported, both in teaching and in fund-raising activities, since the mid-

1970s. David may be a wonderfully enthusiastic film producer, but his eyes light up every time he talks of his Film School work. The jibes that he does it for the purpose of personal glorification are surely unjust. Any glory that accrues would be a consequence of his actions, not the driving force behind them.

Perhaps Patsy provides a glimpse into the future. "I'd like to see him take a bigger role in the whole conservation issue," she says. "I think he's a visionary in many ways, and the ecology has to come first in all of our lives. I don't want him to give up on filmmaking, but it's possible he could run in parallel with that. He could bring some real wisdom to the ecology debate. I think it's the standpoint, the platform to be on, and if anybody could do it, he could. Perhaps you can't juggle the two balls, but I think it is *the* major subject of the end of the twentieth century, and I would very much encourage him to get involved in that."

With Patsy's help, and a new mature outlook that will evolve when he is finally able to assess the last couple of years objectively, David could well handle both. Hollywood saw the worst of the man. The best can be found in the aspirations inherent in a letter he wrote to the crew of *The Killing Fields* on May 6, 1983:

On Sunday we all start to make a very difficult but worthwhile film. It is by far and away the most ambitious that I have ever attempted to produce, and it will, by the time we get through, have thoroughly tested us all. I'm sure that, like me, you constantly get asked what movies you've worked on. I always *hope* that the one I'm presently working on will instantly top the list when answering that question. All too often it doesn't work out that way. However, by nature, by sheer scope and theme, *The Killing Fields* is one of those few movies by which all our careers will undoubtedly be judged.

Roland and I found a speech of President Kennedy's this week in which he said, "I realize that the pursuit of peace is not as dramatic as the pursuit of war. And frequently the words of the pursuer fall on deaf ears. But we have no more urgent task." Those words, spoken twenty years ago, have never been more relevant. We have a unique opportunity with this film to make our contribution. In the years to come, it is my honest belief that *The Killing Fields* will be the very first we mention in explaining and justifying the way we spent the best and most difficult years of our lives.

For my part, I'll always be around to help if things go ugly. But in the final analysis all I can do is stand back, support Roland to the hilt and hope that luck and good sense run with us. All the best to all of us. This story deserves to be told and told well. If we pull that off then every form of possible reward will undoubtedly follow, and we will deserve it.

David Puttnam

Although the "blitz baby" has come a long way, he still has a long way to go. The direction David takes will indicate whether the expediency that has so often been his prime motivation has finally been overcome. The emotional and psychological catharsis that will yet emerge from the Columbia adventure will be painful, but ultimately a learning and healing process. One thing is certain: this is a man, for all his human failings, *never* to be underestimated.

INDEX